The Cambridge Introduction to
Robert Frost

Robert Frost is one of the most popular of American poets and remains
widely read. His work is deceptively simple, but reveals its complexities
upon close reading. This *Introduction* provides a comprehensive but
intensive look at his remarkable oeuvre. The poetry is discussed in detail
in relation to ancient and modern traditions as well as to Frost's
particular interests in language and sound, metaphor, science, religion,
and politics. Faggen looks back to the literary traditions that shape
Frost's use of form and language, and forward to examine his influence
on poets writing today. The recent controversies in Frost criticism and in
particular in Frost biography are brought into sharp focus as they have
shaped the poet's legacy and legend. The most accessible overview
available, this book will be invaluable to students, readers, and admirers
of Frost.

Robert Faggen is Barton Evans and H. Andrea Neves Professor of
Literature at Claremont McKenna College.

The Cambridge Introduction to
Robert Frost

ROBERT FAGGEN

CAMBRIDGE
UNIVERSITY PRESS

CAMBRIDGE UNIVERSITY PRESS
Cambridge, New York, Melbourne, Madrid, Cape Town, Singapore,
São Paulo, Delhi, Dubai, Tokyo, Mexico City

Cambridge University Press
The Edinburgh Building, Cambridge CB2 8RU, UK

Published in the United States of America by Cambridge University Press, New York

www.cambridge.org
Information on this title: www.cambridge.org/9780521670067

First published 2008

A catalogue record for this publication is available from the British Library

Library of Congress Cataloguing in Publication data

Faggen, Robert.
The Cambridge introduction to Robert Frost / Robert Faggen.
    p. cm.
Includes bibliographical references and index.
ISBN 978-0-521-85411-5 (hbk.) – ISBN 978-0-521-67006-7 (pbk.) 1. Frost, Robert,
1874–1963 – Criticism and interpretation. I. Title.
PS3511.R94Z5595   2008
811.52 – dc22   2008025531

ISBN 978-0-521-85411-5 Hardback
ISBN 978-0-521-67006-7 Paperback

Contents

Preface   *page* vii
Acknowledgments   viii
List of abbreviations   ix

1 Life   1

2 Contexts   13

3 Works   25

  Frost's poetics   25
    The sound of sense   26
    Poetry and metaphor   36
    Pastoral   49
  "Men work together"   64
  Labor and beauty   83
  Women, nature, and home   92
  The dialogue of home   98
  Frost and the poetry of nature   109
  Frost and believing-in   133
    Journeys into matter   136
    Sacrifice   149
    Belief and truth   154
    Justice, mercy, and passionate preference   158

4 Reception   162

  1920s–1940s   165
  1947–1963   167
  Frost and the postmodern   173

Notes   175
Guide to further reading   179
Index   185

Preface

Robert Frost became an American sage. His public popularity as well as the approachability and renown of a few of his justly brilliant lyrics – "The Road Not Taken," "Fire and Ice," "Stopping by Woods on a Snowy Evening" – have obscured the immense range of his achievement and subtlety as an artist and his complexity as a thinker. This was partly Frost's own doing as he enjoyed the evasions strangely made possible by the great fame in his later years that had eluded him in his early decades. At first a shy performer, Frost became a charming reader of his own work. The sound of a poem was so important to him that he insisted on "saying" a poem, never "reading" it. Each performance could become a slightly new interpretation. He was also a masterful talker, and he cultivated a brilliant way of sounding off-handed while being incisive and profound. For many, Frost the figure of the genial farmer-poet and prophet of American individualism became one of the great acts of American literary culture; the real Frost was a far more elusive shapeshifter and trickster, a learned and trenchant intellect with a sometimes terrifyingly bleak vision of human existence.

This Introduction will focus on Frost's major poetry, from his earliest lyrics to the complex dramatic narratives rarely discussed but which are part of his most important work. Frost's ideas about prosody and metaphor will be considered in terms of both the poems themselves and how they developed in relation to some of the thinking of his contemporaries. His major thematic concerns – labor, democracy, home, nature, and belief – will be considered in the context of ancient poetic traditions such as the pastoral, and modern intellectual and political questions such as science, immigration, and the New Deal.

The Frost that is still to be discovered is a consummate craftsman and maker of some of the most psychologically engaging and artistically beguiling poetry of his or any time.

Acknowledgments

For years of ongoing fruitful discussion and collaboration, I am grateful to Mark Richardson, Don Sheehy, Lisa Seale, Jonathan Barron, Tim Steele, and Paul Muldoon. The fellowship and kindness of John Lancaster, Jack Hagstrom, John Ridland, Philip Cronenwett, Lesley Francis, Peter Gilbert, and Edward Lathem have been invaluable. Connie Bartling and Tim Geaghan were of great help in completing this project. I am particularly indebted to Barton Evans, Andrea Neves, Perry Lerner, and Claremont McKenna College for their appreciation and support.

The author gratefully acknowledges the Estate of Robert Lee Frost for permission to quote from Frost's poetry and prose.

Abbreviations

CP   *The Collected Prose of Robert Frost*, ed. Mark Richardson. Cambridge, Mass.: Harvard University Press, 2007.

CPPP   *Robert Frost: Collected Poems, Prose, and Plays*, ed. Richard Poirier and Mark Richardson. New York: Library of America, 1997.

LU   *The Letters of Robert Frost to Louis Untermeyer*. New York: Holt, Rinehart and Winston, 1964.

I   *Interviews with Robert Frost*, ed. Edward Connery Lathem. New York: Holt Rinehart, and Winston, 1968.

N   *The Notebooks of Robert Frost*, ed. Robert Faggen. Cambridge, Mass.: Harvard University Press, 2007.

SL   *Selected Letters of Robert Frost*, ed. Lawrance Thompson. New York: Holt, Rinehart, and Winston, 1964.

Chapter 1

Life

Robert Frost became a legend in his own long lifetime and participated in the shaping of the legend of his life's story. In addition to the dozens of interviews conducted from his return to the United States in 1915, we have Robert Newdick's incomplete *Season of Frost* (1939; published in 1976) and Elizabeth Shepley Sergeant's *A Swinger of Birches* (1960), which was intended mostly as a critical study though Frost cooperated and provided a variety of information. Lawrance Thompson's official biography, begun in the 1940s and completed posthumously in the early 1970s, remains an invaluable source of information, if a troubling and self-consciously troubled interpretation of its subject and especially of the poetry. Thompson left more than 15,000 pages of notes for yet another book on the writing of a biography, which provide useful material for anyone wishing to delve deeply into the nuances of Frost's life. In more recent years, William Pritchard's *Robert Frost: A Literary Life Reconsidered* and Stanley Burnshaw's *Robert Frost Himself* have presented counters to some of the legends created by the Thompson biography. Pritchard's biography, in particular, has focused more on Frost's literary contexts. John Evangelist Walsh's *Into My Own: The English Years of Robert Frost* focused on that period in Frost's life, while Jay Parini's *Robert Frost* has also provided a balanced, comprehensive, one-volume study vision of the poet's working life.

More than almost any American poet of the twentieth century and even of the nineteenth century, Robert Frost became an icon in his own time, an almost granite-like figure worthy of a place on Rushmore or a similar pantheon of poets. To many he came to represent values of individualism, independence, agrarian New England, country values. The image of his reading a poem at John F. Kennedy's inauguration, the first poet in American history to do so, remains etched in the national imagination. However much John F. Kennedy or Lionel Trilling or Randall Jarrell alluded or flat out pointed to Frost's darker truths and terrors, Frost himself had managed very well to project an image of an avuncular, sometimes rambling and witty talker. But not the master of tragic fate, Sophocles, nor the continental intellectual and prophet of shattered sensibilities, T. S. Eliot. The deep thinking, the immense skill and thought of the poetry, and – above all – the tragedies of his life were matters he kept very close to himself and revealed only to a few friends.

When Thompson's biography started to appear in the 1970s and depicted Frost as an egotistical monster to his family and friends, many were either horrified or all too eager to see this sage of American letters knocked from his pedestal. Yet, Frost's moods, envies, jealousies in the end could be attributed to the tortured relationship his biographer had with him and in part to Thompson's inability to interpret Frost's tone and sense of irony. Frost would hardly be the first or the last artist to have been difficult, moody, or even depressed, and no doubt he was at times all of those. Sentimental expectations about his personal life or conduct probably went hand in hand with sentimental and naïve interpretations of his poetry, which persist miraculously despite years of finely tuned and attentive scholarship and criticism. Be that as may be, Frost's personal story was filled with what will appear to anyone to be a great number of hardships as well as triumphs, though it remains a risky enterprise to read any but a few of the poems biographically. By any measure Frost's biography embraces more than an ordinary share of horrors. He lived to see the deaths of four of his children; two suffered severely from mental illness, and one committed suicide. He long outlived his only wife, Elinor, whom he had met at high school, and then fell into an affair with a married woman who would not leave her husband. Through it all, Frost – wounded and no doubt tortured – remained by all accounts devoted to his family and to his art. One should not be surprised by the darker passions that suffused his life nor by his immense humor; both and much more are in the poetry as he seemed to face relentlessly the bleakest questions of existence.

The great farmer-poet of New England actually spent most of his childhood in two cities. Robert Lee Frost was born in San Francisco, on March 26, 1874, the first son of William Prescott Frost, Jr. and Isabelle Moodie. Frost's father had been born in Kingston, New Hampshire, the only son of an old New England farming family. His mother had been born in Scotland, the daughter of a sea captain, who died soon after her birth. Frost was named for Robert E. Lee, the Confederate general, because his father had run away as a teenager during the Civil War and joined the Confederate Army of Northern Virginia under Lee before he was sent home. Later, he attended Harvard University and was graduated Phi Beta Kappa. He married Belle Moodie in 1873 and for a while they were both school teachers in Lewiston, Pennsylvania, before moving to San Francisco. There he became city editor of the San Francisco *Daily Evening Post*, edited by the social reformer Henry George.

The first decade of Frost's life was in part a tempest created by his father and the extraordinary and eccentric teaching of his mother. His sister, Jeanie

Florence, was born during a trip with his mother back east in 1876. Frost did not enjoy his early schooling, often complaining of nervous abdominal pain. His mother was a conscientious and forceful educational influence, and by second grade Frost was baptized into her Swedenborgian Church. She also read aloud to him from Emerson, Shakespeare, Poe, the Bible, classical myths, and romantic poetry. Soon after their return to California, Frost's father was diagnosed with consumption after being declared champion in a six-day walking race. He also challenged himself by swimming in San Francisco Bay while young Robert watched terrified. His father also became deeply involved in politics, first as a delegate to the Democratic National Convention in Cincinnati in 1880, and later in 1884 when he resigned his job on the newspaper to run for city tax collector on the Democratic ticket. Both times, he was on the losing side, and fell into depressions exacerbated by drinking. Often out of work and in rapidly declining health, he died of tuberculosis in 1885, leaving the family virtually broke.

Frost and his family would be bailed out by his paternal grandfather, William Prescott, Sr., a retired mill supervisor, who would continue to be a looming financial presence in his life for more than two decades. Frost's father was buried in Lawrence, Massachusetts, where Frost began to attend school commuting by train from nearby Salem, where his mother was teaching. Frost's graduating class consisted of only 32 students, though more than 70 had been members of his class freshman year. Some accounts of Frost's Lawrence years give the impression that his family suffered severe economic hardship. While it may be true that Belle Moodie was not wealthy, Frost never endured poverty while in Lawrence. He was also able to pursue his studies relatively free of external hardships.

The early 1890s saw important growth in both Frost's indoor and outdoor schooling. At the top of his class in 1889 and 1890, Frost studied algebra, Greek and Roman history, European history, Latin, and, of course, English literature. Befriending an older student named Carl Burrell, Frost developed a lifelong interest in botany, astronomy, and evolutionary theory. His favorite reading at the time included Prescott's *The Conquest of Mexico and Peru*, Jane Porter's *The Scottish Chiefs*, and Richard Proctor's *Our Place Among the Infinities*. In addition to learning haying on Loren Bailey's farm, Frost also earned enough money to buy his first telescope by selling subscriptions to *The Youth's Companion*.

A poem inspired by Prescott's *Conquest of Mexico*, entitled "La Noche Triste," became Frost's first published verse and appeared in the Lawrence High School *Bulletin* in April 1890. More poems followed, including "A Dream of Julius Caesar," and Frost became editor of the *Bulletin* as he prepared to graduate and enter Harvard. In his senior year he met and fell in love with his classmate

Elinor Miriam White, beginning what would be a tempestuous courtship and the most important relationship of his life.

Elinor and Robert were co-valedictorians at their graduation; Robert's address was entitled "A Monument to After-Thought Unveiled" and Elinor's "Conversation as a Force in Life." After graduation, Robert worked as a clerical assistant in the Lawrence mill. He became engaged to Elinor in a private exchange of rings. Because he was dependent upon his paternal grandfather's support, Robert was persuaded to go to Dartmouth instead of Harvard. His grandfather argued that Dartmouth was both less expensive and less likely to do the kind of damage to him that he believed Harvard had done to his father. Bored, restless, and focused on Elinor, he left Dartmouth before the end of the first semester.

What happened to Frost after he returned to Salem, Massachusetts, in 1893 has become one of the most wild and mysterious episodes of his biography. He briefly helped his mother with unruly students at her school and then took a job in Arlington Woolen Mill in Lawrence changing carbon filaments in ceiling lamps and studying Shakespeare in his spare hours. Elinor had returned from studying at St. Lawrence University in Canton, New York, and Frost had asked her to marry him. But she would not leave college as he asked, and she returned in September. Frost quit his job in the mill in February 1893 and began teaching grade school in Salem. He also learned that *The Independent*, edited by Susan Hayes Ward, would be publishing his poem "My Butterfly: An Elegy," and paying him $15 for it (the poem would later be collected in *A Boy's Will*). Frost again tried unsuccessfully to persuade Elinor to marry him, and prepared a privately printed selection of poems for her entitled *Twilight* ("My Butterfly: An Elegy," "Summering," "The Falls," and "An Unhistoric Spot"). He traveled to St. Lawrence to present her with a copy and, presumably, inspire her to elope. But her icy response sent him back to Salem. In a state of despair, he traveled to the Dismal Swamp in November by train and walked for miles into the swamp, presumably with the intention of drowning himself. Instead, he allowed a group of boatmen to take him to Nags Head on the Atlantic coast, where he jumped freight cars to Baltimore. His mother sent him the train fare that allowed him to return to Lawrence by the end of November.

Despite the near-tragic trip to Virginia, Elinor and Robert were married in Lawrence in December 1895 in a ceremony presided over by a Swedenborgian pastor. He and Elinor, who had graduated from St. Lawrence, lived with Frost's mother and sister. Both continued teaching school, Frost for a while at his mother's school house in Lawrence. His first child, a son, Elliot was born in September 1896. Though Frost was writing, he seemed to want to have the necessary credentials in classics to teach at a good school in order to earn a decent income. He passed the Harvard College entrance examinations in Latin, Greek, ancient history, and physical sciences, and with money borrowed from his grandfather entered Harvard as a freshman.

Frost studied at Harvard during its golden age of philosophy, and took courses with George Santayana, Josiah Royce, the classicist George Herbert Palmer, and Hugo Munsterberg. He had wanted to study with William James, who was on medical leave, but read his *Principles of Psychology* under the tutelage of Munsterberg. He also studied evolutionary geology under Nathaniel Southgate Shaler (the Steven Jay Gould of his era), and English literature as well as classics and the requisite German, with which he struggled slightly. An excellent student, he withdrew, after he felt he had enough, and as doctors warned him about concerns about too much sedentary work.

At the dawn of the century, Frost turned from the life of student-teacher to farmer-poet. He took up poultry farming early in 1899 with financial help from his grandfather, but family pressures began to change his life in drastic ways. His daughter Lesley was born in December 1899 but his mother was diagnosed with terminal cancer just a few months later. In July 1900 Elliot died of cholera, and Frost began to suffer symptoms of depression that would plague him for years. The family moved to a 30-acre farm in Derry, in southern New Hampshire, purchased by William Prescott Frost. Frost's mother died shortly thereafter.

Though not the most assiduous of farmers, Frost worked the Derry farm full time from 1901 to 1906. He also worked intensely on his poetry at night, filling his notebooks with drafts that would eventually become a number of the poems of his first four books. When his grandfather died in 1901, he willed him an annuity of $500 and use of the farm for ten years, after which the annuity was to be increased to $800 and Frost would have ownership of the farm. Frost was hardly wealthy but he was not pressed. He kept up his poultry business and published stories based on the poultry business in *Farm-Poultry* and *Poultryman* (the poem "The Housekeeper" and "A Blue Ribbon at Amesbury" also reflect his experience with poultry breeders). The Frost family also grew in these years; his son Carol (b. 1902), Irma (b. 1903), and Marjorie (b. 1906).

From 1906 to 1911, Frost made a transition back from farming to teaching, while still working on his poetry. He assumed a post teaching English at the Pinkerton Academy in 1906, and he would develop a reputation for an innovative, conversational teaching style with an emphasis on "the influence of great books and the satisfactions of superior speech." Frost's teaching impressed the New Hampshire superintendent of schools sufficiently to invite him in 1909 to lecture before assemblies of New Hampshire state teachers. He did so but was so nervous that he put rocks in his shoes to create pain to distract him from the audience. Frost also directed students in plays by Marlowe, Sheridan, and Yeats. A particular favorite of his was a production of Milton's masque *Comus*.

By 1911, Frost had sold the rest of his poultry and moved the family from the Derry farm, first to nearby Derry Village and then to Plymouth. He began teaching psychology and education at the Plymouth State Normal School, assigning works by William James including *Psychology: Briefer Course* and *Talks to Teachers on Psychology and to Students on Some of Life's Ideals*. He also taught works by Herbert Spencer, Rousseau, Pestalozzi, and Plato. Though Frost had published several of his poems in *The Independent, New England Magazine*, and the Derry *Enterprise*, he had no success interesting New York or major American publishers in his poetry.

Elinor and Robert decided together that the family needed to move on from Derry in some kind of adventure. Frost wanted to devote himself entirely to writing and thought that getting away from Derry might be a good idea. The choice was between journeying out west or going to England, and they chose the latter. With the money from the sale of the farm, the Frosts planned to live modestly in England for a few years where Robert could write.

By 1911, Frost had decided to sell his farm in Derry and move away – somewhere, away. He later described the decision about where to go as a coin toss between Canada and England, with the latter winning. But there were probably a number of reasons for choosing England, including both its literary climate and relatively low cost of living. Sale of the farm in New Hampshire and an annual annuity of $800 from his paternal grandfather would provide the funding for Robert and Elinor and the four children to live very modestly in England while Robert continued to write. Elinor was attracted to the romance of living in a thatched-roof English cottage. Frost hoped their money would last as long as four or five years but ultimately it did not. On the other hand, Frost's literary fortunes developed unexpectedly well within only a few years, enabling him to return to the United States with both publishing and teaching opportunities. They sailed from Boston in August 1912, stayed in London for a week, and rented a cottage in Beaconsfield, twenty miles north of London. Within a few months, Frost prepared the manuscript of his first book, *A Boy's Will*, and found a publisher, David Nutt, who accepted it. Robert Frost's first book was published on April 1, 1913 in London. He was thirty-eight years old. When he left for England he was a hard working but not particularly successful farmer and an unknown and virtually unpublished poet. When he returned, he was on his way to one of the most remarkable careers (if such a term can be used to describe Frost's remarkable life) in literary history.

Whatever Frost's motives, he did not appear overeager to ingratiate himself in the London literary scene. Living in Beaconsfield, Frost focused on his writing but also sought out a publisher and managed to spend some time amongst the literary lions of modernism. Traveling into London, Frost met and sparred with W. B. Yeats, Ford Madox Ford, and Ezra Pound as well Rupert Brooke, Jacob Epstein, T. E. Hulme, Laurence Binyon, Robert Bridges, Walter de la Mare, and Robert Graves. As his funds grew low and some of his and his family's patience with literary London wore thin, Frost eventually moved to rural Gloucestershire where he intensified his friendship with the Georgian poets, devoted more like himself to country things, Wilfred Gibson, Lascelles Abercrombie, and, perhaps most important, Edward Thomas. Thomas and Frost developed a deep friendship through which both men, especially Thomas, grew as poets. It ended, tragically, with Thomas's death in combat in 1917.

It would be wrong to simplify Frost's complex relationship with literary London. He spent time at Harold Monro's Poetry Bookshop and with sculptor Jacob Epstein through whom he met the critic and philosopher T. E. Hulme.

Frost was conscious from the beginning of being an outsider to literary London. On January 8, 1913, Harold Monro, editor of *Poetry and Drama* and publisher of *Georgian Poetry*, opened his Poetry Bookshop in London. Frost was present at this literary event. On the occasion, poet Frank Flint asked Frost whether he was American. Surprised, Frost responded, "Yes, How'd you know?" Flint simply replied: "Shoes."[1] It was Flint who made the introduction between Pound and Frost and a number of the London literary elite. In an amusing way, Frost was first identified in London as an American by his square-toed shoes more suited to a New Englander.

Hulme and Frost had numerous fruitful conversations about a range of philosophical and aesthetic matters including Henri Bergson's *Creative Evolution* and imagism at Hulme's flat on Frith Street. He found an admirer in Robert Graves, who would later call Frost "one of the very few poets alive whom I respected and loved."[2] Through Pound, Frost met Yeats twice at his Bloomsbury apartment and discussed the Irish poet's plays he had put on with students while teaching at the Pinkerton Academy. But he also found Yeats to be a "false soul" (*N*, 457), engaged in too much of a masquerade in and out of his poetry. Yeats's holding forth seriously about leprechauns and fairies as well as treating Frost, as Pound did, with mild condescension also fueled Frost's animosity.

Frost's most complex relationship was with Pound, the Idaho-born poet who became a latter-day European troubadour and a father of literary high modernism. At the urging of his new London acquaintances, Frost came calling on Pound who quickly secured an advanced copy of the first edition of *A*

Boy's Will, about to be published by David Nutt. Though Frost shared Pound's belief that poetry should be every bit as well written as prose (or, at least as prose could be), Frost came to have little patience for Pound's cosmopolitan championing of literary rebellion, the cult of making it new. Frost preferred "the old fashioned way to be new," a phrase Frost used in his remarkable appreciation of E. A. Robinson, his Introduction to *King Jasper*. Though Pound wrote two insightful and largely positive reviews of *A Boy's Will*, Frost also became sorely annoyed by Pound's patronizing and condescending attitude toward him. Pound, Frost's junior, had taken the attitude that he had virtually discovered this "VURRY Amur'k'n" writer,[3] whom he once also went so far as to call a "backwoods, even a barnyard poet,"[4] unfair indeed given Frost's dramatic and metric sophistication; his great knowledge of Roman and Greek poetry in the original was a classicism that Pound could at best only fake. Although *North of Boston* was largely assembled when Frost met him, Pound took enormous credit from friends for having encouraged Frost to publish this book of eclogues and georgics.

Frost's letters from late in 1913 indicate that though he was comfortable in England, money was running low. Beaconsfield had none of the appeal of rural England, and by March, the Frosts had decided to move to the village of Dymock in the heart of the Gloucestershire countryside to be near Wilfred Gibson, Lascelles Abercrombie and "those that spoke our language and understood our thoughts."[5] Frost admired Gibson and described him in a letter to a friend back in the States as "my best friend. Probably you know his work. He much talked about in America at the present time. He's just one of the plain folks with none of the marks of the literary poseur about him – none of the wrongheadedness of the professional literary man."[6] Surely he imagined Gibson in marked contrast to both Yeats and Pound.

In England, in the midst of conversations about poets with Hulme and Flint, Frost made his most pointed formulations about the sound of sense in letters to his friends and former students in America, John Bartlett and Sidney Cox.

The publication of *North of Boston* in 1915 by David Nutt was met by favorable reviews in *The Nation* (London), *The Outlook*, *The Times Literary Supplement*, *Pall Mall Gazette*, *The English Review*, *The Bookman*, *The Daily News*, and other journals. Frost's literary reputation had now grown as his financial resources dwindled. He prepared to move back to the United States determined not to become part of the elite group of modernist literary ex-patriates writing for a limited audience. However much Frost insisted on his subtlety and integrity, he also disdained obscurity.

Frost returned to the United States in February 1915. Henry Holt published *North of Boston* in the same month, followed by *A Boy's Will* in April. Both received remarkably strong reviews. The Frosts settled on a farm in Franconia, New Hampshire. It was a moment in which Frost had to make choices among teaching, farming, and writing as he indicated to a bemused reporter who visited him at his farm:

> You know, I like farming, but I'm not much of a success at it. Some day I'll have a big farm where I can do what I please and where I can divide my time between farming and writing . . . I always go to farming when I can. I always make a failure, and then I have to go to teaching. I'm a good teacher, but it doesn't allow me time to write. I must either teach or write: can't do both together. But I have to live, you see?   (*I*, 12)

With growing fame from the reputation of his books, Frost began an on-and-off career of teaching and giving public talks that would continue for the rest of his life. In 1916, Henry Holt published his third book, *Mountain Interval*, and Frost read "The Bonfire" and "The Ax-Helve" at Harvard College and also gave readings in New York, New Hampshire, and Pennsylvania. He also accepted an offer to teach at Amherst College for one semester per year, and began in the fall of 1917 with courses on poetry appreciation and pre-Shakespearean drama. The initial relationship with Amherst lasted only three years. Frost wanted to spend more time writing and less time teaching, and in 1920 he resigned. He also had a fallout with Amherst President Alexander Meiklejohn over personnel matters in the English department (Frost appeared to regard Meiklejohn as too morally permissive). He moved from Amherst and sold the Franconia property, buying an eighteenth-century stone farmhouse in South Shaftsbury, Vermont. Consulting for Henry Holt involved occasional trips to New York with Elinor, but he also continued public talks and readings, including an inaugural reading at the new Bread Loaf School of English in Ripton (near Middlebury College), with which he would have a life-long affiliation. Frost also planted an apple orchard and pine trees with his son Carol. His sister Jeanie, who was living in Maine, was suffering from mental illness, and needed hospitalization.

Frost could not keep himself completely out of academe for long. In 1921, he accepted a position as Fellow in Letters at the University of Michigan, a position that required advising students and giving talks for one semester but no teaching. He held the post for two years before returning to Amherst in 1923 after President Meiklejohn had been fired. Frost taught courses on literature and one on critical judgment. His discussions at Amherst on quantum mechanics with Danish physicist Niels Bohr became an important inspiration for "Education by Poetry" (1930), his essay on metaphor and belief.

New Hampshire, Frost's fourth book, published late in 1924, included the title poem, a long work with "notes and grace notes." Frost was awarded his first Pulitzer Prize for the volume, and he also received honorary doctorates from Middlebury and Yale. The tennis match between Amherst and Michigan continued when Frost accepted a lifetime appointment from the University of Michigan, with no teaching obligations, beginning in the fall of 1925. Frost left his family in New England while he taught in Michigan. His daughter Marjorie suffered from severe physical ailments, while her sister Irma's mental health also deteriorated. The strain of Frost's tenure in Michigan proved too great. When Amherst President George Wilson Olds visited Michigan and offered Frost a new position, he accepted and started teaching again in January 1927, along with his summer affiliation with the new Bread Loaf Writers' Conference.

The next decade saw great professional triumph for Frost and deep personal loss. In 1928, *West-Running Brook* and an expanded edition of his *Selected Poems* were published by Holt, with whom Frost was now able to negotiate a higher percentage of both royalties and monthly payments. On a trip to Europe with Elinor, Frost traveled to Dublin to visit Yeats, Padraic Colum, and George Russell and also met T. S. Eliot for the first time in London. Frost was awarded his second Pulitzer Prize for his *Collected Poems* (1930), and he was inducted into the American Academy of Arts and Letters. When Edwin Arlington Robinson died in 1936, Frost wrote a remarkable Introduction to his final book, *King Jasper*. In 1936, Harvard honored Frost with an appointment as the Charles Eliot Norton Professor of Poetry, which required him to deliver a series of lectures. Frost's lectures focused on "The Renewal of Words," and were delivered to audiences of thousands at Memorial Hall. Although the lectures were intended for publication, no manuscript or transcription of them survives. *A Further Range* (1936) won Frost his third Pulitzer Prize in 1937.

Frost had kept a breakneck lecturing schedule during these years, very often to help pay for the medical expenses of his family. His sister Jeanie had been committed to a state mental hospital in Augusta, Maine, and died there in 1929. His daughter Marjorie suffered on and off from a variety of severe ailments including a pericardiac infection and pneumonia. After she married and had a daughter in 1934, she contracted puerperal fever and died, despite Frost's efforts to have her treated. Elinor underwent cancer surgery late in October 1937. The Frosts went to Florida for her recuperation but she died in Gainesville after a series of heart attacks in March 1938.

Frost resigned from his position at Amherst College. He had become close friends with Theodore Morrison, director of the Bread Loaf Writers' Conference, and his wife, Kathleen, "Kay," Morrison, in 1936. In the turmoil after the death of his wife, Frost began a tumultuous relationship with Kay Morrison that started with a sudden marriage proposal and then settled into her becoming his professional assistant for the rest of his life. By 1939, Frost had taken an apartment in Boston and purchased the Homer Noble Farm, which was within walking distance of Bread Loaf. He also accepted the position of Ralph Waldo Emerson Fellow in Poetry at Harvard, giving informal seminars. Though his emotional turmoil was still palpable to many around him, he had taken steps to settle down. In 1940 Frost traveled from his South Shaftsbury farm to visit his son Carol who was suffering from severe depression and entertaining suicidal thoughts. He returned to Boston only to learn that Carol had committed suicide with a deer-hunting rifle.

During World War II, Frost divided his time between his house on Brewster Street in Cambridge, Pencil Pines in Florida, and the Homer Noble Farm. Dedicated to Kay Morrison, *A Witness Tree* was published in 1942 and includes a variety of different kinds of lyrics including "Never Again Would Birds' Song Be the Same," "The Subverted Flower," "The Most of It," "To a Moth Seen in Winter," and "The Gift Outright." Some of the poems reach back to experiences much earlier in Frost's life. It was awarded a Pulitzer Prize, Frost's fourth. Frost's friendship with Rabbi Victor Reichert appeared to nurture *A Masque of Reason*, based on the Book of Job and published in 1945. Its companion, *A Masque of Mercy*, more focused on the legend of Jonah, was published in 1947 along with another collection of lyrics, *Steeple Bush*, which includes "Directive." *Steeple Bush* received sharp reviews largely because of its "editorial" poems. However, *Complete Poems, 1949* received strong reviews and sold well. It was, however, only complete as of 1949 – there was yet one more book to come.

Frost was now not only a poet but a statesman and sage of American letters. In 1950 the US Senate adopted a resolution honoring him on his seventy-fifth birthday (which had actually been the previous year). Following a series of gala celebrations of his eightieth birthday in 1954, he accompanied his daughter Lesley to Brazil as a delegate to the World Congress of Writers. The Vermont State Legislature named a mountain in Ripton after him in 1955. He received honorary degrees from Oxford and Cambridge in the same year. Frost had received so many honorary degrees, in fact, that he made a patchwork quilt from them.

Despite his irritations with Ezra Pound's condescension and politics, Frost joined a powerful group of fellow writers including Eliot and Ernest Hemingway campaigning to drop treason charges against Ezra Pound. He also supported Pound's release from St. Elizabeth's mental hospital in Washington. Despite Frost's criticism of the New Deal, he remained, as he once said, a disappointed democrat. After predicting the election of John F. Kennedy in 1960, he became the first poet asked to write a poem for a presidential inauguration. He did not read the poem he wrote, ostensibly because of glare and wind, and recited instead "The Gift Outright." At the height of the cold war, Kennedy sent Frost as a goodwill ambassador to the Soviet Union, where he gave readings in Leningrad and Moscow and met a number of Soviet poets including Anna Akhmatova, Andrei Voznesensky, Yevgeny Yevtushenko, and Andrei Tvardovsky. He traveled to Gagra, a resort on the Black Sea, to meet Soviet Premier Nikita Khruschev. Upon returning to the United States, Frost claimed that Khruschev said that "the United States was too weak to defend itself," angering Kennedy from whom he remained estranged. Frost was still busy at his writing. He published his final book of poems, *In the Clearing*, in March 1962, and continued to give readings and talks until December 1962.

On December 3, 1962 Frost entered Peter Brent Brigham Hospital and was soon operated on for cancer. He suffered a pulmonary embolism in late December. In January 1963, he was honored with the Bollingen Prize for Poetry, and though ailing, continued correspondence and seeing visitors. He died on January 29, shortly after midnight, at the age of eighty-eight. Frost's ashes were interred in the family plot in Old Bennington on June 16, 1963.

Chapter 2

Contexts

Frost has always stood a large but solitary figure in the landscape of twentieth-century American poets. Unlike almost all of his luminary contemporaries and near-contemporaries – Eliot, Pound, Stevens, Williams, cummings, and Moore – Frost enjoyed an unrivaled popularity with a general readership. At the same time, at least for a long period, Frost had the respect of his peers and of critics as one of the great artists of his era. Yet he has often baffled some critics, scholars, and readers for his appearance of both artistic and political conservatism, a refusal to participate in the ferment of modernist and postmodernist preoccupations with either self-defined ideas of the new or the self-reflexive attitudes toward language. A great craftsman, he seemed to believe in values of individualism, order, and human agency in an age when it had become simply naïve to do so. Yet many readers have, even during his life, perceived his subtle and acute insight into human psychology, and a vision of life in the poetry that though couched sometimes in humor and wit was, without question, terrifying and bleak. Frost developed a way both within and outside his poetry of seeming offhanded if not, sometimes, funny (in all senses of the word) and humorous, often joking with his readers and referring to his poems as jokes. But irony works in many different strategic ways in Frost:

> I own any form of humor show fear and inferiority. Irony is simply a kind of guardedness. So is a twinkle. It keeps the reader from criticism . . . Belief is better than anything else, and it is best when rapt, above paying its respects to anybody's doubt whatsoever. At bottom the world isn't a joke. We only joke about it to avoid an issue with someone to let someone know we know that he's there with his questions: to disarm him by seeming to have heard and done justice to his side of the standing argument. Humor is the most engaging cowardice. With it myself I have been able to hold some of my enemy in play far out of gunshot. (*LU*, 166)

At bottom, Frost's world isn't a joke, or one that can be hard at times to take. A couplet Frost published tells us that all kinds of learning – far inside and outside books – may be necessary as we approach the world of his "fooling": "It takes all sorts of in and outdoor schooling / To get adapted to my kind of fooling."

Frost always kept both his learning and his intellectual interests muted. His posture as pastoral and somewhat untutored rural sage grew more pronounced as his fame increased – his immense learning of the classics, his great knowledge of science, theology, and philosophy, were matters that he kept largely to himself and to which he sometimes only hinted in his public talks. But his wickedly playful, shape-shifting evasiveness goes to the heart of the ethical force of much of his poetry. Rather than provide the simple order and closure for which it has become popular, his poetry often has the propulsive and disturbing effect that Frost suggested in a 1927 letter his writing might have on the attentive reader:

> I was asked in yesterdays mail by a New Yorker: in my Mending Wall was my intention fulfilled with the characters portrayed and the atmosphere of the place? You might be amused by my answer. I should be sorry if a single one of my poems stopped with either of those things – stopped anywhere in fact. My poems – I should suppose everybody's poems – are all set to trip the reader head foremost into the boundless. Ever since infancy I have had the habit of leaving my blocks carts chairs and such like ordinaries where people would be pretty sure to fall forward over them in the dark. Forward, you understand, *and* in the dark. I may leave my toys in the wrong place and so in vain. It is my intention we are speaking of – my innate mischievousness.   (*SL*, 344)

When Frost arrived in England in 1912 and encountered Ezra Pound and eventually W. B. Yeats, T. E. Hulme, and Ford Madox Ford, the poems if not the poetic vision of what would soon be published as *A Boy's Will* and, to a large extent, *North of Boston*, had already been formed. He may have written some of the poems in England but we know that he had already begun and published a few of the innovative, longer narratives in *North of Boston* while in the United States ("A Hundred Collars," "The Black Cottage, and "The Housekeeper," among others). Frost developed intellectually and artistically in considerable isolation, as a young student in Massachusetts both at Lawrence and, then, Harvard and while living as a poultry farmer in Derry, New Hampshire, in the first decade of the twentieth century. This does not mean that he did not react to the ferment of modernism or remain impervious to his time in England, to World War I, the Great Depression, the New Deal, World War II, and the cold war. But Frost rarely allowed himself to be swayed easily by the moment and tended to absorb both politics and artistic currents carefully, subtly, and often ironically into the existing eddy of his poetic and intellectual preoccupations and symbolic landscapes. Frost distrusted intellectual currents and fashions. Many, though, have mistaken his approachability and lucidity for simplicity, innocence, or naïvety. Though Frost wrote lyrics within recognizable traditions, his innovations in meter, particularly blank verse, subject matter, and form, made him one of the most unusual, if not iconoclastic poets of his time.

Frost had the modernist preoccupation with refreshing the language, purging it of some of its early Victorian literariness. We can often hear Frost talking about poetry and poetic practices in terms of the new and the casting off of the old. In this respect, he sounds not only American but Emersonian in his advocacy of discarding the sepulchers of the European fathers:

> I must have registered the pious wish I wished in 1915 when the
> Germans were being execrated for having destroyed Reims Cathedral. I
> wish they could with one shell blow Shakespeare out of the English
> language. The past overawes us too much in art. If America has any
> advantage of Europe it is in being less clogged with the products of art.
> We aren't in the same danger of seeing anywhere around us already done
> the thing we were just about to do. That's why I think America was
> invented not discovered to give us a chance to extricate ourselves from
> what we had materialized out of our minds and natures. Our most
> precious heritage is what we haven't in our possession – what we haven't
> made and so have still to make.   (*N*, 179)

Yet, Frost held great respect for traditions and institutions and could in another thought go against Emerson's ideal, expressed at the end of "Give All to Love," of superseding the old in favor of the new:

> I must have taken it as a truth accepted that a thing of beauty will never
> cease to be beautiful. Its beauty will in fact increase. Which is the
> opposite doctrine to Emersons in "Verily know when the half gods go
> the gods arrive": the poets and poems we have loved and ceased to love
> are to be regarded as stepping stones of our dead selves to higher things.
> Growth is a distressful change of taste for the better. Taste improving is
> on the way upward to creation. Nay-nay. It is more likely on the way to
> dissatisfaction and ineffectuality. A person who has found out young
> from Aldous Huxley how really bad Poe is will hardly from the
> superiority of the position this gives him be able to go far with anything
> he himself attempts . . .   (*N*, 49)

Frost once said that the way he became a poet was "by following the procession down the ages." Classical poets including Horace, Virgil, Lucretius, and Ovid as well as the great English poets, Shakespeare, Donne, Marvell, Milton, Pope, Smart, Keats, Wordsworth, Tennyson, and Browning among many formed part of Frost's own canon; he knew thousands of their lines by heart. He also immersed himself in American poets. He gave his future fiancée, Elinor, the iconoclastic Emily Dickinson's *Poems, First Series* (1890) (although, at the time, much of Dickinson's strange practices of punctuation had been edited out). Frost's interest in metaphor's way of saying one thing in terms of another as well as one thing and meaning another may reflect Dickinson's sense of circumference and her methods of telling the truth slant. When Frost wrote "A Fountain, a Bottle, a Donkey's Ears, and Some Books," he may well have had Dickinson in mind as a model of the home-bound poet. In reading "The Road Not Taken," it would be hard to imagine that, in addition to Dante, Frost did not have this poem by Dickinson in mind:

> Our journey had advanced;
> Out feet were almost come
> To that odd fork in Being's road,
> Eternity by term.
>
> Our pace took sudden awe,
> Our feet reluctant led,
> Before were cities, but between,
> The forest of the dead.
>
> Retreat was out of hope,–
> Behind, a sealed route,
> Eternity's a white flag before,
> And God at every gate.

Frost may be less inclined to meditate beyond the grave but both he and Dickinson had penetrating minds, exploring the conflict of knowledge and faith.

Frost also read and admired the poetry of William Cullen Bryant, Emerson, Longfellow, and, of course, Edwin Arlington Robinson, all poets known and popular in their own times. It might be true that Frost sought to align himself with a New England tradition and sense of place associated with these poets. The chords often strike deeper. Frost no doubt loved both the thought and the wit of Emerson's appeal to the vernacular in *Monadnoc*: "I can spare the college bell, / And the learned lecture, well; / Spare the clergy and libraries, / Institutes and dictionaries, / For that hardy English root / Thrives here, unvalued, underfoot." Writing of this passage in 1918 to Regis Michaud, a Smith College Professor, Frost stressed both its emphasis on the colloquial and its inspiration of the local in poetry:

> I am as sure that the colloquial is the root of every good poem as I am that the national is the root of all thought and art. It may shoot up as

high as you please and flourish as widely abroad in the air, if only the roots are what and where they should be. One half of individuality is locality; and I was about venturing to say the other half was colloquiality.   (*SL*, 228)

Other notable Frost poems appear to work in some dialogue with poems by Emerson. For example, Emerson's "Hamatreya" begins with a vision of men who once "possessed the land which rendered to their toil / Hay, corn, roots, hemp, flax, apples, wool, and wood." But the speaker goes on to ask "Where are these men? Asleep beneath their grounds; / And strangers, fond as they, their furrows plough." Frost's "The Gift Outright" continues the meditation on who and how we "possess" the land and how it possesses us. Frost, too, though in a different way from Emerson, leaves open the question of the future of its possession.

Though Longfellow became the *bête noire* of Pound's modernist poetics, Frost never condescended to him. While one would be hard-pressed to find the kind of sentiment in Frost one finds in Longfellow, the interest in writing memorable poetry in meter and in form no doubt attracted Frost to Longfellow's shorter lyrics. The pastoral world of such longer poems as *Evangeline*, the world of the "forest primeval" where the village of Acadian farmers has gone to waste and "the farmers forever departed," no doubt resonated with the decaying New England landscape that haunted so many poems in *North of Boston* and other books. The title of Frost's *A Boy's Will* is a phrase from a line of Longfellow's 1858 poem "My Lost Youth": "A boy's will is the wind's will, / And the thoughts of youth are long, long thoughts." It may be worth keeping in mind that the line in Longfellow to which Frost alludes is itself actually a translation of a line from a Finnish folk poem; the allusion may provide an interesting comment on originality as well as on the notion of "will" itself.

A number of the attitudes and practices of high modernism became anathema to Frost. In a remarkable 1934 letter to his daughter, Lesley, largely about Ezra Pound and modernism, Frost defined five aspects of the modernist movement he found objectionable. First, he thought that modernism overvalued imagism over the play of rhythm and meter. Second, he believed that modernist fascination with fractured form and fragments sacrificed the inner form and organic integrity of the whole poem. He stated rather succinctly that everything, including a work of art, has two "compulsions": the movement to inner form, driven by the spiritual or individual, "formity"; and the pressure from without, which may be social, "conformity." All poetry, Frost thought, followed those two principles, except for "poetry according to the Pound–Eliot–Richard Reed school of art. For me I should be as satisfied to play tennis with the net down as to write verse with no verse set to stay me."[1] A third, and related, aspect of modernism that troubled Frost was the way the emphasis on the image allowed for disassociation among the images or no great attempt to create connections among them. Fourth, Frost found the modernist poem became a kind of a self-referential game, "intimation, implication, insinuation, and innuendo as an object in itself."[2] Fifth, and related, Frost found much of modernist poetry a game of literary allusions, "They quote to see if you can place the quotations."[3]

The tension in Frost between innovation and tradition remained throughout his work. In his sly Introduction to E. A. Robinson's *King Jasper*, Frost begins by summarizing many of the trends of modernism, "new ways to be new," but seems to praise Robinson for having found "the old fashioned way to be new." Frost made an ambivalent response to Pound's and the modernist mantra of "make it new." Perhaps his difference from Pound and other high modernists also had something to do with his attitude toward success and toward his audience. Frost wanted to succeed by being read by a larger circle than those acclimated to the limited objectives of his own highly specialized ideas about poetics. Writing in 1913 from England to his former student John Bartlett, Frost emphasized his desire to "reach out" and, if possible, by "taking thought":

> There is one qualifying fact always to bear in mind: there is a kind of success called "of esteem" and it butters no parsnips. It means a success with the critical few who are supposed to know. But really to arrive where I can stand on my legs as a poet and nothing else I must get outside that circle to the general reader who buys books in their thousands. I may not be able to do that. I believe in doing it – dont you doubt me there. I want to be a poet for all sorts and kinds. I could never make a merit of being caviare to the crowd the way my quasi-friend Pound does. I want to reach out, and would if it were a thing I could do by taking thought. (*CPPP*, 667–668)

Frost was consonant with some of the attitudes of his contemporaries in his sense of the limits of self-expression in poetry. Dickinson presented a luminous but powerful lyric ego in circumference and Whitman an operatic ego. For all Whitman's emphasis on self-song, he is not really more personally revealing than was Dickinson in her poetry. Though we are often tempted to identify Frost's biographical persona with the lyric "I" of his poetry, Frost also resisted turning his poetry into self-expression, much less confession:

> Poetry is measured in more senses than one: it is measured feet but more important still it is a measured amount of all we could say an we would. We shall be judged finally by the delicacy of our feeling of where to stop

short. The right people know, and we artists should know better than they know. There is no greater fallacy going than art is expression – an undertaking to tell all to the last scrapings of the brain pan . . . Im never so desperate for material that I have to trench on the confidential for one thing, nor on the private for another nor on the personal, nor in general on the sacred.   (*SL*, 361)

Frost's comment does not veer far from, though it is by no means the same as, T. S. Eliot's assertion in "Tradition and the Individual Talent" that poetry is an escape from personality. Frost may be drawing on emotions and thought, what he liked to call (from the Roman poet Catullus) the *mens animi*, or the "thought of his emotions," but not from the raw and unvarnished scraps of his personal life.

Frost took the "scrapings of the brain pan," or at least his intellect, quite seriously. Frost's way of "taking thought" in poetry took many forms. He once wrote that the mind is a dangerous thing in poetry and must be left in:

Too many poets delude themselves by thinking the mind is dangerous and should be left out. Well, the mind is a dangerous thing and should be left in . . . If a writer were to say he planned a long poem dealing with Darwin and evolution, we would say it's going to be terrible. And yet you remember Lucretius. He admired Epicurus as I admire, let's say, Darwin. It's in and out: sometimes it's poetry, sometimes intelligent doggerel, sometimes quaint. But a great poem. Yes, the poet can use the mind – in fear and trembling. But he must use it.[4]   (*I*, 124)

Frost rigorously engaged some of the most difficult intellectual problems of his time, particularly the conflict between science and faith, as well as lasting human ethical problems of justice and mercy, freedom and fate. Perhaps the most challenging intellectual problem of the age into which Frost delved as a writer was natural science in general and Darwin in particular. Two years after Frost's birth, Melville began his conclusion to *Clarel*, his epic poetic pilgrimage in the Holy Land, "If Luther's day expand to Darwin's year, / Shall that exclude the hope – foreclose the fear?" In "New Hampshire," Frost wrote somewhat wryly (conflating the scientist with great pugilist John L. Sullivan), "The matter with the Mid-Victorians / Seems to have been a man named John L. Darwin." For the young, avid botanist and astronomer, the questions raised about nature in light of natural selection did not go unnoticed. The early books he read on both subjects, Dana's *How to Know the Wild Flowers* and Richard Proctor's *Our Place among the Infinities*, contain detailed discussions about the impact of Darwinian thought on their subjects.

Much of the discussion of science and Darwin had focused on the conflict between science and religion or science and faith. Romantic writers such as Wordsworth, Emerson, and Thoreau, each in their own way, had allowed for a confluence between the mind and nature that led somehow to revelations of spirit. Darwin himself was an avid reader of Wordsworth's poetry. Darwin altered and threatened much of this way of thinking by introducing a vast amount of waste into an uncertain, fluid, and clumsy game of chance and violence. Nature included human nature in the animal kingdom. Natural history and natural selection threatened science itself by including the human mind in the process of change, bringing enormous skepticism to the enterprise of scientific and positivistic certainty.

Frost hardly rejected Wordsworth, Emerson, or Thoreau. A reader of Frost's poetry will recognize his dialogue with Wordsworth in "The Mountain" and "The Black Cottage"; with Thoreau's account of the loons in *Walden* in "The Demiurge's Laugh" or the French Canadian woodchopper in "The Ax-Helve." But the dialogue remains complex. In one interview with Reginald Cook, Frost praised *Walden* as a favorite book but then wryly called himself "Thorosian," suggestive of the way Thoreau tends to lose himself in his details (*I*, 143–144). In another interview, Frost also insisted "I am not a 'back-to-the-lander.' I am not interested in the Thoreau business" (*I*, 78). As full of praise as Frost could be about Emerson's writing, particularly his style ("one of the noblest least egotistical styles," *LU*, 166), Frost also wrote in his notebooks "Emerson's Mistake about Nature" (*N*, 162).

That entry could have referred to many things but it is reasonable to assume that by the end of the nineteenth century, nature did not remain the same symbol of the spirit that Emerson had suggested in his first essays. Emerson read nature emblematically and symbolically in terms of correspondences between the mind of man and nature. Natural facts could be transformed and sublimated by man into spiritual facts. Darwin may have made man too much part of nature to make that kind of upward correspondence and symbolic reading possible. While one senses skepticism in Emerson's later essays (particularly those produced after the death of his son and the publication of *On the Origin of Species*), one senses a limit to how radical his thinking about nature becomes. Darwin and science had driven many of faith entirely away from nature. One path for artists was that of despair at the disappearance of God. Another path could be the way of pure aestheticism. This duality became something of the major division among Victorian writers. Frost would eventually say of Emerson that he was "too Platonic about evil," referring to Emerson's essay "Circles" and his line in the poem "Uriel" that "unit and universe are round" (*CP*, 204). Frost added that "ideally in thought only is a circle round. In practice, in nature, the circle becomes an oval. As a circle it has one center – Good. As an oval it has two centers – Good and Evil" (*CP*, 205). While Frost did not portray himself as a moralist ("Never mind about my morality . . . I don't care whether the world is good or bad – not any particular day" *CP*, 106), he did continually suggest and dramatize a duality of conflict in which the poles of good and evil could be hard to discern. "We look for the line between good and evil and see it only imperfectly for the reason that we are the line ourselves," Frost wrote (*N*, 169).

The rift created between Darwin and religion remained complex. For many Christian fundamentalists, Darwin and natural selection remained incompatible ways of viewing creation and divinity. Some Protestant intellectuals attempted to reconcile evolutionary theory and Christianity, either through the misguided idea that evolution meant progress or by considering that Darwin's concept of our humble beginnings was compatible with an idea of original sin. Frost himself certainly thought deeply about the challenge of the Darwinian conception of nature and man's place in it to his own religious inclinations. Frost held science as another form of poetry, both created and limited by metaphor. He admired it greatly, and though never a positivist, his inclinations, as we shall see, went strongly with the empirical and experiential tendencies of science. Though it would be simple and wrong to say Frost was not swayed and moved by instincts and intuitions for which science had no names.

When Frost decided to attend Harvard in 1896, he had hoped to study with William James, who was on medical leave. James was a physiologist who eventually became a psychologist and philosopher, deeply and positively influenced by Darwin's theories. James found in Darwin's concept of natural selection an alternative to a deterministic view of life. Yet James's search for and belief in religious experience would also lead him into the strange domain of spiritualism. Nevertheless, James represented a major strain in American thought that attempted to heal the rift between science and faith. As a polymath who had developed new paths in the study of psychology, he had also been part of a group of Cambridge philosophers known as "The Metaphysical Club," including Charles Sanders Peirce, Chauncey Wright, and Oliver Wendell Holmes. James's development of pragmatism owed a great deal to Darwin and actually used Darwin's theory of natural selection to combat overly deterministic views of human action and will. James championed the human "will to believe" within the framework of the scientific worldview, and he also maintained faith in the reality of religious experience. James welcomed a vision of reality that was always in flux, and in which theories were merely instruments for an ongoing process of work:

"God," "Matter," "Reason," "the Absolute," "Energy," are so many solving names. You can rest when you have them. You are at the end of your metaphysical quest.

But if you follow the pragmatic method, you cannot look on any such word as closing your quest. You must bring out each word its practical cash-value, set it at work within the stream of your experience. It appears less as a solution, then, than as a program for more work, and more particularly of the ways in which existing realities may be *changed*.

Theories thus become instruments, not answers to enigmas, in which we can rest.[5]

James's instrumental theory of consciousness and language put man in the position of imposing truth on a constantly fluctuating reality:

In our cognitive life as well as in our active life we are creative. We *add*, both to the subject and to the predicate part of reality. The world stands readily malleable, waiting to receive its final touches at our hands. Like the kingdom of heaven, it suffers human violence willingly. Man *engenders* truth upon it.[6]

Frost did actually study philosophy at Harvard with two men worlds apart in their thinking: Josiah Royce and George Santayana. Irving Babbitt, with whom Frost did not study, also exerted considerable influence on the intellectual debate about science and religion of the time. Babbitt advocated humanism against romanticism, and he went to great lengths to define both of these terms carefully in his early lectures and his most famous book *Rousseau and Romanticism*. Babbitt's aristocratic humanism insisted on perfecting the individual rather than the humanitarian elevation of the group and in maintaining a balance between sympathy and selection. More important, Babbitt strove to delimit the impact of empiricism and materialism. Babbitt viewed Francis Bacon as one kind of corrosive influence, whose thinking "unkinged" man in the name of scientific law and progress. Rousseau, in Babbitt's view, allowed for an excess of liberty, in the advocacy of unfettered action.[7] Both tendencies, Babbitt thought, could be found not only in Emerson but also in William James and Henri Bergson, the French philosopher, whose widely influential *Creative Evolution* Frost read in 1911. Babbitt's advocacy of classical restraint and balance made him fear the possible consequences of severe religiosity or social chaos; he hated both theology and science. While some in Frost's lifetime would identify him with some of Babbitt's views, Frost never missed a chance to distance himself from "humanists," and to ally himself at least to some degree with those of both a scientific and religious temperament.

Frost had little to say about Royce's idealism in his later years. But Royce's lectures would have given him ample exposure to the history of German idealism and to the problems it faced by evolution and contemporary science. In a lecture later published as "The Rise of the Doctrine of Evolution," Royce characterized the significant shift in nineteenth-century thinking, which he characterized in terms of flow and change:

> But for our nineteenth century it is just the change, the flow, the growth of things that is the most interesting feature of the universe. Old-fashioned science used to go about classifying things. There were live things and dead things; of live things there were classes, orders, families, genera, species, – all permanent facts of nature. As for man, he had one characteristic type of inner life, that was in all ages and stations essentially the same, – in the king and in the peasant, in the master and in the slave, in the man of the city and in the savage . . . The dignity of human nature, too, lay in just this its permanence. Because of such permanence one could prove all men to be naturally equal, and our own Declaration of Independence is thus founded upon speculative principles that, as they are stated, have been rendered meaningless by the modern doctrine of evolution.[8]

Royce's last statement about evolution's threat to Jefferson's "speculative principles" or natural law resonates strongly with the debate that goes on about Jefferson's principles and the Civil War in Frost's "The Black Cottage."

George Santayana also taught with Royce the same philosophy survey that Frost took. Frost had a strong and apparently contrary reaction to Santayana, who seemed to him too much of an aesthete. Santayana approached the problem of science, scientific psychology, and religion by proposing the ultimate power of beauty and aesthetic pleasure and preference. He offered a radical skepticism that tended to glorify the power of the mind and place all constructs in the realm, happily so, of illusion. When writing of religion in *The Sense of Beauty* (1896), Santayana encouraged trust of the supremely imaginative beyond any veracity:

> For, if we are hopeful, why should we not believe the best we can fancy is also the truest; and why should if we are distrustful in general of our prophetic gifts, why should we cling only to the most mean and formless of our illusions? From the beginning and end of our perceptive and imaginative activity, we are synthesizing the material of experience into unities independent of reality of which is beyond proof nay beyond the possibility of evidence . . . The most perfect of these forms, judged by its affinity to our powers and its stability in the presence of our experience, is the one with which we should be content; no other veracity could add to its value.[9]

Illusion, then, exalted to its highest form of imagination became Santayana's reaction to the scientific worldview. This satisfied Wallace Stevens in part but Frost found it anathema. In his notebooks, Frost remained critical of Santayana's sense of imagination and spirit dissociated from matter: "All Santayana thinks is that almost all natural basis for spirit can be done away with – not quite all: almost all virtue can be stated in terms of taste – not quite all. The spirit needs not personality nor nationality nor any place of order at all. But it must have place. Be it no more than chaos" (*N*, 254). Referring to them by initials, Frost in his notebooks criticized the masks of Yeats and the aesthetic illusions of Santayana. Poetry becomes the shedding of "dead selves" and "illusions" in the pursuit of reality. Frost's metaphor of the "stream that runs away" suggests the figure he uses in "West-Running Brook," a figure of consciousness and duration that he appears to have adapted from both William James and the French philosopher Henri Bergson:

> There is such a thing as sincerity. It is hard to define but is probably nothing but your highest liveliness escaping from a succession of dead selves. Miraculously. It is the same with illusions. Any belief you sink into when you should be leaving it behind is an illusion. Reality is the cold feeling on the end of the trout's nose from the stream that runs away. WBY and G. Santa. are two false souls.   (*N*, 456–457)

This severe comment does at least give some indication that Frost maintained a sense of the real outside of the human imagination. He wrestled with the relationship of poetic knowledge and scientific knowledge of the world, acknowledging an interesting, if uneasy, relationship between the two seemingly disparate realms.

Yet it would be wrong to assume that Frost, a consummate craftsman, whose most intense preoccupations were with the tones of voice in poetry and with the power of instinct and "passionate preference" in ethics, would be indifferent to Santayana's sense of beauty.[10] Frost's sense of aesthetic pleasure always led to life beyond the poem: "My object is true form – is was and always will be – form true to any chance bit of true life" (*SL*, 361).[11]

Chapter 3

Works

Frost's poetics

Frost's elaboration of his poetics came in the form of relatively short essays and often letters. Unlike Eliot, Pound, and, to some extent, Stevens, Frost deliberately avoided deflecting attention away from his poetry by the enterprise of literary criticism or critical theory. Nevertheless, he left an impressive body of critical prose, and many of his concepts "sound of sense," "education by metaphor," poetry as "a momentary stay against confusion," have come to define not only his own work but also some of the most salient problems of modern poetics. His later essays on poetry are, by most standards, extremely short and published in what would be considered unlikely venues for a world-famous poet intent on having his views brought forth to world. "Education by Poetry," his richest statement on the nature of metaphor, was a talk given to an Amherst Alumni Association meeting. One of his most important statements on history, nature, and poetic form was a short letter of thanks to the Amherst student newspaper for their salutation on his sixtieth birthday, now known as "Letter to *The Amherst Student*." His Norton Lectures on Poetry, delivered at Harvard before audiences of thousands of students and faculty, were never published, and not so much as a draft of them survives.

However Frost's comments – in letters, essays, and interviews – found their ways into the culture and his thoughts on poetics have remained resonant, and not only as interpretive tools for reading his own poetry. His ideas about sound, figurative language, and cosmology continue to provoke poets and writers throughout the world. Frost's poetics can be considered around three major areas, all related to the rather elusive notion of form. First, Frost emphasized sound in poetry and particularly what he called the "sound of sense." Second, Frost also talked often of figurative language, particularly metaphor, which he provocatively considered not only the whole of poetry but nearly the whole of thought. Third, in setting so much of his poetry in the country, Frost invoked the ancient mode of the pastoral, a symbolic landscape which often sets the world of contemplation of the rural against the tumult and sophistication of the urban. The pastoral mode has always been burdened with symbolic and political complications, and Frost's poetry adds greatly to this tradition. He chose to write in the pastoral mode at a time when almost all of his modernist contemporaries had become urban or cosmopolitan in their symbolic strategies. Confusions and simplifications arise from taking Frost's statements about his poetics straight up or without recognizing the difficulties of seeing them as ideas that work somewhat differently in practical discussion of his work. Frost's concept of sound and metaphor as well as his overarching insistence on locality and the particularity of rural New England should be discussed not as theories but as persistent and deeply developed preoccupations in his work.

The sound of sense

Frost began "The Figure a Poem Makes," his preface to *Collected Poems, 1939*, with some comments on abstraction in modern art: "Abstraction is an old story with the philosophers, but it has been like a new toy in the hands of the artists of our day" (*CP*, 131). While Frost hardly seemed allied with modern abstractionism, he often sounded close on the matter of sound in poetry. As he continued in the preface, "Granted no one but a humanist much cares how sound a poem is if it is only *a* sound. Then we will have the sound out alone and dispense with the inessential . . ." (*CP*, 131). But Frost added that to make each poem as different as possible from another "We need the help of context – meaning – subject matter" (*CP*, 131). From the early stages of his writing, when he developed the unusual blank verse eclogues of *North of Boston*, Frost's interest in sound as "pure form" came to dominate his thinking about poetics.

On July 4, 1913, just before the publication of his first books, Frost wrote a letter to his former Pinkerton Academy student John Bartlett and made his own declaration of independence from the Victorian poetics of assonance. This is the first appearance of his concept of the "sound of sense," the notion that sentences have meaningful tones that precede the words, "abstract vitality" and "pure form":

> I am possibly the only person going who works on any but a worn out
> theory (principle I had better say) of versification. You see the great
> successes in recent poetry have been made on the assumption that the
> music of words was a matter of harmonized vowels and consonants.
> Both Swinburne and Tennyson arrived largely at effects in assonation.
> But they were on the wrong track or at any rate on a short track. They
> went the length of it. Any one else who goes that way must go after them.
> And that's where most are going. I alone of English writers have

consciously set myself to make music out of what I may call the sound of sense. Now it is possible to have the sense without the sound of sense (as in much prose that is supposed to pass muster but makes very dull reading) and the sound of sense without sense (as in Alice in Wonderland which makes anything but dull reading). The best place to get the abstract sound of sense is from voices behind a door that cuts off the words . . . The sound of sense, then. You get that. It is the abstract vitality of our speech. It is pure sound – pure form.   (*CPPP*, 664)

Was Frost interested in the "pure form"? Later in the letter, he provides a more complete sense of how this notion of the sound of sense will be worked into verse in practice:

But if one is to be a poet he must learn to get cadences by skillfully breaking the sounds of sense with all their irregularity of accent across the regular beat of the metre. Verse in which there is nothing but the beat of the metre furnished by the accents of the polysyllabic words we call doggerel. Verse is not that. Neither is it the sound of sense alone. It is a resultant from those two.   (*CPPP*, 665)

Frost was indeed advocating something different not only from Victorian poets but also from modernist poets, particularly Eliot and Pound, who often saw only a divorce possible between rhythm and meter. What Frost formulated here was an intricate entangling of rhythm and meter. Meter, of course, is the very regular alternation between stressed and unstressed syllables in a line. Iambic pentameter, a line of five feet of unstressed/stressed pairs of syllables, was a favored, though certainly not exclusive meter in which Frost liked to write. It should also be emphasized now that Frost introduced very skillful, *subtle* variations within the regularity of a given meter without resorting to wild eccentricities. I will return to how this works in his poetry.

Frost's interest in the "sound of sense" kept in step with the poetic revolutions of his time, particularly the desire to shed the perceived archaic literariness of Victorian and Edwardian verse. In this respect, Frost was closer than is often thought to his slightly younger contemporaries, Pound and Eliot (and some-what ahead of them), and very much attuned to the innovations of Edwin Arlington Robinson, who was so skillful at bringing natural syntax and diction into precisely crafted formal verse. Frost discusses the "sound of sense" and "tones of voice" in the context of a strong interest in human intimacy, in people, and in the colloquial as the source of knowledge. Writing to Sidney Cox in 1914, Frost inveighs against modernist tendencies, symbolist and imagist: "Of course the great fight of any poet is against the people who want him to write in a special language that has gradually separated from spoken language" (*CPPP*, 682).

It needs to be stressed that Frost was most interested in the complexities of ordinary language, and those complexities, of course, must include everyday speech. "I like the actuality of gossip the intimacy of it," he wrote to Braithwaite in 1915. Nothing that vital can be understood on a purely semantic or lexical level. This is one of Frost's great insights. Frost evoked Wordsworth's goal of summoning experience fresh from life: "As language only exists in the mouths of men, here again Wordsworth was right in trying to reproduce in his poetry not only the words – and in their limited range, too actually used in common speech – but their sound" (*I*, 7). One cannot separate Frost's interest in "common speech" from aspects of his pastoral fascination with not just rural but common men and women in extraordinary situations. He took "common speech" much farther than Wordsworth or, for that matter, almost any other poet before him, bringing as much as he could the crudity of remote New England into poetry.

In the interview of 1915 in which he discussed Wordsworth and common speech, Frost also emphasized two other aspects of his principle of "sound of sense": its primitive quality and its elusiveness that cannot be codified the way Sidney Lanier attempted in *Science of English Verse*. Note again Frost's use of the word "actuality," linking sound to action and deed:

> All folk speech is musical. In primitive conditions man has not at his aid reactions by which he can quickly and easily convey his ideas and emotions. Consequently, he has to think more deeply to call up the image for the communication of his meaning. It was the actuality he sought; and thinking more deeply, not in the speculative sense of science or scholarship, he carried out Carlyle's assertion "that if you think deep enough you think musically."
>
> Poetry has seized on this sound of speech and carried it to artificial and meaningless lengths. We have it exemplified in Sidney Lanier's musical notation of verse, where all the tones of the human voice in natural speech are entirely eliminated, leaving the sound of sense without root in experience.   (*I*, 7–8)

Frost's readings in evolutionary biology and psychology, which included Charles Darwin, Herbert Spencer, William James, and Henri Bergson, had all contributed to the view behind this view of the primitive origins of language in sound and music. With this came a conception of the poet not as an originator but as a summoner of what had been so very long in existence:

> Just so many sentence sounds belong to man as just so many vocal runs belong to one kind of bird. We come into the world with them and create none of them. What we feel as a creation is only selection and grouping.

We summon them from heaven knows where under excitement with the audile imagination. And unless we are in an imaginative mood it is no use trying to make them, they will not rise.   (*SL*, 140)

A year later, Frost wrote to Walter Prichard Eaton that his particular interest in "sentence" tones ran against the grain of what was generally considered "poetical," and probably "beautiful," and also against the grain of modern ideas of originality. The tones are "real cave things," prior to words, in the cave of the mouth and in the caves of our primitive ancestors:

> I am only interesting to myself for having ventured to try to make poetry out of tones that if you can judge from the practice of other poets are not usually regarded as poetical. You can get enough of those sentence tones that suggest grandeur and sweetness everywhere in poetry. What bothers people in my blank verse is that I have tried to see what I could do with boasting tones and quizzical tones and shrugging tones (for there are such) and forty eleven other tones. All I care a cent for is to catch sentence tones that havent been brought to book. I dont say to make them, mind you, but to catch them. No one makes them. They are always there – living in the cave of the mouth. They are real cave things: they were before words were. And they are as definitely things as any image of sight. The most creative imagination is only their summoner.   (*CPPP*, 690–691)

Once summoned, how did he capture these tones and get them onto the page? "It is one thing to hear the tones in the mind's ear. Another to give them accurately at the mouth. Still another to implicate them in sentences and fasten them to the page. The second is the actor's gift. The third is the writer's" (*N*, 645). Frost believed, as he wrote to Sydney Cox, that this could be accomplished only within the context of metrical verse: "They [sentence sounds] are only lovely when thrown and drawn and displayed across the spaces of the footed line. Everyone knows that except a free-verster" (*CPPP*, 691). Frost's dislike of free verse had very much to with what he considered its inability "to catch" the fundamental sentence sounds or speech rhythms. In a 1914 letter to John Cournos, Frost defined his versification as breaking rhythm across established meter:

> It is as simple as this: there are the very regular preestablished accent and measure of blank verse; and there are the very irregular accent and measure of speaking intonation. I am never more pleased than when I can get these into strained relation. I like to drag and break the intonation across the metre as waves first comb and then break stumbling on the shingle.   (*CCCP*, 680)

Frost's interest in writing metered verse had very little to do with a conservative cast of mind. In fact, like many of his contemporaries, he was responding to a great deal of the ferment in both anthropology and science that suggested new, primordial roots of human consciousness and language. But Frost's view that the tones of human speech were not "original" and ultimately limited in number was to some extent not congenial to certain concepts of far-flung originality. Frost enjoyed a subtle play and tension of voice against the regularity of meter. Meter remained part of the artist's apparatus of order against the complex variety of life.

Frost wrote in his 1939 preface "The Figure a Poem Makes":

> All that can be done with words is soon told. So with also meters –
> particularly in our language where there are virtually but two, strict
> iambic and loose iambic. The ancients with many were still poor if they
> depended on meters for all tune. It is painful to watch our
> sprung-rhythmists straining at the point of omitting one short from a
> foot for relief from monotony. The possibilities for tune from the
> dramatic tones of meaning struck across the rigidity of a limited meter
> are endless.   (*CP*, 131)

"Strict and loose iambic" became Frost's essential theory of meter. But it should be kept in mind that while Frost introduces interesting variations into strict iambic meters, one should not go too far interpreting how loose he can become or to confuse rhythmic stress with metric variation.[1]

There is tremendous tonal variety among Frost's poems, a fact easy to overlook if one focuses on only a few well-known lyrics or even if one has heard those lyrics frequently without careful attention to the subtlety of their craft. Some of the confusion about Frost's concept of "the sound of sense" and its embodiment in his poetry comes from recognizing that while the colloquial and dialogue are an essential part of his poetry, it is not always perfectly clear from the poems themselves what the tones of voice should be at any given moment.

The tendency for some readers of the poems becomes to scan the lines of the poems according to their interpretations of the speech rhythms rather than according to the regularity of an expected iambic meter. This is not to say that Frost did not vary the iambic line: he most certainly did. He said that there are really only two meters in English, "strict iambic and loose iambic." Frost, along with every other major modern poet, strove to break the bonds of writing predictable verse stuffed with tortured syntax into fixed forms and sing-song meters. In order to do this, he decided not to go the route of free verse and decided to work within the possibilities of syllabic-stress verse and iambic meters. For him, this created wonderful possibilities of dramatic tension: a line set to an underlying meter but the expectations of its spoken rhythms pulling in a slightly or possibly completely different direction, creating the possibility of irony. "In fact a good sentence does double duty: it conveys one meaning with words and syntax another by the tone of voice it indicates. In irony the words may say one thing, the tone of voice the opposite" (*N*, 645).

Frost's theory of "the sound of sense" becomes relational in the practice of the poems. Whether in short lyrics, dramatic or blank-verse poems, Frost attempted to create bodies of sound in which the fundamental components – sentences – varied in tone one from the other but always *dramatically*. The limits of iambic meter, and often of the pentameter line, enabled him to create remarkable variations. While it is fundamentally impossible to determine precisely the tone demanded of any given line, Frost was certainly able to give a strong sense of the difference of one line from another – indeed, that a different tone was at least at work. It's not hard to notice the slight metrical variations in the following lines from "Birches." Slight though they are, the effect on the rhythm and, therefore, the tone of the lines is likely to be considerable:

> Then he flung outward, feet first, with a swish,
> Kicking his way down through the air to the ground.
> So was I once myself a swinger of birches.
> And so I dream of going back to be.
> It's when I'm weary of considerations,
> And life is too much like a pathless wood
> Where your face burns and tickles with the cobwebs
> Broken across it, and one eye is weeping
> From a twig's having lashed across it open.

Frost carefully enjambs one sentence over four lines, intensifying the sense of "pathless" wandering. Trochaic inversions also slow down the pace of the iambic pentameter, underscoring the resistance of the woods. But all the lines work within the range of blank verse, and it is that form and underlying metric that gives the variations so much dramatic power.

An equally great, and better-known, example of this kind of flexibility occurs in the beginning of "Mending Wall," also in blank verse. Some have argued that Frost mimes the disordered quality of the wall in the opening lines with not only an initial trochaic substitution for an iamb but with additional spondees and pyrrhic substitutions. Many try to scan the opening lines with all manner of pyrrhics or spondees. The initial trochaic substitution aside ("Something," of course, is trochaic, and so is "under" in the second line), the lines remain regularly blank verse: unrhymed iambic pentameter. The reader hears the difference in relative stress pulling against that in the rhythm. The breaks in the feet of the second and third lines, the words being completed in the following feet, suggest falling rhythms. But the essential iambic meter is there all the way through. Frost ingeniously plays with different sentences across this basic grid, in a way that encourages, if not forces, attention to the rhythms of the voice. You cannot comfortably read the lines as strictly iambic:

> Something there is that doesn't love a wall,
> That sends the frozen-ground-swell under it,
> And spills the upper boulders in the sun;
> And makes gaps even two can pass abreast.
> The work of hunters is another thing:
> I have come after them and made repair
> Where they have left not one stone on a stone,
> Bu they would have the rabbit out of hiding,
> To please the yelping dogs. The gaps I mean . . .

Frost skillfully keeps the tonal drama in tension with the meter in his narrative dramatic poems.

Frost contributed to the confusion about the interpretation of how his prosody works by some of his own comments. For example, he defined a sentence as "a sound in itself on which other sounds called words may be strung." For any writer, this can be a useful way to think about the unit of a sentence. Frost imagined the tonal shape or posture of a sentence without the words. And occasionally in a lecture he would actually state what those tones were *to him*, as he did in a 1915 talk to students (*CPPP*, 687–689). But one should never confuse tonal interpretation or voice stress with metrical scansion. What cannot be overemphasized is the way the regularity of the meter in Frost often works against what must be the rhythms and stresses of speech. But those rhythmic stresses and the ultimate tonal interpretation of any phrase or sentence may be left open to interpretation.

Another known instance of readers confusing rhythm and meter in Frost occurs in the opening line of the lyric "Desert Places," which has often been scanned as a spondee, pyrrhic, iamb, and limping spondee: "Snow falling and night falling fast, oh, fast." That would be imposing rhythmic stresses, stresses of speech, on the very regular iambic pentameter meter. The tension between the two gives the line its power.

"In the Home Stretch" provides a powerful dialogue, really a series of questions and answers, within the confines of "loose iambic" between husband and wife about beginnings and ends, new and old in life. Pentameter lines are

broken between them as the conversation builds to the wife's lyric and metri-
cally regular expression of recurrence:

> "What is this?"

> > "This life?
> Our sitting here by lantern light together
> Amid the wreckage of a former home?
> You won't deny the lantern isn't new.
> The stove is not, and you are not to me,
> Nor I to you."
> > > "Perhaps you never were?"

> "It would take me forever to recite
> All that's not new in where we find ourselves.
> New is a word for fools in towns who think
> Style upon style in dress and thought at last
> Must get somewhere. I've heard you say as much.
> No, this is no beginning."
> > > "Then an end?"

> "End is a gloomy word."

Frost works in many other meters and forms than blank verse, even though he
made a considerable contribution to that form. The excellence of his principle
works stunningly in the rhymed tetrameters of "Stopping by Woods on a Snowy
Evening." The iambic tetrameter lines are very clearly in place. But one would
never read the lines strictly according to the meter – you simply can't do it
without sounding spooky. In the case of the third stanza, Frost has the words
break across the feet as if to emphasize the downward movement of snow and
wind:

> The only other sound's the sweep
> Of easy wind and downy flake.

Frost also created more complex variations in "loose iambic" meter in such
poems, for example, as "The Draft Horse," a poem predominantly iambic but
with interesting anapestic variations. The anapestic meter combined with the
series of prepositional phrases creates a tension between the forward movement
of the horse and buggy and their awkwardness and frailty:

> With a lantern that wouldn't burn
> In too frail a buggy we drove
> Behind too heavy a horse
> Through a pitch-dark limitless grove.

Frost brings anapestic meter and rhymed couplets into a different kind of play in the narrative eclogue "Blueberries." The lightness of anapestic rhythm in this case draws us into the playful pasture scene, even though the tensions between the two narrators and the Lorens may grow less than amusing, as we shall see later.

This is not to say that Frost does not take great risk with meters, and often with great success. "After Apple-Picking" may be one of his greatest lyric poems, and has predominantly iambic pentameter lines. It begins, however, with an irregular, hypermetric line, the beginning of a sentence enjambed over four lines. He gives the feeling of uncertainty, stress, exhaustion, and swaying. When the meter settles into iambic pentameter in the fifth line, it gives that line enormous weight, a great finality enforced by the rhyming couplet:

> My long two-pointed ladder's sticking through a tree
> Toward heaven still,
> And there's a barrel that I didn't fill
> Beside it, and there may be two or three
> Apples I didn't pick upon some bough.
> But I am done with apple-picking now.

However iambic the first line may be, Frost knows that colloquial speech will dictate that we read "sticking through a tree" as a single phrase, rushing into the next line "Toward heaven still." Nevertheless, the iambic beats are still holding the poem in check and sway and eventually giving it its underlying vocal tension. The poem unfolds with remarkable variations in line lengths, irregular rhymes but hovering around iambic pentameter in order to give the poem its formal tension. Most of the following lines are pentameter but each remarkably different in rhythm:

> For I have had too much
> Of apple-picking: I am overtired
> Of the great harvest I myself desired.
> There were ten thousand thousand fruit to touch,
> Cherish in hand, lift down, and not let fall.

Frost creates a similar effect in "The Most of It," in which three successive lines of iambic pentameter are as different rhythmically as could be:

> He would cry out on life, that what it wants
> Is not its own love back in copy speech
> But counter-love, original response.

The conceptually paradoxical phrases in the third of the three lines, and the caesura separating them, contribute to the difference.

His handling of the one-sentence "Dust of Snow," a poem predominantly in iambic dimeter, shows skillful loosening of the meter with interesting effects. The first stanza is almost entirely iambic but the possibility holds that "Shook down" could be a trochaic inversion, rather than a difference in rhythmic stress emphasis. The first stanza ends with the inclusion of an anapest:

> The way a crow
> Shook down on me
> The dust of snow
> From a hemlock tree
>
> Has given my heart
> A change of mood
> And saved some part
> Of a day I had rued.

The anapests in the first and final lines of the second stanza also add subtle variations to the predictable iambic rhythm. Though "rued" is stressed, its finality has a kind of bitterness, and the lightness of the anapests may or may not work against the sense of what is evoked by the phrase "Of a day I had rued."

Frost also worked in a great variety of forms. He wrote blank-verse narratives that ranged from the dramatic monologue ("A Servant to Servants" and "The Pauper Witch of Grafton") to dialogues with third-person narrators ("Home Burial" or "The Death of the Hired Man") or dramatic narratives in which the narrator may be implicated in the drama, such as "The Housekeeper" or "The Mountain." Among his lyrics, Frost could work deftly in short, three-beat lines such as "Kitty-Hawk" or the hendecasyllables of "For Once, Then, Something."

Perhaps no form so greatly exhibited the variety of his skill as the seemingly limiting one of the sonnet.[2] The sonnet usually takes the form of fourteen lines of rhymed iambic pentameter. If the poem breaks into an octave (eight lines) followed by a sestet, rhyming abba abba cde cde, we have a Petrarchan sonnet. If fourteen lines, with three quatrains and a couplet, rhyming abab cdcd efef gg, then the poem would be a Shakespearean sonnet. Of course, Frost produced several dozen poems that appear to be sonnets and have elements of both Petrarchan and Shakespearean sonnet forms. As one might expect, he frustrates strict taxonomists. "Mowing," for example, might fit both categories. "The Oven Bird" has a particularly strange rhyme scheme (aa bcb dcd ee fgfg), but Frost's subtle variation may well underscore that the bird knows "in singing not to sing." "Hyla Brook," the preceding poem, appears to be a sonnet except that it has fifteen rather than fourteen lines, and the fifteenth line seems to leap the boundaries of the observable when it asserts "We love the things we love for what they are." One of Frost's most stunning achievements in the sonnet form may be "Acquainted with the Night," in part because the rhyme scheme is *terza rima*, difficult in English. The separation of the tercets distracts the reader from seeing immediately that the poem is a sonnet, a song of wandering that recalls Dante but seems devoid of love and goal.

Poetry and metaphor

Though in his letters he was forceful about his formal interests, Frost rarely discussed his thematic interests in any explicit way. At best, he talked around them. In his lectures, essays, and prefaces of the 1920s and 1930s, Frost discussed his interest in metaphor and figurative language. In these discussions, he comes closest to accounting for the way a poem comes into being and for the relationship between the form and themes of his poems. In probing the nature of metaphor, Frost made highly provocative and insightful claims about the nature of figurative language and, ultimately, about poetry itself.

Frost made a strong and unapologetic case for the importance of metaphor in poetry. One of his most concise statements appeared in the essay "The Constant Symbol," published in *The Atlantic* in 1946:

> ... there are many other things I have found myself saying about poetry, but the chiefest of these is that it is metaphor, saying one thing and meaning another, saying one thing in terms of another, the pleasure of ulteriority. Poetry is simply made of metaphor. So also is philosophy – and science, too, for that matter, if it will take the soft impeachment from a friend. Every poem is a new metaphor inside or it is nothing. And there is a sense in which all poems are the same old metaphor always.   (*CP*, 147)

Frost gives summary here to many things that he had been saying for a number of years. In defining metaphor in a clear and straightforward way, "saying one thing in terms of another," Frost also allows in qualification the possibility of irony, "saying one thing and meaning another." This recalls his discussion of the potential irony created in the tension between the semantic meaning of a sentence and the tone with which it might be spoken. The main point thrust is that the poem provides "the pleasure of ulteriority," and in reading the poem it is the work of the reader to know just how ulterior things are. What, precisely, is being said in terms of something else? Can that something be stated at all in other terms? Frost once said, "I like to say, guardedly, that I could define poetry this way: It is that which is lost out of both prose and verse in translation" (*CPPP*, 856).

Frost also significantly aligns poetry with other fields of knowledge – philosophy and science – on the basis of their common reliance upon metaphor. This represents the summation of a discussion that Frost himself had been having, but it had been part of a debate within western culture for hundreds of years ever since Plato in Book V of *The Republic* declared poets to be mere imitators of eternal forms. When Frost gave his remarkable talk "Education by Poetry," which is primarily education by metaphor, he was writing his own twentieth-century apology for poetry.

Perhaps most intriguing, Frost asserts that every poem "is a new metaphor inside" and then appears, perhaps, to contradict this by saying that "all poems are the same old metaphor always." What metaphor would that be? "The Constant Symbol" provides something of an answer, a mythos that merits consideration at least in the context of Frost's poems. What he says is both about the making of poems and about living:

> Every single poem written regular is a symbol small or great of the way the will has to pitch into commitments deep and deeper to a rounded conclusion and then be judged for whether any original intention it had has been strongly spent or weakly lost; be it in art, politics, school, church, business, love or marriage – in a piece of work or in a career. Strongly spent is synonymous with kept.   (*CP*, 147)

Much can, and has been, said about the economic metaphors and implications of the concluding aphorism. It dovetails with his sense of the necessity of waste and the necessity of taking great risk. The sense of ethical commitment, the way one has acted, has more to do with the worthiness and integrity of the enterprise than its outcome. In some way, all enterprises in Frost's world can be viewed as failures: "Failure is failure but success is failure," Paul says in *A Masque of Mercy*, probably giving voice to Frost's sense of the psychology of religion. Frost uses shifts from "metaphor" in the previous paragraph to "symbol" here but the essential subject matter remains the same: a story of the will taking risks. A paragraph later he writes, "Every poem is an epitome of the great predicament; a figure of the will braving alien entanglements" (*CP*, 148). In this instance, "epitome" serves Frost's purposes instead of "metaphor" or "symbol."

In what ways does this mythos serve to illuminate the nearly five decades of work that Frost had by then written? What does it say about Frost's concept of metaphor? In what ways is such a statement also conditioned by his dialogue with the cultural prestige of philosophy and, especially, science? Looking at a few poems from various moments in Frost's life may illuminate some of the pleasures in ulteriority that developed into the larger sense of predicament he expressed in "The Constant Symbol."

Frost's thinking about metaphor and his approach to the subject matter of his poetry reaches back to the debate between Plato and his disciple Aristotle over the nature of eternal forms and their realization on earth. Whereas Plato saw everything on earth, and certainly all artists' representations, as merely imperfect copies of eternal types in heaven, Aristotle saw the study of forms in nature as emanations in a continuum from the eternal. Frost saw this as the beginning not only of science but related to Aristotle's appreciation of *mimesis*, the art of representation and of form in his treatise the *Poetics*. Perhaps more significant is the connection Frost makes between this form of observing "traits" in nature, the romantic poetry of Wordsworth, and the development of modern science, something that historians of modern science such as Alfred North Whitehead also made in his *Science in the Modern World*. The tendency, as Frost describes it, is a movement *into* matter, and *then* up, "down up," "out in":

> Ever since I began to see the relation of Aristotle to Plato I have had a growing suspicion that it is even worse than Aristotle when he we must reject not only the a priori but equally the a posteriori: what comes up is as important as what comes down. Plato would have it that nothing down here below but is an imperfect copy of the ideal idea above. Aristotle broke that when he turned to study nature with the same respect reverence piety that he used in thinking the thoughts Plato believed nature derived from. One day in my reading it was revealed to me that what Wordsworth meant by "days bound each to each by natural piety"[3] was by nature piety. In a loose way he had been taken (by me perhaps by nobody else) as meaning a religious piety that was natural for all of us to feel. He was talking an Aristotelian philosophy contrary to the Platonic. Maybe Rousseau set him in the right way. But Aristotle should have set us all long ago. I have a growing suspicion that might line me up in disloyalty to the humanists that nothing comes down from above but what has so long since come up from below that we have forgotten its origin. All is observation of nature (human nature included) consciously or unconsciously made by our eyes and minds developed from the ground up. We notice traits of nature – thats all we do. The so called nature poet so tiresome to some toils not neither does he spin like a natural scientist but it is to the natural scientist he is nearest of kin in his fresh noticing of the details that prove he has "been there" as the expression is (low down). Little to choose he finds

background nature (rocks and trees and wild animals) and foreground
nature the portrait of a man neither laughing nor weeping but with
features qualified by having laughed and wept: The proud humanists
would be right if they said they held themselves above the part of nature
not yet human. Or nearer right, when they put on airs of disdain for the
praise of out doors that without exclamation of wonderful and beautiful
pays tribute by reporting details not previously mentioned. Thats nature
poetry and nature science. You have to be careful with the word natural –
with all words in fact. You have to play the words close to the realities.
And the realities are from below upward and from outside inward. There
is such a reservoir such a stock pile accumulated above to do our
thinking from that it gives the illusion of always having been up there of
itself absolutely. My growing suspicion is that practically all is from
down up and from out in. The great difference to discriminate between
is the old and seasoned harvest or vintage and the new harvest or vintage
and the new harvest green from the garden before it has time to wilt
spoil and ferment into inspiration that has no flavor of its derivation.
(*N*, 493–495)

The "low down" facts of nature, then, whatever great importance they may
have to Frost as the basis of metaphor, are the things from which one derives
ulteriority. This would not be the only time that Frost expressed contempt
for proud humanists who felt themselves above the complexities of nature,
observation, and science.

In locating himself within the context of other moderns, Frost enjoyed calling
himself a "Synecdochist." "I prefer the synecdoche in poetry – that figure
of speech in which we use the part for the whole." In the context of Pound
and others he said, perhaps somewhat facetiously, "I started calling myself
a Synecdochist when others called themselves Imagists or Vorticists. Always,
always a larger significance. A little thing touches a larger thing."[4] The last
phrase illuminates best why Frost liked the term because it reveals his interest
in observing traits and in moving from the low down and the little thing to see
its connectedness to, the way it "touches," a larger thing. This should definitely
not be taken to mean that poetic figures are simply emblems or symbols of
spiritual facts, as has often been a mistake of critics too ready to associate Frost
simply with dicta of Emerson's early essay "Nature."

Of "Mowing," one of the most compelling poems of *A Boy's Will* and one of
Frost's most beguiling sonnets, one could ask how do the facts become figures?
What thing is being said in terms of another? The central figure is the labor of
the mower as well as the sound created by his scythe. That activity seems as
much a mystery for interpretation to him as it may be for the reader:

> There was never a sound beside the wood but one,
> And that was my long scythe whispering to the ground.
> What was it it whispered? I knew not well myself;
> Perhaps it was something about the heat of the sun,
> Something, perhaps, about the lack of sound –
> And that was why it whispered and did not speak.

The octave of this somewhat modified Petrarchan sonnet poses the problem of the meaning of the scythe's sound. The instrument of his labor takes on a life of its own in the sound it makes. One might be tempted to answer too readily, as some critics have, that the answer may be poetry itself. The scythe becomes a figure for the pen or the instrument that interacts with the world by whispering but leaving ultimate meaning ulterior and open-ended.

Such a reading would not readily be able to account for this repeated emphasis on the preverbal, the "whispered," in response to the conditions of the "heat." There are facts here, as Frost said in comments quoted earlier, that come from "out in," from the drama of the will "braving alien entanglements," and not simply from the imagination imposing itself on the world. Whatever the "something" is

> It was no dream of the gift of idle hours,
> Or easy gold at the hand of fay or elf:
> Anything more than the truth would have seemed too weak
> To the earnest love that laid the swale in rows,
> Not without feeble-pointed spikes of flowers
> (Pale orchises), and scared a bright green snake.

The narrator-mower reflects on many things that he observed and yet does not quite state explicitly how they all touch upon each other. Frost published a couplet in *In the Clearing*, his last book, that could be instructive about how to consider "facts" that appear in his poems: "It takes all sorts of in and outdoor schooling / To get adapted to my kind of fooling." Outdoor schooling, of the kind Frost had as a farmer, would tell a reader that flowers, however beautiful, are weeds to farmers, and the ones that grow back after each mowing are generally more persistent. Greenness usually keeps snakes camouflaged from predators but here it does little good. What do all these facts have to do with each other? What kinds of associations do we have with the scythe? How does the tone seem to work in relation to the meter of some of the lines?

The sonnet concludes with one of Frost's stunning aphoristic utterances followed by a beautiful dramatic coda:

> The fact is the sweetest dream that labor knows.
> My long scythe whispered and left the hay to make.

The aphorism appears to posit an analogy and paradox: the fact is the sweetest dream, something uncovered, strangely, that "labor knows." What this means requires deeper consideration and, I don't think, can readily be taken in reverse to mean that dreams have the status of facts. The laborer has cut the hay in windrows and left it "to make," a farm term that means to dry, but also a word that forms the root meaning of *poesis*, poetry, "making." In some respects, his role may be to create sound and for others to make something of its meaning.

"Mowing" can be read as a metaphor but also by analogy to other poems. The last phrase, "and left the hay to make," almost suggests that the mow is left to be made something of, to be completed at another time, *after* the whispering sound of the scythe. Despite the apparent finish of the sonnet form, Frost did not regard the poem as a final act nor the interpretation of a poem as a closed procedure. To read Frost, and probably any other poet, is to become entangled among the poems, and to read them in light of each other. Each poem, in Frost's view, bore a metaphoric relation to another. There was no steady progressive way to read the poems as a narrative development. As he wrote in a short preface "The Prerequisites":

> A poem is best read in the light of all the other poems ever written. We read A the better to read B (we have to start somewhere; we may get very little out of A). We read B the better to read C, C the better to read D, D the better to go back and get something more out of A. Progress is not the aim, but circulation. The thing is to get among the poems where they hold each other apart in their place as the stars do.   (*CP*, 174)

"Mowing," for example, can be read in light of Andrew Marvell's "mower" poems or Wordsworth's "The Solitary Reaper," and Edwin Arlington Robinson's "The Sheaves." But it can also be read in light of Frost's own poems including "The Tuft of Flowers," and "The Last Mowing," because they play with the figure of mowing. Those poems lead to other poems that may lead back to "Mowing." One aspect of "Mowing" that may resonate with a number of other Frost poems is labor, waste, and technology as well as sound. The figure of the mower could be seen as a figure of that which cuts down things which have no particular use, a grim reaper. That may be somewhat different from the figure of the maker of sound.

How far does one take the metaphor? How much larger a thing does it suggest? Frost was particularly sensitive to this question. In 1935, he gave a talk to Amherst alumni in which he addressed the importance of poetry by pointing out that all discourse, not only poetry, was made of metaphor:

> I have wanted in late years to go further and further in making metaphor the whole of thinking. I find someone now and then to agree with me that all thinking, except mathematical thinking, is metaphorical, or all thinking except scientific thinking. The mathematical might be difficult for me to bring in, but the scientific is easy enough.
>
> Once on a time all the Greeks were busy telling each other what the All was – or was like unto. All was three elements, air, earth, and water (we once thought it was ninety elements; now we think it is only one). All was substance, said another. All was change, said a third. But best and most fruitful was Pythagoras' comparison of the universe with number. Number of what? Number of feet, pounds, and seconds was the answer, and we had science and all that has followed in science. The metaphor has held and held, breaking down only when it came to the spiritual and psychological or the out of the way places of the physical.   (*CP*, 104)

Frost, on the basis of the universality of metaphor in thought, makes all forms of knowledge a subspecies of poetry. But he always recognized that metaphor had limitations and that it did not encompass the whole of reality. "Metaphor may not be far but it is our farthest forth" (*N*, 29), he wrote in an early notebook. Metaphors, like all constructs and all living organisms, break down:

> What I am pointing out is that unless you are at home in the metaphor, unless you have had your proper poetical education in the metaphor, you are not safe anywhere. Because you are not at ease with figurative values: you don't know the metaphor in its strength and its weakness. You don't know how far you may expect to *ride it* and when it may break down with you. You are not safe in science; you are not safe in history . . . All metaphor breaks down somewhere. That is the beauty of it. It is touch and go with the metaphor, and until you have lived with it long enough you don't know when it is going. You don't know how much you can get out of it and when it will cease to yield. It is a very living thing. It is as life itself.   (*CP*, 106–107) [emphasis mine]

Of course, Frost knew as well as anyone that his discussion of metaphor could not, and perhaps should not, escape metaphor. His own principle of the limits of metaphor may be suggested in some of the poetry. Consider, the metaphor of "riding" in this passage from "Birches," in which the boy "subdued his father's trees / By riding them down over and over again / Until he took the stiffness out of them, / And not one but hung limp, not one was left / For him to conquer." While it would be too reductive to call "Birches" a poem about metaphor, it certainly provokes certain very profound questions about analogy, especially in light of other comments Frost makes on the subject. The first part of the poem envisions trees as personified, trees as people, who have succumbed to life. The second part of the poem imagines the birches as the plaything of a boy. The sense of analogy or metaphor has changed. The boy must also learn how to play with these "living things," how to "ride them."

The way the boy learns to climb the tree demands skill and art to avoid driving the tree to the ground, as though a figure itself for taking something too far:

> He learned all there was
> To learn about not launching out too soon
> And so not carrying the tree away
> Clear to the ground. He always kept his poise
> To the top branches, climbing carefully
> With the same pains you use to fill a cup
> Up to the brim, and even above the brim.
> Then he flung outward, feet first, with a swish,
> Kicking his way down through the air to the ground.

By the poem's conclusion, there is some suggestion in this figure of transcendence, of climbing upward, of being "carried across," which, of course, is what the very term metaphor, means. Again, the speaker resists going beyond the world:

> Earth's the right place for love:
> I don't know where it's likely to go better.
> I'd like to go by climbing a birch tree,
> And climb black branches up a snow-white trunk
> *Toward* heaven, till the tree could bear no more,
> But dipped its top and set me down again.
> That would be good both going and coming back.
> One could do worse than be a swinger of birches.

A great deal could be said of Frost's very suggestive use of the word "go" here, or the interplay of black and white, and the phrase "snow-white" to describe the trunk, or the almost magical way the tree seems to act in setting the boy down. Other smaller metaphors within the poem suggest more; he rides his "father's trees"; the reference to Shelley's "Adonais" when he says "such heaps of broken glass you'd think the inner dome of Heav'n had fallen." The modest satisfaction in the tone of the final line and the immense suffering that seems to have inspired so much of its vision cannot be ignored. "Earth's the right place for love / I don't know where it's likely to go better," seem spoken by someone who may have indeed wished at some point to find a better place. Frost, however, allows the central figure of the poem to become a metaphor of metaphors, that pushes us not only to contemplate the work itself but beyond it into different realms of thought.

In a reading to students at Yale University in 1961, Frost said that poetry "moves us to a higher plane of regard" but he was careful to emphasize that this did not mean "a higher plane."[5] In emphasizing the role of metaphor in education, Frost clearly recognized the tendency to move from analogy to transcendence, from saying one thing in terms of another, to saying the spiritual in term of the material. In "Education by Poetry," this becomes one of the most complex and vexing aspects of Frost's thinking about metaphor:

> We still ask boys in college to think, as in the nineties, but we seldom tell them what thinking means; we seldom tell them it is just putting this and that together; it is just saying one thing in terms of another. To tell them is to set their feet on the first rung of a ladder the top of which sticks through the sky.
>
> Greatest of all attempts to say one thing in terms of another is the philosophical attempt to say matter in terms of spirit, or spirit in terms of matter, to make the final unity. That is the greatest attempt that ever failed. We stop just short there.   (*CP*, 107)

Frost's tossed-in analogy about the ladder cannot help but evoke the image of one his finest lyrics, "After Apple-Picking." Perhaps he mentioned it provocatively to send readers back to the poem. The poem in both tone and form suggests so much that it would be impossible here to consider the full range of its ulteriority. Nevertheless, it begins with the sure voice of the speaker invoking the ladder against the tree. We could, then, considering "The Prerequisites," read this earlier poem very well in light of the later poem "Birches" – the human figure ascending the swaying tree. Unlike "Birches," the means of ascent here is a ladder, a common farm tool. It resonates with the tools in other Frost poems, scythes, grindstones, ax-helves, walls, as metaphors of technology and control at once consonant and in some discord with nature:

> My long two-pointed ladder's sticking through a tree
> Toward heaven still,
> And there's a barrel that I didn't fill
> Beside it, and there may be two or three
> Apples I didn't pick upon some bough.
> But I am done with apple-picking now.

Frost breaks the exquisite rhythms of the first sentence over five lines of varying lengths, intensifying the effect of a ladder swaying with the tree. The sixth line, a complete sentence unto itself, falls into pentameter and underscores the finality it states. The weight of that line suggests that a great deal more is at stake here than a day in the orchard, though Frost would be the last person to deprecate the labor in its own literal vitality.

The imagery of the poem is, of course, suggestive – picking fruit from the tree and then the ache of the instep arch accompanied by a vision evoke Adam and Jacob wrestling with angels. A number of images may be suggestive of biblical passages. But we might also wonder whether that means carrying the analogy of the poem too far into the realm of allegory. It may be in dialogue with such images but creating its own vision in its own world, one of labor, and dream, and waste:

> Essence of winter sleep is on the night,
> The scent of apples: I am drowsing off.
> I cannot rub the strangeness from my sight
> I got from looking through a pane of glass
> I skimmed this morning through the drinking trough
> And held against the world of hoary grass.
> It melted, and I let it fall and break.
> But I was well
> Upon my way to sleep before it fell,
> And I could tell
> What form my dreaming was about to take.
> Magnified apples appear and disappear,
> Stem end and blossom end,
> And every fleck of russet showing clear.
> My instep arch not only keeps the ache,
> It keeps the pressure of a ladder-round.
> I feel the ladder sway as the boughs bend.
> And I keep hearing from the cellar bin
> The rumbling sound
> Of load on load of apples coming in.
> For I have had too much
> Of apple-picking: I am overtired
> Of the great harvest I myself desired.

The reader can decide what the speaker means by "the great harvest," and what the visions of the magnified apples and the rumbling sound signify. It is by no means certain how far one should take the metaphors of the poem. The poem itself dramatizes the state of someone who has been on the ladder "toward heaven" too long, become "overtired" by the "harvest" he has "desired." On one, and only one, level, there is something of a story here of the limits of how far one can go into matter on the "two-pointed ladder" of metaphor before recognizing that he has gone too far.

Though in "Education by Poetry" Frost spoke of metaphor as the first rung on the ladder that leads to heaven, in the context of "After Apple-Picking," one can see how much more deeply complex the venture of saying matter in terms of spirit and spirit and terms of matter can be. As the poem concludes, we become aware of a world, numerous and other, that seems threatening and beyond the speaker's human grasp given both in the form of the apples and then the woodchuck, already gone to hibernation:

> There were ten thousand thousand fruit to touch,
> Cherish in hand, lift down, and not let fall.
> For all
> That struck the earth,
> No matter if not bruised or spiked with stubble,
> Went surely to the cider-apple heap
> As of no worth.
> One can see what will trouble
> This sleep of mine, whatever sleep it is.
> Were he not gone,
> The woodchuck could say whether it's like his
> Long sleep, as I describe its coming on,
> Or just some human sleep.

We cannot even be sure by the end of the lyric when the dreaming begins, since the speaker suggests that it was about to begin as the poem commences, had already begun "this morning," and is coming on at the end of the poem. The temporal boundaries and the boundaries between sleep and dream subtly elide. "Sleep" repeats as a cadence four times in the last five lines, rounding the lyric to a close.

What, then, does poetry and metaphor specifically do in negotiating the realms of the material and non-material or spiritual worlds? How is meaning of any kind achieved for Frost?

Frost made distinction between "materialism" and "materiality." While he rarely allowed himself flights from the latter, from rootedness in the drama of life and things of the earth, he would not quite allow himself to be classified as a "materialist." He saw metaphor, and this is very much an inheritance of an aspect of pragmatism, as an instrument of order against chaos:

> But it is the height of poetry, the height of all thinking, the height of all poetic thinking, that attempt to say matter in terms of spirit and spirit in terms of matter. It is wrong to call anybody a materialist simply because

he tries to say spirit in terms of matter, as if that were a sin. Materialism is not the attempt to say all in terms of matter. The only materialist – be he poet, teacher, scientist, politician, or statesman – is the man who gets lost in his material without a gathering metaphor to throw it into shape and order. He is the lost soul.   (*CP*, 107)

Frost sometimes expressed his conception of metaphor as an instrumental ordering principle against chaos, as he did in "Letter to *The Amherst Student*." Notice his retreat, though, from the sublime language of terror into the twinkling language of pleasure in the small, well-made thing. He appears to enjoy the challenge of hugeness and confusion, probably underscored by such an adjective as "utter." He also enjoys digging at humanists and Platonists dissatisfied with art as less than so-called eternal forms:

> The background is hugeness and confusion shading away from where we stand into black and utter chaos; and against the background any small man-made figure of order and concentration. What pleasanter than that this should be so? Unless we are novelists or economists we don't worry about this confusion; we look out on it with an instrument or tackle it or reduce it. It is partly because we are afraid it might prove too much for us and our blend of democratic-republican-socialist-communist-anarchist party. But it is more because we like it, we were born to it, born used to it and have practical reasons for wanting it there. To me any little form I assert upon it is velvet, as the saying is, and to be considered for how much more it is than nothing. If I were a Platonist I should have to consider it, I suppose, for how much less it is than everything. (*CP*, 115)

The poem itself, then, became Frost's figure or metaphor of life and love. In his 1939 preface "The Figure a Poem Makes," Frost adds another important concept to the conversation: "clarification" (related to a word that he had used in the poem that prefaced all his books, "The Pasture": "And wait to watch the water clear I may" and that he would take as the title for his last book, *In the Clearing*). A poem ends "in a clarification of life . . . not necessarily a great clarification . . . but in a momentary stay against confusion":

> The figure a poem makes. It begins in delight and ends in wisdom. The figure is the same as for love. No one can really hold that the ecstasy should be static and stand still in one place. It begins in delight, it inclines to the impulse, it assumes direction with the first line laid down, it runs a course of lucky events, and ends in a clarification of life – not necessarily a great clarification, such as sects and cults are founded on, but in a momentary stay against confusion.   (*CP*, 131–132)

Some of Frost's poems appear to be metaphors or to focus on metaphors, others take on more the quality of synecdoche. Taken in the context of other poems they have an ulteriority and suggest bigger things than at first they may seem to do. "The Rose Family," for example, begins with a play on a line from Gertrude Stein, "a rose is a rose is a rose," and the realist notion from Shakespeare that "a rose by any other name would smell as sweet." But as Frost's poem goes, matters of analogy become more complex:

> The rose is a rose,
> And was always a rose.
> But the theory now goes
> That the apple's a rose,
> And the pear is, and so's
> The plum, I suppose.
> The dear only knows
> What will next prove a rose.
> You, of course, are a rose –
> But were always a rose.

Frost's knowledge of botany and taxonomy tells him (and us) that not only by analogy but by biological descent, the apple is a member of the rose family and so are other fruit. The tree of knowledge is a shadowy figure in the poem growing in uncertain directions and making eternal correspondences unstable. Against this, the poet asserts to his beloved "You, of course, are a rose – / But were always a rose."

The problem of analogy appeared to have been troubling Frost by the 1920s. "The Door in the Dark," another poem in *West-Running Brook*, also focuses on the problem rift between the mind and the world in making analogies:

> In going from room to room in the dark,
> I reached out blindly to save my face,
> But neglected, however lightly, to lace
> My fingers and close my arms in an arc.
> A slim door got in past my guard,
> And hit me a blow in the head so hard
> I had my native simile jarred.
> So people and things don't pair any more
> With what they used to pair with before.

This highly skeptical little drama of trying to make analogies by going blindly around in the dark also resonates with the title poem, "West-Running Brook," in which a couple who seem to be lost first attempt to locate themselves and, in the process, name a brook. But the naming process may be entirely circular.

We may ask what really prompts the woman to ask the initial question "where is north?" More important, with what real certainty does Fred answer the question and claim the brook runs west? She then names brooks, and we get a parenthetical comment from the narrator that "*men call it*" by that name today. But is that any indication that the brook actually runs west?

> "Fred, where is north?"
>
> 　　　　　　"North? North is there, my love.
> The brook runs west."
>
> 　　　　　　"West-running Brook then call it."
> (West-running Brook men call it to this day.)
> "What does it think it's doing running west
> When all the other country brooks flow east
> To reach the ocean? It must be the brook
> Can trust itself to go by contraries
> The way I can with you – and you with me –
> Because we're – we're – I don't know what we are.
> What are we?"

The naming process sets a profound dialogue in motion about contraries; about contraries between Fred and his love. Their correspondence with each other may be as delicate, tentative, and shifting as language's shifting representation of an already fluid reality. The poem begins and ends with a dialogue again about naming, reminding each other that so much of what is real may be what is said to be real.

Pastoral

Frost's work plays in and out of ancient literary traditions in subtle ways. He wrote poems distinctly in the pastoral and georgic mode, and it is useful to recognize some of these traditions at work in his poetry. His dialogue with the tradition became but one way of creating meaning.[6] Discussions of pastoral literature usually focus on classical origins in the Hellenistic era and the Sicilian poet Theocritus, who drew on the folk traditions of Sicilian shepherds. Centuries later, the Roman poet Virgil developed the tradition of Theocritus and also of Bion and wrote his *Eclogues*, ten beautifully crafted poems on rustic and bucolic subjects, including the competition of shepherds, the loss, and love. There has been much detailed scholarly discussion about what constitutes the essence of pastoral. One important element has been the presence of shepherds or rustic figures. Perhaps more important has been the idea of a *locus amoenus* or "beautiful place," often an idealized pasture or garden set in contrast to the sophistication or corruption of the city. It should of course be understood that any such conception almost always implies an existing sense of estrangement or loss and a gentrified person's fascination with return to a state of relative simplicity or, perhaps, innocence. For the Greeks, this state was known as Arcadia and governed by the god Pan. In the Judeo-Christian tradition, representations alternate among Eden, the pasture, and versions of purifying desert and wilderness.

The longing for a past which may have never existed and therefore is itself part of a powerfully imagined present can be the source of great art. The tension between the remnants of the past and our imagination of them gives power to pastoral art. One of the dramatic motifs of pastoral literature has been described as "escape," or the desire to escape the boundaries of the corrupt or civilized world and enter or return to the world of innocence in the *locus amoenus*. However, one can regard the movement synchronically as "escape" or, perhaps, as "retreat," the latter implying a return to the life of the country from the life of the city or one of sophistication. (One meaning of "sophistication" is adulteration, so return to the country can be associated with purity as well as simplicity.)

Perhaps an even more troubling question evoked by pastoral art becomes the possibility of attaining, achieving, or maintaining innocence at all. What does the natural, devoid of the corruptions of civilization, hold? It became a more intense hope of some thinkers after Rousseau that man could be liberated from the bonds and corruptions of civilization and delivered back to the purity of the natural. To what extent, however, can nature be said to be either pure or liberating? Wordsworth came to believe, following Marvell's transcendent vision of a "green thought in a green shade" of "The Garden," in a deep consonance between the mind of man and the natural world:

> Speaking of nothing more than what we are –
> How exquisitely the individual Mind
> (And the progressive powers perhaps no less
> Of the whole species) to the external world
> Is fitted; and how exquisitely too –
> Theme this little heard of among men –
> The external world is fitted to the mind;
> And the creation (by no lower name
> Can it be called) which they with blended might
> Accomplish.

Frost lived in and confronted the complexities of the post-Darwinian world. Man's "mind" had been created from the rest of nature and, as part of it, may possess an uncertain ability in deciphering the world. The delicate, reciprocal relationship between mind and nature in Frost becomes beautifully dramatized in "Tree at My Window." The tree comes to the speaker's attention from outside but also holds the possibility of becoming a "window tree," a portal to seeing. Yet not "all" its "tongues talking aloud / Could be profound." Yet both the mind's inner world of dreams and the tree's outer world obey conditions of existence, "weather":

> That day she put our heads together,
> Fate had her imagination about her,
> Your head so much concerned with outer,
> Mine with inner, weather.

What can we know of nature and of the country? Is nature itself inherently innocent or a blank upon which we project our wishes and fantasies? To what extent is nature a creation of civilization, an externalization of man, dependent upon human projections and the inscription of human language? Frost appeared to explore such problems in many of his poems, both narratives and lyrics.

From the outset, Frost's poetry plays with the conventions and questions of pastoral in profound and interesting ways. "Into My Own" and "Ghost House," the first two poems of *A Boy's Will*, raise the pastoral themes of retreat and *locus amoenus* but in peculiar ways that add to the tradition. In "Into My Own," the speaker expresses only his wish to "steal away, / Fearless of ever finding open land, / Or highway where the slow wheel pours the sand." The wilderness of the forest fascinates him but he also appears as much interested in threatening or at least wondering whether those who love him would seek him. And he concludes by suggesting if not a return, an experience that would leave him unchanged:

> I do not see why I should e'er turn back,
> Or those should not set forth upon my track
> To overtake me, who should miss me here
> And long to know if still I held them dear.
>
> They would not find me changed from him they knew –
> Only more sure of all I thought was true.

"Ghost House," the poem that follows "Into My Own," meditates upon a landscape of extinction. It is a keynote poem in the book and for Frost's work generally because what it describes so haunts his work. The speaker has situated himself in the cellar of a vanished house: it and the farm of which it was once a part are now part of a wilderness that has grown back. He describes the fences in the first line of the second stanza as "ruined" but characterizes the now overgrown footpath as "healed":

> O'er ruined fences the grapevines shield
> The woods come back to the mowing field;
>> The orchard tree has grown one copse
>> Of new wood and old where the woodpecker chops;
> The footpath down to the well is healed.

There is an emotional ambivalence about where he is, though it is hard to tell whether from his imagined sense of loss of the house and the lives or from his own estrangement from others:

> I dwell with a strangely aching heart
> In that vanished abode there far apart
>> On that disused and forgotten road
>> That has no dust-bath now for the toad.

The life in the country bears a *memento mori*, a remembrance of death, yet even the names have become obscured by growth:

> It is under the small, dim, summer star.
> I know not who these mute folk are
>> Who share the unlit place with me –
>> These stones under the low-limbed tree
> Doubtless bear names that the mosses mar.

He must, instead, imagine love starting fertile life somehow surviving and starting anew despite the recognition from the past that the future leads to oblivion. One wonders what in the speaker's life would be such, "in view of how many things," would make these ghostly companions "as sweet . . . as might be had":

> They are tireless folk, but slow and sad,
> Though two, close-keeping, are lass and lad,–
>> With none among them that ever sings,
>> And yet, in view of how many things,
> As sweet companions as might be had.

So many Frost poems meditate upon the fragility of the home, looking synchronically and diachronically into the lives of forgotten and abandoned rural New England. Frost's focus was particularly poignant as New England farm populations were dwindling rapidly at the end of the nineteenth and the beginning of the twentieth century, abandoning farm life, and moving increasingly into urban areas. "Ghost House" strikes a chord that Frost will develop in many poems including "The Generations of Men," "Home Burial," "In the Home Stretch," "The Black Cottage," "The Wood Pile," "The Need of Being Versed in Country Things," "The Census Taker," "A Fountain, a Bottle, a Donkey's Ears and Some Books," and, "Directive." All of these poems evoke the loss or abandonment of home, the threat and fragility of human life with extinction, and the difficulty of country life.

A Boy's Will provides differing *loci amoenae*, each erotically charged in a different way. "Rose Pogonias," takes us far off the civilized path to "A saturated meadow, / Sun-shaped and jewel-small, / A circle scarcely wider / Than the trees around were tall . . ." In this little paradise of a bog has sprung "a thousand" of the delicate "bearded lady" orchids, also known as rose pogonias. The speaker, perhaps with his lover or perhaps with a fellow worker, treats the spot as holy, to be left untouched "in the general mowing," by which perhaps more is suggested than the literal harvest:

> We raised a simple prayer
>   Before we left the spot,
> That in the general mowing
>   That place might be forgot;
> Or if not all so favored,
>   Obtain such grace of hours,
> That none should mow the grass there
>   While so confused with flowers.

One might ask of the final line whether the place or the mowers may be the ones "confused" with flowers. Be that as may be, the orchid came to occupy a special place in Frost's imagination. Hardly an unusual preoccupation in the late nineteenth or early twentieth century, the fascination with orchids became associated with obsessions with rare beauty. Orchid hunters would go to great lengths to find and preserve rare and beautiful breeds. Frost made a point that he was interested in wild orchids and not in the cultivation of orchids for sale. But orchids in the nineteenth century also came to represent the scientific aspect of botany. Darwin's famous study of orchids initiated all those who studied wild flowers in the knowledge that beauty was part of the engine for the dissemination of seeds. "Rose Pogonias" has the feel less of something religious than of submission to the inevitable worship and heat of the erotic.

The steamy bog temple of "Rose Pogonias" has a sultry quality. Seasons cycle in *A Boy's Will* and the possibility of a *locus amoenus* appears to fade. It may not be the change in season, alone, that produces some skepticism about the pastoral. The double perspective always appears present in Frost as in "The Vantage Point." The sonnet surprises even within the octave: we learn that when "tired of trees," and seeking mankind, he does so at a distance. What he sees of mankind brings homes into focus with graves:

> If tired of trees I seek again mankind,
>> Well I know where to hie me – in the dawn,
>> To a slope where the cattle keep the lawn.
> There amid the lolling juniper reclined,
> Myself unseen, I see in white defined
>> Far off the homes of men, and farther still,
>> The graves of men on an opposing hill,
> Living or dead, whichever are to mind.

His restlessness with even this distance turns with the sestet. What kind of alternative does nature provide? Noonday heat has for centuries been a trope of the moment of contemplation for the pastoral poet. Here it has the quality of something more actual and empirical: a sun-burned hillside. The poem ends with three sensuous acts, the last of which appears to call attention to an almost lunar insect analogy to the dwellings of men:

> And if by noon I have too much of these,
>> I have but to turn my arm, and lo,
>> The sun-burned hillside sets my face aglow,
> My breathing shakes the bluet like a breeze,
>> I smell the earth, I smell the bruised plant,
>> I look into the crater of the ant.

Pan had been the classical god of the pastoral world, a figure empowered through his erotic power and his skill at piping to transform the world around him. In the mysterious lyric "Pan with Us," Frost depicts the god emerging from the woods satisfied at the remoteness of the pasture he surveys:

> He stood in the zephyr, pipes in hand,
> On a height of naked pasture land;
> In all the country he did command
>> He saw no smoke and he saw no roof.
>> That was well! and he stamped a hoof.

But something causes him to "toss his pipes," perhaps satisfied with the sounds of birds, perhaps dissatisfied with the remoteness of anyone else to teach:

> He tossed his pipes, too hard to teach
> A new-world song, far out of reach,
> For a sylvan sign that the blue jay's screech
>> And the whimper of hawks beside the sun
>> Were music enough for him, for one.

The elusive and pressing question is what is meant by "a new-world song"? By "new-world" does Frost mean America and its preoccupations with industry as opposed to art and play? Or does he mean something more general and perhaps figurative by "new-world," one indifferent to thinking about pagan gods in nature and more about empirical facts, chance, and the "new terms of worth" of science? The landscape with which the poem concludes no longer seems fertile but "sun-burned," and deeply subjected to the forces of the elements:

> Times were changed from what they were:
> Such pipes kept less of power to stir
> The fruited Dough of the juniper
>   And the fragile bluets clustered there
>   Than the merest aimless breath of air.
>
> They were pipes of pagan mirth,
> And the world had found new terms of worth.
> He laid him down on the sun-burned earth
>   And ravelled a flower and looked away –
>   Play? Play? – What should he play?

The repetition of "play" in the final line underscores an important aspect of pastoral thought, the realm of play in opposition to labor and struggle, "work and play," "*labor* and *otium*." But Frost's poetry dramatizes as much the world of labor as it does of play and often seems to struggle to bridge those two seemingly incommensurate realms. This blending of work and play has an ancient tradition, too, that extends as far back as Hesiod's *Theogony* and, most particularly, to Virgil's four extended poems about farming, the *Georgics*. The *Georgics* may be about farming on one level but suggest much more about politics, history, and man's place in nature. In those poems, too, no clear boundary exists between contemplation and labor. In Virgil's Second *Georgic*, he extols the life of the farmer, the explorer-scientists who would investigate the causes of things, and the contemplative who knows the gods of the countryside. Virgil embraces somewhat the Epicureanism that would form the basis of the great Roman poem of Lucretius *De Rerum Natura*, "On the Nature of Things." Lucretius tends to deflate the romanticized and rustic tales of Pan in favor of naturalized explanations of a completely material universe:

> I have observed places tossing back six or seven utterances when you have launched a single one: with the tendency to rebound, the words were reverberated and reiterated from hill to hill. According to local legend, these places were haunted by goat-footed Satyrs and Nymphs. Tales are told of Fauns, whose noisy revels and merry pranks shatter the mute hush of night for miles around; of twanging lyre strings and

> plaintive melodies pouted out by flutes at the touch of the players' finger; of music far-heard by the country-folk when Pan, tossing the pine-branches that wreathe his brutish head, runs his arched lips again and again along the wind-mouthed reeds, so that the pipe's wildwood rhapsody flows unbroken. Many such fantasies are related by rustics. Perhaps, in boasting of these marvels, they hope to dispel the notion that they live in a backwood abandoned by the gods. Perhaps they have some other motive, since mankind everywhere has greedy ears for such romancing.[7]

Whatever diminishment Pan suffers in "Pan with Us," it may be part of a worldview that recognizes the difficulty of the landscape and the environment, the sun-burned earth, the struggle of screeching blue jays or whimpering hawks, or the force of wind and rain. We may also discuss what kind of "demiurge" may be at work in "The Demiurge's Laugh." In "Mowing," perhaps the most remarkable sonnet of *A Boy's Will*, Frost's pastoral music-making comes through labor. He introduces work as an inextricable part of contemplation and knowledge. In this particular poem, the work and the sound it produces are solitary and of the speaker's own making. Its meaning seems mysterious to him. The silence, related to the intense heat, and the fact of difficult labor, distinguish this pastoral dream from "the easy gold at hand of fay or elf" of contemplative rustics.

Frost's poetry draws the reader into a rustic, mysterious, and, to a large extent, lost New England landscape. Frost's New England – particularly New Hampshire and Vermont – may be both part real and part invented. Place names – Bow, Coos, Lancaster, Woodsville, and Mount Hor – beguile us with their literary and mythic resonances. One would not want to say that the worlds of *North of Boston* and *Mountain Interval* are imagined landscapes; Frost's vanishing, turn-of-the-twentieth-century New England could be recognized by many. But it begins with the local and extends widely beyond itself. Frost once said that he "first heard the speaking voice in poetry in Virgil's *Eclogues*," a group of ten dialogues or dramatic monologues of shepherds dwelling in Arcadia, a land of innocence and beauty. Virgil's *Eclogues* stand in decided contrast to his great poem of empire and heroic power, the *Aeneid*. They also complement another important set of his poems, the *Georgics*, which appear to be four treatises on farming but which also have allegorical significance, particularly in the realm of politics. Ezra Pound shrewdly called Frost's poems "modern georgics," and he no doubt was referring to the overarching themes of labor and work, usually associated with georgics as opposed to pastoral poems or eclogues, which are more often associated with contemplation.

Was there something political in his choice to write primarily in the pastoral mode? It might be asked why a poet of Frost's energy and skill did not write epic poetry (a question often asked of modern poets). Frost wrote in the mode of Virgil's *Eclogues* and *Georgics*. In a dialogue with the English Poet Laureate Cecil Day Lewis, Frost wrote of the significance of the hero in poetry but emphasized what he called "the unconsidered person":

> *Day Lewis*: And I suppose that anyone who is going to write a narrative poem now has to have the kind of interest in human beings that often comes out as hero-worship.
> *Frost*: That's it. It is hero-worship, you see, and one of the things that makes you go is making a hero out of somebody else had never noticed was a hero . . . You pick up the unconsidered person.
> *Day Lewis*: Yes, and of course that is what gossip does, in a small community: it makes heroes, doesn't it – or villains – out of our neighbors? But they're big anyway.
> *Frost*: Yes . . . (*I*, 176)

Frost thought of the intimacy of gossip about the unconsidered person as a new way or rather *his* way of writing narrative poetry about heroes, and many of the narrative poems from *North of Boston* blend elements of pastoral and georgic traditions to depict these characters.

Writing in the pastoral mode, authors from Theocritus and Virgil to Dante and Milton as well as Wordsworth and Thoreau have explored questions of human equality, man's place in nature, and the nature of faith. Though focused on country life or rural life, both pastoral and georgic have long been known as modes written by and appealing to those of immense learning and sophistication. It should not be surprising that pastoral and georgic modes consider the country from the perspective of those who live in or at least have had some experience of the city. A tension between city and country, innocence of one kind and experience or learning and sophistication of another, has always been a part of the pastoral and georgic mode.

The pastoral has had an important place in American ideology but by no means a singular meaning. The puritan pursuit of renewal through rebellion against ecclesiastical corruption invokes what may be called a pastoral longing for perfection through simplicity. Thomas Jefferson praised the way of agrarianism, echoing Greek ideals of the independent farmer. Frost's complex version of the pastoral does not involve a complete retreat into wilderness (one version), nor a faith in pure agrarianism, nor social reform. He once said, distinguishing himself from Thoreau's version of the pastoral: "I am not a 'back-to-the-lander.' I am not interested in the Thoreau business. Only a few can do what Thoreau did. We must use the modern tools at our disposal" (*I*, 78). Shortly after his *Collected Poems* were published in 1930, Frost affirmed the relationship of his poetry to a fundamental pastoral ideal, the praise of rustic over urban life:

> Poetry is more often of the country than of the city. Poetry is very, very rural – rustic . . . It might be taken as a symbol of a man, taking its rise from individuality and seclusion – written first for the person that writes and then going out into its social appeal and use. Just so the race lives best to itself – first to itself, storing strength in the more individual life of the country, of the farm – then going to market in the industrial city. (*I*, 75–76)

Frost saw an analogy between the development of poetry, the individual, and the society from the nascent and isolated world of the country to the more sophisticated or adulterated, world of the city.

The poems may raise questions though of how one should take the rustic world of New England and to consider the reality of that world. The turn-of-the-twentieth-century New England in which Frost wrote was hardly an idyllic place. Beautiful though it may have been then and now, it was hardly an idyllic place for farmers, particularly independent farmers. The independent, hillside farms that characterized much of Vermont in the popular imagination declined to only six percent of the total state farms by 1930. In the first decades of the new century, one could commonly see abandoned farms or run-down independent farms near run-down communities in contrast to the growing number of farms that had given themselves over to larger production of meat, fruit, and vegetable agricultural operations. Scientific management of agriculture as well as such movements as Theodore Roosevelt's Commission on Country Life, convened in 1908, attempted to restore a healthful agricultural world to a now fading and increasingly impoverished backwater New England. Further, a strong tourist industry developed that sold a nostalgic world "North of Boston," and many living in New Hampshire and Vermont were encouraged to board people and keep up appearances for those visiting with high expectations. Frost living in the midst of these changes witnessed the dissonance between the way New England was imagined by outsiders and the way it was in its deepest recesses, filled with all manner of tensions – economic, racial, domestic. It is important to keep this context in mind when reading "A Servant to Servants," "The Mountain," "The Self-Seeker," "A Hundred Collars," "Blueberries," "The Ax-Helve," or "The Generations of Men," where we see real rural isolation, pain, suffering, racial tension, and madness.

By 1930, Frost definitely regretted the tendency toward industrialization in farming and the loss of independent farms:

> We are now at a moment when we are getting too far out into the social-industrial and are at the point of drawing back – drawing back in to renew ourselves. The country life we are going back to I can't describe in advance, but I am pretty sure it will not be the country life we came out of years ago. Farming, what survives of it, has demeaned itself in an attempt to imitate industrialism. It has lost its self-respect. It has wished itself other than what it is.   (*I*, 76)

Frost's pointed attack on this renewal was the ultimate lack of integrity it created within the culture. Echoing the puritanical language of Nathaniel Hawthorne, he stated "That is the only unpardonable sin: to wish you are something you are not, something other people are. It is so in the arts and in everything else" (*I*, 76). The only psychological solution for Frost appeared to be a severe retreat. "I think a person has to be withdrawn into himself to gather inspiration so that he is somebody when he comes out again among folks – when he 'comes to market' with himself. He learns that he's got to be almost wastefully alone" (*I*, 76). The theme "waste" recurs frequently in Frost, and one should consider carefully what he means by being "wastefully alone." Frost expresses here a complex version of a traditional pastoral topos of retreat. "The farm is a base of operations – a stronghold. You can withdraw into yourself there" (*I*, 76). But Frost had a sense of limits to retreating into that stronghold. "If a man is wastefully alone, he should be better company when he comes out . . . The real thing that you do is a lonely thing. And remember the paradox that you become more social in order that you may become more of an individual" (*I*, 78).

Frost's published poems appear to be framed by poems embodying the pastoral mythology of retreat. His signature poem "The Pasture," with its refrain, "I shan't be long," prefaced his collected and complete poems. The phrase in that poem "and wait to watch the water clear I may" became the keynote for his final volume, *In the Clearing* (1962), as well as for an important concept in Frost's notion of what a poem does in providing "a clarification of life but not a great clarification such as sects and cults are founded on." The concluding poem of *In the Clearing* also provides a powerful image of retreat and being "wastefully alone":

> In winter in the woods alone
> Against the trees I go.
> I mark a maple for my own
> And lay the maple low.

. . .
I see for Nature no defeat
In one tree's overthrow
Or for myself in my retreat
For yet another blow.

One might ask whether "nature" and "defeat" includes both the tree's "over-throw" (battle-rich metaphors) and the speaker's retreat from cutting down the maple (one kind of blow) as well as from one of life's blows that sends him returning to the woods for yet another maple?

Is this cutting down the maple an act of labor or one of pleasure? The question seems beside the point in this poem or perhaps the answer is obvious – it is both. In "Two Tramps in Mud Time," one of Frost's most famous and controversial poems about the relationship of labor and leisure, the narrator also contemplates the meaning of striking blows for pleasure with his axe. It is one of a number of poems that Frost wrote in the 1930s, including "Build Soil: A Political Pastoral," that drew strong criticism for their apparent stance against the New Deal.

Much of the criticism directed against Frost came from his lack of political activism and his obvious irritation with much of the New Deal. For those whose sympathies became directed toward the plight of the poor and, from the poor, toward socialism, Frost appeared in his poetry and in his other statements to be indifferent, if not cruel. Frost certainly was not a political activist, and his attitude toward the New Deal seemed to stem from a variety of attitudes about human history and human nature. First, he thought it arrogant to assume that any age was the worst in human history, something he articulated strongly in the "Letter to *The Amherst Student*" (1935). Second, he refused to regard the poor as an oppressed group morally superior to the rich. His temperament was to distrust, if not hate, all classes and to be contemptuous of all forms of power taken to extremes:

> The New Deal has so dealt as to demonstrate incontrovertibly that the rich are all bad. I have lived with the poor and know that they are greedy and dishonest – in a word bad. Take my word for it . . . So much for the upper and the lower end. Both the upper and lower class are bad. There is left the middle class to consider. But the middle class is the bourgeoisie, our favorite black beast, that has been tried and found out by all the literature of the last fifty years. Communists and all the intelligentsia are agreed that the middle class is bad. Both ends then and the middle – they are all bad. We are arrived at a conclusion that means nothing. When all is bad it makes no difference whether it is called good or bad. Be it all called good and lets start over. (*N*, 47)

Frost could not see any merit to the notion of dialectical materialism or of progress, given his assumption of the inherent badness of all classes, including the oppressed. In another notebook entry he wrote, "Don't talk to me about getting rid of poverty. All principles are bad except as they are checked in *about* mid career by contrary principles" (*N*, 35). This kind of thinking produced such editorial poems in *A Witness Tree* as "An Equalizer" and "A Semi-Revolution." Frost's objection to the attempts of cosmic justice were that they might, of course, create injustice: "Handicapping needed if the human race is to be a race of justice and mercy. Mercy to the weak is handicapping the strong" (*N*, 485). In a 1937 address, *Poverty and Poetry*, Frost asked the question "What *is* the relationship between poverty and poetry?" He used the Bible, specifically the New Testament, for an answer. Frost always regarded the New Testament as a book focused on both mercy and the poor. But in this instance, he referred to something Jesus says in Matthew and elsewhere, "The poor you will always have with you but you will not always have me," as an argument against too much focus on the poor and poverty in poetry:

> But what *is* the relation of poverty and poetry? I know once in
> self-defense I did come near to swearing. It says in the Bible, you think –
> I don't – it says in the Bible that you always have the poor with you. That
> isn't what it says. It says, "For Christ's sake, forget the poor some of the
> time." There are many beautiful things in the world besides poverty. I
> have praised poverty and spoken of its beauty and its use for the arts, but
> there are other things.   (*CPPP*, 761)

The poems of *A Further Range*, particularly "Two Tramps in Mud Time," "A Lone Striker," and "A Roadside Stand," and "Provide, Provide," appear to address most directly the ethos of the New Deal but some of them have been read with little subtlety and often with too much focus on political context. The speaker of "Two Tramps in Mud Time" has been all-too readily identified with Frost because of the strength of his rhetoric and the memorable summation uniting vocation and avocation by which he hopes to live:

> But yield who will to their separation,
> My object in living is to unite
> My avocation and my vocation
> As my two eyes make one in sight.
> Only where love and need are one,
> And the work is play for mortal stakes,
> Is the deed ever really done
> For Heaven and the future's sakes.

The problem of uniting work and play, *labor* and *otium*, has always been one of the great challenges of pastoral thought and human life. What readers and critics seemed to find objectionable is the speaker's attitude toward the two tramps and their need to work for pay. The entire poem, however, is about balance, between seasons and between men and between "love" and "need." He admits that theirs "was the better right." The fact that he has to admit this may trouble some, especially in an era when so many suffered from unemployment. Frost does not give us an uncomplicated speaker untroubled by irony. The speaker somewhat condescendingly presumes to know what the two tramps are all about but assumes that they don't know his motives. Does he know himself that well? We find him splitting wood as a kind of ethical activity of "self-control" but the purpose remains ambiguous:

> Good blocks of oak it was I split,
> As large around as the chopping block;
> And every piece I squarely hit
> Fell splinterless as cloven rock.
> The blows that a life of self-control
> Spares to strike for the common good
> That day, giving a loose to my soul,
> I spent on the unimportant wood.

We might ask what does the speaker really think is best for "the common good" – striking blows or sparing to strike them? Why? Is it because all human action is ultimately suspect, possibly violent? His chopping the wood as he does may be a way of displacing such violence. At this moment, "mud time," he tells us "Be glad of water, but don't forget / The lurking frost in the earth beneath / That will steal forth after the sun is set / And show on the water its crystal teeth."

In "A Roadside Stand," a tonally complex poem, the problem of poverty in the New Deal appears from the side of the country poor and an observer. The "roadside stand" is both a fruit and vegetable stand ignored by city drivers and a figure of a last "stand" against absolute poverty doomed to failure. An extremely dark stanza describes the beneficent plans to bring these impoverished poor into the city according to a welfare plan, as merely "calculated to soothe them out of their wits," presumably by destroying their impetus to work and think:

> It is in the news that all these pitiful kin
> Are to be bought out and mercifully gathered in
> To live in villages next to the theater and store
> Where they won't have to think for themselves any more;

> While greedy good-doers, beneficent beasts of prey,
> Swarm over their lives enforcing benefits
> That are calculated to soothe them out of their wits,
> And by teaching them how to sleep the sleep all day,
> Destroy their sleeping at night the ancient way.

As cruel as the narrator sounds, he concludes the poem with a cruel cancellation of both the country-folk's pain and then his own cruelty, which he has recognized as nearly insane:

> I can't help owning the great relief it would be
> To put these people at one stroke out of their pain.
> And then next day as I come back into the sane,
> I wonder how I should like you to come to me
> And offer to put me gently out of my pain.

Frost had little sympathy for, and deep suspicions of, the enforced ideals of the New Deal. But he also thought about the problem of human suffering from a broad historical perspective and with a strong sense of the limitations and irony of his own perspective.

The poignancy of "A Roadside Stand" or "Two Tramps in Mud Time" foregrounds an important aspect of the pastoral in Frost that can be illuminated by William Empson's definition of the mode: "the process of putting the complex into the simple."[8] Empson's view of the pastoral had little to do with landscape and more to do with social amelioration and politics, observing that "the essential trick of the old pastoral, which was felt to imply a beautiful relationship between rich and poor, was to make simple people express strong feelings (felt as the most universal subject, something fundamentally true about everybody) in learned and fashionable language." By this analysis, Frost would hardly be "old pastoral." The characters of Frost's narratives are rarely simple. One could hardly call their language learned or fashionable but it often rises to extraordinary eloquence. It may be that we expect them to be simple or straightforward. Frost himself had a genius for fooling people in his work with the appearance of both approachability and simplicity. Whether it be the speaker of "Mending Wall," the farmer of "The Mountain," Lafe of "A Hundred Collars," Baptiste of "The Ax-Helve," or the old woman of "The Witch of Coos," Frost's "rustics" beguile and often baffle their interlocutors. They rise to sharp levels of eloquence and insight which often makes fools of their citified interlocutors. But simple they are not. Frost appears to enjoy the pleasure of how those often taken not to mean much can subvert or undermine the unsuspecting and the witless, no matter what their level of education. The expectation of a beautiful relationship that the speaker hopes for in "The Tuft of Flowers" may be found almost nowhere else in Frost. Almost all other relationships suffer severely from tentativeness, volatility, potential violence, and threat. The possibility of retreat and return to simplicity, consonance with a humanly comprehensible nature, consonance with a fellow humanity, and peace within and without the home all give way in Frost to the subversion and instability of hierarchy, and perpetual loss and struggle to restore order, and an implacable sense of human loneliness in a universe that resists our attempts to project our ideals upon it.

"Men work together"

Though *A Boy's Will*, Frost's first book, consisted primarily of short lyrics, *North of Boston*, his second, developed the complexities of the pastoral in narrative poems of remarkable variety, tonal range, dramatic compression, and psychological depth. As he composed *North of Boston*, Frost revealed to F. S. Flint his concern with generic variety within the pastoral mode:

> You may infer from a list of my subjects how I have tried to get variety in material. I have the following poems in something like shape for my next book:
>
> 1. The Death of the Hired Man – an elegy
> 2. The Hundred Collars – a comedy
> 3. The Black Cottage – a monologue
> 4. The Housekeeper – a tragedy
> 5. The Code – Heroics, a yarn
> 6. The Mountain, a description
> 7. Arrival Home, an idyl
> 8. Blueberries, an eclogue
>
> But variety of material will not excuse me for lack of it in treatment.[9]

He continued to publish these dramatic eclogues and georgics in his subsequent books – *Mountain Interval, New Hampshire*, and *West-Running Brook* – though those subsequent volumes contained many more shorter lyrics. In fact, *North of Boston* has only one lyric that "intones," namely "After Apple-Picking." Their characters inhabit a local world little known and not readily accessible to all readers, even if the ultimate insights into their suffering radiate out and touch a much greater human world. The form of these longer poems varies from appearing as strongly dramatic with significant though relatively subtle intrusion of the narrator, such as "Home Burial," "The Fear," or "The Death of the Hired Man," to poems that work as hybrids of narrative, drama, and dialogue with several voices, such as "Snow" and "The Self-Seeker," or dramatic narratives in which the narrator may play a significant role, such as "The Housekeeper," "The Grindstone," "The Ax-Helve," or "A Fountain, a Bottle, a Donkey's Ears and Some Books." Frost also wrote a number of stunning narrative poems and dramatic monologues, such as "Paul's Wife," "The Pauper Witch of Grafton," and, perhaps best of all, "A Servant to Servants." The nuances of the forms of these poems, the way they tell stories and reveal characters, and from which emerge moments of elevated lyric tell us a great deal about Frost's full sense of the poetic universe, one which is always charged by the give and take of human relationships, the desirability of maintaining boundaries, as well as our ultimate inability to maintain them.

The drama often centers on an object which becomes a synecdoche or form teasing or drawing out the relationships between the speakers or conflicting characters of the poem. Their ability to understand that thing – a tuft of flowers, a wall, a cellar hole, an ax-helve, a grindstone, a brook, or a house or home itself – becomes inextricably bound to their ability to understand one another. The poems penetrate to the limits of individuality and the demands of community in the creation of meaning. Frost's dramatic poems often allow outsiders to "see what we were up to sooner and better than ourselves," as the characters move each other and us subtly toward psychological revelation:

> The ruling passion in man is not as Viennese as is claimed. It is rather a gregarious instinct to keep together by minding each other's business. Grex rather than sex. We *must* be preserved from becoming egregious. The beauty of socialism is that it will end the individuality that is always crying out mind your own business. Terence's answer would be all human business is my business. No more invisible means of support, no more invisible motives, no more invisible anything. The ultimate commitment is giving in to it that an outsider may see what we were up to sooner and better than we ourselves . . . Every poem is an epitome of the great predicament; a figure of the will braving alien entanglements. (*CP*, 147–148)

As an artist, Frost sought to capture the human voice as a means to understanding drama. "I like the actuality of gossip, the intimacy of it," he wrote in 1914, discussing the importance of tones of speech, "Say what you will effects of actuality and intimacy . . . gives the thrill of sincerity. A story must always release a meaning more readily to those who read than life itself as it goes ever releases meaning" (*SL*, 159). As he moved from *A Boy's Will* to his second book, he originally thought of calling it "New England Eclogues" (*SL*, 89). In an unpublished expanded preface to *North of Boston,* Frost reiterated his interest in Virgil, noting that the book

> was written as scattered poems in a form suggested by the eclogues of Virgil. Beginning with one about Julius Caesar in the year I was reading about Aenius and Meliboeus, luckily (I consider) in no vain attempt to Anglicize Virgil's versification, dactylic hexameter. It gathered itself together in retrospect and found a name for itself in the real estate advertising of the *Boston Globe . . .* Some of them are a little nearer one act plays than eclogues but they seem to have something in common that I don't want to seek a better name for. I like it's being locative. (*CPPP,* 849)

Frost explored the intimacy of human psychology and the tensions between labor and contemplation as well as the anxiety of human inequality and strife in an idyllic and remote world.

One sees the highly dramatic impulse in all of Frost's lyrics. But the desire of one farmer to speak deeply to the heart of another and to challenge boundaries of solitude and power becomes a definite theme in the early lyric of *A Boy's Will,* "The Tuft of Flowers." The loneliness or perhaps solitude of the mower's "scythe whispering to the ground" in "Mowing," becomes the impetus for a meditation on the community of labor in "The Tuft of Flowers." The speaker, a farmer who rakes hay, imagines that the mower has spared the flowers because he, too, recognizes their value beyond the grass that must be cut down. By chance, a butterfly, seeking nectar, draws the speaker's attention to the flowers, and he hesitantly imagines why they had been spared:

> I thought of questions that have no reply,
> And would have turned to toss the grass to dry;
>
> But he turned first, and led my eye to look
> At a tall tuft of grass flowers beside a brook,
>
> A leaping tongue of bloom the scythe had spared
> Beside a reedy brook the scythe had bared.
>
> The mower in the dew had loved them thus,
> By leaving them to flourish, not for us,
>
> Nor yet to draw one thought of ours to him,
> But from sheer morning gladness at the brim.

By simply imagining the mower's "sheer morning gladness at the brim," the speaker can perceive, though not state, "a message from the dawn," and can hear the mower's "long scythe whispering the ground" and "feel a spirit kindred to my own." No longer feeling that men are inevitably "alone," "whether they work together or apart," the speaker can imagine a dialogue of "brotherly speech":

> And dreaming, as it were, held brotherly speech
> With one whose thought I had not hoped to reach.
>
> "Men work together," I told him from the heart,
> "Whether they work together or apart."

The couplets underscore the poem's general theme of coupling and of bringing together in the imagination those who seemed isolated as well as the disassociated worlds of work and contemplation in the heart of the speaker.

In a prefatory note to the first edition of *North of Boston*, Frost alerted readers that the keynote poem, "Mending Wall," picked up on themes first laid down in "The Tuft of Flowers." The provocative note points to an aspect of the poem that can be overlooked in overeager moral or political readings of it, namely, that there are two laborers who understand each other "whether they work together or apart." Readers will often remember "Mending Wall" for either one of its two main aphorisms but not *both* of them. It begins with "Something there is that doesn't love a wall," spoken by the narrator. It ends with "Good fences make good neighbors." Both sayings are repeated by the narrator twice in the course of the poem. It would be naïve to say that either view is Frost's, and Frost did actually leave quite a bit of significant evidence in his notebooks, poems, and interviews to suggest that he viewed the matter, so to speak, from both sides of the fence. But Frost warned against reading himself into any one of the characters: "I make it a rule not to take any 'character's' side in anything I write," he cautioned Sidney Cox in a 1914 letter discussing "The Black Cottage" (*SL*, 138).

Frost himself later published poems – "A Cow in Apple Time" and "Triple Bronze" – that, taken in the context of "Mending Wall," make any simple ethical reading of it problematic. *In the Clearing* contains the couplet "From Iron," "Nature within her inmost self divides / To trouble men with having to take sides." Frost also said in his notebooks: "All life is cellular physically and socially" and also "One chief disposition in life is cell walls breaking and cell walls making. Health is a period called peace in the balance between the two. Sickness a period of war" (*N*, 280–281). In an interview Frost added: "We live by the breaking down of cells and the building up of new cells. Change is constant and unavoidable. That is the way it is with human beings and with nations, so why deplore it?" (*I*, 179). Cells both contain within themselves and build into larger units; their walls are barriers but also permeable thresholds and points of division. Looked at from this plane of figurative regard, "Mending Wall" may have greater possibilities than the perspective of the narrator.

The rhetorical strength of the speaker of "Mending Wall" makes a crafty, wise case for openness against what appears to be the crude creator of barriers and boundaries. The speaker betrays his own rhetoric several times in the course of trying to be persuasive in ways that make one wonder. For one thing, the speaker lets the neighbor know that it is time to fix the wall: "I let my neighbour know beyond the hill; / And on a day we meet to walk the line / And set the wall between us once again. / We keep the wall between us as we go." At this moment, the speaker and his neighbor may be separated by the membrane of the wall but they are also brought together by it at the same time. The fact remains that the wall gets "repaired" annually as much as the speaker becomes "re-paired" with his antagonist.

Does the speaker hope for a utopian world without boundaries? When he describes his neighbor as an "old stone savage armed" who "moves in darkness as it seems to me / not of trees only" his worst crime may be an inability to think and to renew language, "to go behind his father's saying." But the speaker also repeats his saying "something there is that doesn't love a wall." What is that "something"? He insists that it should be left unsaid. The speaker does show particular disaffection for the obvious or crude. "I could say 'Elves' to him, / But it's not elves exactly, and I'd rather / He said it for himself." The speaker's aside early in the poem about the hunters reveals a good deal about his own pleasure in concealment:

> The work of hunters is another thing:
> I have come after them and made repair
> When they have left not one stone on a stone,
> But they would have the rabbit out of hiding,
> To please the yelping dogs.

We may ask here whether "the work of hunters," which presumably participates in the general work that includes mending walls, is something entirely other from the ice that breaks up the wall – another thing altogether – or just another thing. He calls what the hunters do "work," yet as if to belittle the annual process of rebuilding the wall or perhaps his neighbor's enthusiasm for it, he calls the process ". . . just another kind of out-door game, / One on a side. It comes to little more." All this work may also be play. And all that may be culture may also be nature. If so, then a reader should not be too ready to assume an opposition between nature and human nature. The narrator, in the case of the hunters, on repairing the wall, not leaving it down. Why? Only because the hunters destroyed it? He seems to have contempt for their desire to "have the rabbit out of hiding" and, worse, "to please the yelping dogs." Lack of subtlety, complete openness, and literalness seem worse offenses than perpetual dialogue. Yet he insists on drawing out his rather laconic neighbor and on putting notions in his head. There may be something to the fact that the final utterance of the poem is the neighbor's "Good fences make good neighbors," with some strange recognition that it is one of two truths in conflict that cannot and do not have to be resolved. "Life is that which beguiles us into taking sides in the conflict of pressure and resistance, force and control. Art is that which disengages us to concern ourselves with the tremor of the universal deadlock" (*N*, 168). Frost wrote of poetry: "Your Fist in your hand. A great force strongly held. Poetry is neither the force nor the check. It is the tremor of the deadlock" (*N*, 265).

One could see that both hunters and frozen groundswells (frost) are things that subvert walls. It would be something of a problem to say which side Frost himself was on or whether he truly appealed to nature. His notebook writings reveal how complex and shifting his thinking on these matters really was. One entry succinctly pits nature against humanity with the individual ordering force between the two:

> Nature is a chaos. Humanity is a ruck. The ruck is the medium of kings. They assert themselves on it to give it some semblance of order. They build it into gradations narrowing upward to the throne. There are periods of felicity when the state stands [lasts] for a reign and even two or three reigns or a dynasty. The people are persuaded to accept their subordinations. But the ruck is a discouraging medium to work in. Form is only roughly achieved there and at best leaves in the mind a dissatisfaction and a fear of impermanence and a relative confusion. It is always as transitional as rolling clouds where a figure never quite takes shape before it begins to be another figure. Contemplation turns from it in mental distress to the physicians. The true revolt from it is not into madness or into a reform. It is onward in the line projected by nature to human nature and so on to individual nature. It is the one man working in a medium of paint words or notes – or wood or iron. Nothing composes the mind like composing composition. Let a mere man attempt no more than he is meant for. Other men are too much for him to count on organizing. Let him compose words into a poem.   (*N*, 46)

Frost does not appeal to nature as Emerson or Wordsworth might have done, at least in this passage. Here it represents the incessantly formless. Frost also regards "humanity" as a "ruck," a pile or another form of chaos. Either way, this perspective does not align readily with the more liberal and social rhetoric of the phrase of "even two can pass abreast" or the wall-subverting mischief of the speaker of "Mending Wall." If anything, Frost would seem to be arguing for the making of some simple form of order against chaos, somewhat closer to the wisdom of "Good fences make good neighbors." On the other hand, Frost seems acutely aware and attuned to the fact of waste in the world, a fact which he sees complementary to the creation of order. The movement from the raw formlessness of nature into form remains only temporary in Frost's imagination.

Tension about human hierarchy and human equality remains an important aspect of "Mending Wall" but it becomes an unquestionably strong theme throughout Frost's dramatic poems. When the narrator calls his neighbor "an old stone-savage armed," he turns his wall-building into an anthropological, if not racial, fantasy. The character was apparently based on Frost's French Canadian neighbor, Napoleon Guay. Though nothing in the poem indicates that he was French Canadian, several French Canadian figures appear in the dramatic poems: Lafe in "A Hundred Collars," Tofille Lajway in "The Witch of Coos," and Baptiste in "The Ax-Helve." Though not as recognizable now, in the early part of the twentieth century, French Canadians would have been regarded certainly as an often despised ethnic minority in New England. What, precisely, does the hierarchy of civilized and savage mean? Is the "old stone-savage" really more crude than the narrator of "Mending Wall"? This precarious ethical relationship of qualities which we value as high and low at once create some of Frost's greatest dramatic tension. Those regarded as low, untutored or rustic may bear seductively a subversive form of insight, if not wisdom.

After he had sent early drafts of the poems of *North of Boston* in 1913 to his friend F. S. Flint, he asked about the effect of his people, clearly indicating the pleasure he takes in the "contemplation of equality," without being a propagandist:

> Did I give you a feeling for the independent-dependence of the kind of
> people I like to write about. I am not propagandist of equality. But I
> enjoy above all things the contemplation of equality where it happily
> exists. I am no snob. I may be several other kinds of fool and rascal but I
> am not that. The John Kline who lost his housekeeper and went down
> like a felled ox was just the person I have described and I never knew a
> man I liked better – damn the world anyway.[10]

Frost's pastoral dramas dramatize tensions between the hierarchy of rural and city and, ultimately, the possibilities of harmony in a democracy. Looked at in another way, Frost puts to the test basic assumptions of cultural difference, communication, boundary and understanding as his characters confront each other. In "The Code," "A Hundred Collars," and "The Mountain," rural characters of baffling intelligence subvert the sophisticated assumptions of their interlocutors.

The title of "The Code" would lead us to think that a set of rules or ethics exists among farmers, and that a town-bred farmer, new to the scene will learn the more obscure limits of the country ways. The opening of the poem reveals a farmer named James fed up and walking off the job while a bewildered, "town-bred" farmer watches, unable to understand what he said or did to precipitate James's anger. The narrator sets the scene against a threatening and violent storm:

> There were three in the meadow by the brook
> Gathering up windrows, piling cocks of hay,
> With an eye always lifted toward the west
> Where an irregular sun-bordered cloud
> Darkly advanced with a perpetual dagger
> Flickering across its bosom. Suddenly
> One helper, thrusting pitchfork in the ground,
> Marched himself off the field and home. One stayed.
> The town-bred farmer failed to understand.

The remaining farmer tries to explain to the "town-bred" farmer what he said to irritate James. There appears to have been a code against urging the workers on because of the oncoming rain:

> "What is there wrong?"
>
> "Something you just now said."
>
> "What did I say?"
>
> "About our taking pains."
>
> "To cock the hay? – because it's going to shower?
> I said that more than half an hour ago.
> I said it to myself as much as to you."
>
> "You didn't know. But James is one big fool.
> He thought you meant to find fault with his work.
> That's what the average farmer would have meant.
> James would take time, of course, to chew it over
> Before he acted: he's just got round to act."
>
> "He is a fool if that's the way he takes me."

The other farmer, also a "local" or "country" farmer, appears sympathetic to the "town-bred" farmer, suggesting that he, of course, did not mean to find fault and would not have intended what "the *average* farmer would have meant."

On the other hand, he depicts James as having thought about it before acting. What didn't the "town-bred" farmer know? Did James take the "town-bred" farmer's meaning as "what the average farmer would have meant"? Was some boundary overstepped?

The country farmer's response opens more possibilities even as he appears to be settling them. He indicates, in fact, that the town farmer did violate a code: *not* to tell a hand two things, "to do work better or faster." Worse, *he* indicates he probably would have acted the same way James did, even though he did call James "a big fool":

> "Don't let it bother you. You've found out something:
> The hand that knows his business won't be told
> To do work better or faster – those two things.
> I'm as particular as any one:
> Most likely I'd have served you just the same.
> But I know you don't understand our ways.
> You were just talking what was in your mind,
> What was in all our minds, and you weren't hinting."

The avuncular country farmer has gone from agreeing that "James is one big fool" to saying that "most likely I'd have served you just the same." Presumably there *is* a code or set of rules that the "town-bred" farmer needed to learn, that hands who know their business will not be told two things. He gives some sympathy to the town farmer who "does not understand our ways." Yet there may be something funny in his suggestion at the same time that his speaking what was in *his* mind was also "in all our minds" and that he, the country farmer, is "as particular as anyone." Perhaps what is interesting is that he was "talking" at all, directly and not "hinting." It raises a question about what *kinds* of differences are *really* at stake between the town and country ways. Did the violation of the country code rest in what was said, the way it was said, or that anything was said at all?

The country farmer proceeds to recount a stunning story of his own experience as a hand working for a man named Sanders in Salem. It would appear at first to be headed in the direction of a cautionary tale or, at least, something meant to illustrate "the code" or principles he had just articulated about not telling an experienced hand to work harder or faster. This story veers from the putative "code" he had just articulated. We learn that Sanders works his hands very hard, while working hard himself, "If by so doing he could get more work / Out of his hired work." Sanders clearly drove his hired hands very hard, and we learn almost brutally so: "Them that he couldn't lead he'd get behind / And drive, the way you can, you know, in mowing – / Keep at their heels and threaten to mow their legs off." It's important to recognize that at this point while Sanders may have been the boss of the hired hands, there is no town–country difference between them. But there is a town–country difference between the speaker and his town-farmer interlocutor, and we can only imagine that he must be sounding just a little shocked about this little revelation in employer–hired hand relations in the country! He must be especially stunned after being chastised for perhaps being a little outspoken in what he said about working harder a little while earlier to James. The farmer goes right along with his story, offering almost as a joke to interpret a country term that doesn't need much translation when the most baffling part of the whole matter remains unexplained:

> I'd seen about enough of his bulling tricks
> (We call that bulling). I'd been watching him.
> So when he paired off with me in the hayfield
> To load the load, thinks I, Look out for trouble.

What happened in the hayfield turned out to be less disturbing than what occurred while loading hay in the barn. Our storyteller recounts how he had the "easy job" of throwing hay down into a bay with Sanders, his boss, down below to catch it. It may not be easy to ascertain what aspect of "the code" had been violated by Sanders when our farmer describes how he felt Sanders seemed to urge him a little with his easy job:

> You wouldn't think a fellow'd need much urging
> Under those circumstances, would you now?
> But the old fool seizes his fork in both hands,
> And looking up bewhiskered out of the pit,
> Shouts like an army captain, 'Let her come!'
> Thinks I, D'ye mean it? 'What was that you said?'
> I asked out loud, so's there'd be no mistake,
> 'Did you say, Let her come?' 'Yes, let her come.'
> He said it over, but he said it softer.
> Never you say a thing like that to a man,
> Not if he values what he is. God, I'd as soon
> Murdered him as left out his middle name.

What code, if any, has been violated by Sanders yelling "Let her come"? Was Sanders crossing so much of a line in urging something that didn't need much urging? In saying something that didn't need saying? Or did the image that the hand makes of there, "the army captain" with the pitchfork shouting orders out of the pit, simply make him an irresistible target of pent-up hatred? Why was that particular command so intolerable as to produce the injunction "Never you say a thing like that to a man, / Not if he values what he is"? Perhaps he was making a joke on Sanders when he made him repeat "Let her come," because the phrase then become a provocation for letting "kingdom come" or "letting all hell break loose." It turns out he was not just joking about murdering him as he quite literally buries him in hay.

The country hand did not wait around to see what happened to Sanders, and others fearful that he was dead kept his wife out of the barn while they dug him out. The hand finds him alive slumped in his kitchen, "slumped way down in a chair, with both his feet / Against the stove, the hottest day that summer." Sanders had escaped, deeply humiliated ". . . but my just trying / To bury him had hurt his dignity." At this point, one may ask, does this tell us anything about a code? Was what the hand did justified? Would one expect Sanders to react the way he did? The town farmer asks the expected uncomprehending question of the hand which is followed by the equally baffling answers that conclude the poem:

> "Weren't you relieved to find he wasn't dead?"
>
> "No! And yet I don't know – it's hard to say.
> I went about to kill him fair enough."
>
> "You took an awkward way. Did he discharge you?"
>
> "Discharge me? No! He knew I did just right."

In the context of "town" logic and "town" right none of what the country hand has told him has made much sense at all. The narrative that followed his outlining of the two rules hardly conforms to the measure of that code or any other code. Any code that could be understood between Sanders and his hand certainly veered on the edge of violence and civility, the funny and the sinister. If the town farmer has sought to understand country ways, the joke may be that the boundaries in power relations remain precarious at all moments. Violence can and will erupt at the least provocation, particularly when one set of men has authority over another set. The town farmer cannot seem to understand this elusive code in his search for rules and order.

Fear, threat, and lack of comprehension across boundaries of sophisticated and rural also inform both "A Hundred Collars" and "The Mountain," the latter, one of Frost's meditations on Wordsworth's "Resolution and Independence." In Wordsworth's pastoral, a wanderer comes upon a leech-gatherer who saves him from his obsessions. Wordsworth compares the leech-gatherer to a stone, a pure and purifying elemental force of nature:

> As a huge stone is sometimes seen to lie
> Couched on the bold top of an eminence;

Wonder to all who do the same espy,
By what means it should thither come, and whence,
So that it seemed a thing endowed with sense:
Like a sea-beast crawled forth, that on a shelf
Of rock or sand reposeth, there to sun itself. –

Though Wordsworth regards the leech-gatherer as a lowly figure, he nevertheless sees in his rustic labor and in his speech loftiness and dignity:

His words came feebly, from a feeble chest,
But each in solemn order followed each.
With something of a lofty utterance drest –
Choice word and measured phrase, above each
Of ordinary mean; a stately speech,
Such as grave do in Scotland use,
Religious men, who give to God and man their dues.

The leech-gatherer embodies both high and low qualities, rising above the
ordinary and the feeble in his speech; and that makes him a compelling figure.

The farmer encountered by the narrator-wanderer in Frost's "The Mountain"
is far more elusive and strange than almost any rustic figure in Wordsworth. He
encounters him as part of the stark, flinty landscape defined by the mountain:

When I walked forth at dawn to see new things,
Were fields, river, and beyond, more fields.
The river at the time was fallen away,
And made a widespread brawl on cobble stones;
But the signs showed what it had done in spring;
Good grass-land gullied out, and in the grass
Ridges of sand, and driftwood stripped of bark.
I crossed the river and swung round the mountain.
And there I met a man who moved so slow
With white-faced oxen in a heavy cart,
It seemed no harm to stop him altogether.

The passage evokes an almost magical entrance into an unknown or hitherto
unseen world by an explorer. The phrase "It seemed no harm" expresses a slight
undercurrent of fear on the part of the narrator in encountering a figure he
does know and may not understand very well.

As it turns out, the narrator learns that he's slightly lost on his "sojourn,"
as he learns from the farmer that he is in "Lunenberg," which is not quite a
town or village but only "scattered farms" that amount to sixty voters and are
completely defined by the presence and ecology of the mountain. In short, they
are a strangely isolated community. The dialogue that follows between them

perplexes the narrator, and probably most readers, because of the farmer's playfulness and sophistication, as well as his apparent lack of interest in what is on the summit of the mountain. The farmer beguiles, if not teases, the narrator *first* by hinting that he's never been up to the top of the mountain, only the sides for trout fishing. Then he teases him further about a brook with its source on the summit with the intriguing facts about its temperatures. He also reveals remarkable eloquence in describing the imagined winter steam and frost:

> "But what would interest you about the brook,
> It's always cold in summer, warm in winter.
> One of the great sights going is to see
> It steam in winter like an ox's breath,
> Until the bushes all along its banks
> Are inch deep with the frosty spines and bristles –
> You know the kind. Then let the sun shine on it!"

Our narrator-wanderer may be baffled or have his mind on grander vistas. He responds to this eloquent vision of the steamy brook with his hope for a great view. His narration then moves to viewing the mountain vegetation as it may move above the tree line, to be scaled and cleared to the top. The farmer softly returns to the less lofty matter of the brook. This drama becomes pastoral dialogue about what kinds of things may be important. The narrator appears only fascinated by the climb and the grand view; the farmer more by the simple fact of the spring and common source:

> "There ought to be a view around the world
> From such a mountain – if it isn't wooded
> Clear to the top." I saw through leafy screens
> Great granite terraces in sun and shadow,
> Shelves one could rest a knee on getting up –
> With depths behind him sheer a hundred feet.
> Or turn and sit on and look out and down,
> With little ferns at his elbow.
>
> "As to that I can't say. But there's the spring.
> Right on the summit, almost like a fountain.
> That ought to be worth seeing."

"Real" for the farmer may have more to do with what can be imagined than experienced. On the other hand, he may also be a trickster, playing with the narrator's idle curiosity.

> "It doesn't seem so much to climb a mountain
> You've worked around the foot of all your life.

What would I do? Go in my overalls,
With a big stick, the same as when the cows
Haven't come down to the bars at milking time?
Or with a shotgun for a stray black bear?
'Twouldn't seem real to climb for climbing it."

The narrator also remains deeply intrigued by the paradox that the brook is
somehow "cold in summer, warm in winter." The farmer has posed this riddle
as a kind of joke: it is really the same all the time:

"I don't suppose the water's changed at all.
You and I know enough to know it's warm
Compared with cold, and cold compared with warm.
But all the fun's in how you say a thing."

The narrator *should* know that but the farmer may be a bit more subtle, if not
playful in talking around the subject of leisure versus labor, about their common
humanity and sensibility, for which the brook has become a metaphor. His
fun, both playful and sinister, is "in how you say a thing," a way of keeping
the sojourner-narrator out of his business. There may be another mythic level
to interplay, in addition to Wordsworth's. The farmer here may be at once
more strange and clever than Wordsworth's leech-gatherer. That mountain,
too, which defines the tiny community has been called Hor, which means
boundary and also evokes the biblical Mount Hor in Numbers. Frost's first
published prose, "Petra and its Surroundings" (1891), begins by evoking the
burial tomb of Moses's brother Aaron, whom God condemned to die on the
summit of Mount Hor. This condemnation, which extended to Moses as well,
stemmed from their lack of faith in God and their transformation from stone
of the waters of Mirabah. There seems to be some echo here, almost a taboo,
of not penetrating too far into the mysterious and the miraculous and about
the relations of brothers. Yet the strange concluding utterance of the farmer,
overheard and broken off, leaves the narrator and readers wondering what
kind of strange isolated consciousness or otherness has developed around the
isolated region of the mountain:

"You've lived here all your life?"

                    "Ever since Hor
Was no bigger than a —" What, I did not hear.
He drew the oxen toward him with light touches
Of his slim goad on nose and offside flank,
Gave them their marching orders and was moving.

A racial fear haunts the pastoral world of *North of Boston*, and this should not be surprising since pastoral has long been a highly political form, though a subtle one. The tension between labor and leisure would always be seen through various lenses of human worth and hierarchy. Well aware of the Jeffersonian ideals of a natural aristocracy rooted in an agrarian society, Frost also witnessed the disintegration of that agrarian ideal in areas of New England challenged by poverty, industry, and changing social conditions. He also witnessed the sometimes strange and fearful responses to this disintegration in the forms of various attempts to capture a fading or old New England. In many respects, this Frost can be looked at and has been regarded as preserving some kind of lost or disappearing New England landscape. That appears to be one aspect of his claim to the pastoral tradition, an affection for contemplation of a fading rural world. But that sentimentality may be precisely what is deceptive about Frost and, indeed, what is deceptive about the pastoral in general.

"A Hundred Collars" should be viewed as a satirical pastoral with strong political overtones. The chance encounter between a professor, Dr. Magoon, and a shady figure, Lafe, short for Lafayette, occurs when Magoon is forced to find a room for the night when he missed his train at Woodsville Junction (the name, of course, is suggestive of the borderland between town and country). When he finds that the only available hotel room in the little village has to be shared with Lafe, the professor learns immediately that his uninhibited roommate likes to drink. Particularly striking, though, is his physical appearance and size, and the ever-expanding girth of his neck in comparison with the professor's:

> The Doctor looked at Lafe and looked away.
> A man? A brute. Naked above the waist,
> He sat there creased and shining in the light,
> Fumbling the buttons in a well-starched shirt.
> "I'm moving into a size-larger shirt.
> I've felt mean lately; mean's no name for it.
> I just found what the matter was tonight:
> I've been a-choking like a nursery tree
> When it outgrows the wire band of its name tag.
> I blamed it on the hot spell we've been having.
> 'Twas nothing but my foolish hanging back
> Not liking to own up I'd grown a size.
> Number eighteen this is. What size you wear?"
>
> The Doctor caught his throat convulsively.
> "Oh – ah – fourteen – fourteen."

> "Fourteen! You say so!
> I can remember when I wore fourteen.
> And come to think of it I must have back at home
> More than a hundred collars, size fourteen.
> Too bad to waste them all. You ought to have them.
> They're yours and welcome; let me send them to you.
> What makes you stand there on one leg like that?
> You're not much furtherer than where Kike left you.
> You act as if you wished you hadn't come.
> Sit down or lie down, friend; you make me nervous."

Surely the joke is on Dr. Magoon, who at this point has been terrified by Lafe, despite his generosity about the collars. Frost conveys much to the reader about what might be frightening about Lafe. His general appearance might be enough – half naked, already a little oiled, fairly irreverent, and quite large – to scare the refined scholar who has insisted on a bed. Other simple social facts would have been obvious to Magoon and to Frost readers. Lafe is French Canadian, and in the early part of the twentieth century in New England and, especially in Vermont, French Canadians were looked down upon as racially inferior, degenerate, and even threatening to the pure Anglo world. This encounter has, in addition, the threat and fear of an ethnic or racial encounter. We might suspect that Lafe knows full well of Magoon's fear and plays with it just a little by underscoring the differences in neck size.

All Lafe's joking about collars, too, makes a joke of the fashion of the time. Lafe has outgrown his shirt, and particularly his collars. He seems a man out of fashion altogether, too big for the constraints of town-imposed form. One notable item of fashion of the turn of the twentieth century was the detachable collar, particularly for men's shirts. Stiff and often made of celluloid, they often came to distinguish business or "white collar" men from working-class men. Frost in his depiction of Lafe outgrowing the collars may have also been satirizing another icon of contemporary American fashion advertising: the Arrow collar man. A handsome figure who appeared in hundreds of advertisements for Arrow shirt collars from 1905 to 1912, the years Frost was most actively engaged in composing the poems for *North of Boston*, he came to represent the ideal of the handsome, athletic, self-confident American. President Roosevelt once called him the portrait of "the common man." The creation of advertising artist J. C. Leyendecker, the Arrow collar man became a vision of the polished Anglo-Saxon figure, and he received as much fan mail as many movie stars.

Lafe, the shirtless French Canadian, becomes the antithesis of the Arrow collar man, at least in so far as he refuses to conform to an image of

Anglo-Saxon perfection. At the turn of the century, Vermont and other areas of the United States were experiencing a resurgence in nostalgia for lost Anglo-Saxon perfection, which many felt had been diluted by immigration and racial degeneration. The birth of the eugenics movement in America coincides with the raging debates about Darwin and the possible application of natural selection and evolutionary theory to the immediate improvement of society. The sentiment that birthed the eugenics movement in Vermont can be seen in a poem of 1897 by Walter M. Rogers entitled "Vermont's Deserted Farms," in which the abandoned farms also suggest lost "races":

> A sound is heard throughout the land
> Which causes vague alarms;
> You hear it oft, on every hand,
> "Vermont's deserted farms."
>
> Where once the strong Green Mountain boy
> Pursued his honest toil,
> And harvests rich were reaped, in joy,
> By tillers of the soil.
>
> You now behold the shattered homes
> All crumbling to decay,
> Like long-neglected catacombs
> Of races passed away.

When Magoon sees Lafe as a "brute," he is certainly not one of those strong "Green Mountain boys" of the old colonial stock but part of the threatening influx of French Canadians who were seen to be undermining the strength of the old.

For all that Lafe may be much more physical, more open than "Professor Square-the-circle-till-you're-tired" Magoon, we might be too hasty in envisioning him as a sensuous figure or one quite of pastoral contemplation, even though he combines work with play, business with fun. He works for a Vermont Republican newspaper, presumably collecting subscriptions. In spite of that, he insists that he is a "double-dyed" Democrat and will not help them re-elect William Howard Taft. His job – such as it is – is to ride around and get the sense of public sentiment. His allegiances appear to shift with his shape. His description of his journeying around to different farms gives a strong sense of his pleasure, but it also conveys the barrenness of some of those farms and the obvious awkwardness, if not fear, those farmers and their families seem to have of him. He says "he likes to find folks" but ultimately they seem rather scarce when he comes around, and he is indifferent to their labor:

I like to find folks getting out in spring,
Raking the dooryard, working near the house.
Later they get out further in the fields.
Everything's shut sometimes except the barn;
The family's all away in some back meadow.
There's a hay load a-coming – when it comes.
And later still they all get driven in:
The fields are stripped to lawn, the garden patches
Stripped to bare ground, the maple trees
To whips and poles. There's nobody about.
The chimney, though, keeps up a good brisk smoking.

His horse naturally turns in at every house because "She thinks I'm sociable. I maybe am." We also learn that he "seldom" gets down "except for meals." What kind of collecting is Lafe truly about? While he represents a spirit of freedom from all manner of constraint, does this portend something slightly threatening about the double-dyed spirit of democracy of the future?

Frost's pastoral mode reaches its darkest and most ironic in "The Vanishing Red." If the perennial theme of "Et in Arcadia Ego" had come to mean "Death is also in Arcadia," this gothic dramatic poem takes that to its extreme, which is nothing less than genocide in rural New England. The title of the poem becomes particularly poignant when taken in the context of the time of its publication, 1916. The phrase "The Vanishing Red," and variants such as "The Vanishing American," had been widely used in North America for more than two centuries in reference to the racial extinction of Indians. Such phrases did not so much describe a statistical reality as express and justify attitudes and, eventually, policies from the mid-eighteenth through the mid-twentieth century. Behind the phrase lies a myth that the Indians are a vanishing race, disappearing before the advance of the white man. And the phrase often embraced a tension: sentimentality toward a noble, savage race that was sadly but inevitably disappearing according to various laws of change and, above all, progress.[11]

Frost published "The Vanishing Red" in 1916, a time when a sense of the inevitability of racial absorption had replaced the frontier hatred and desire to exterminate Indians. Discussions of Indian citizenship also gained momentum because of their service in World War I. Depictions of Thanksgiving, which had formerly focused predominantly on the landing at Plymouth, shifted to the feast of Pilgrims and Indians.[12] But the liberal abolitionist spirit of nineteenth-century New England had also grown decidedly xenophobic by the early twentieth century. Fear of immigrant populations and racial mixing had fueled the growth of interest in eugenics and the rhetoric of Aryan purity. It seems to me that Frost's poem would have been particularly poignant at that moment as an ironic rhetorical gesture. For it would have suggested to New England readers in particular that racial hatred and extermination were neither a thing of the past nor part of some grand process of racial attrition before the inevitable forces of progress but the sum total of individual acts of hatred and sadism. If Frost's "Miller" is supposed to represent progress and technology, he comes off as just about the opposite – brutal and inarticulate. And John – hardly an Indian name – fails to fit James Fennimore Cooper's representations of the Indian as either devil or noble savage. The mill itself is – like grindstones, scythes, and axes – a very old form of technology. Frost's poem thus provides a sharp undoing of much of the traditional sentiment and ideology lurking in the phrase "The Vanishing Red."

When we first encounter the Miller, we learn little about his motives or character except that the narrator barely grants him elevated stature even in his simplest vocal gestures: "And the Miller is said to have laughed– / If you like to call such a sound a laugh." Whatever laugh he might emit, he is hardly generous, and one senses from the very beginning of the poem that he, for reasons that are frighteningly not more but less than anyone can understand, saw it as his grim duty to do the inevitable and exterminate "the last Red Man in Acton":

> But he gave no one else a laughter's license.
> "Whose business – if I take it on myself,
> Whose business – but why talk round the barn? –
> When it's just that I hold with getting a thing done with."

While the narrator does not justify the Miller's intentions, he neither moralizes nor attempts to explain the history of continental relations by casting blame on who started the trouble. It is "just a matter / Of who began it between the two races," which may be to look chillingly on the actors in this little drama as part of an ongoing, brutal drama of extermination.

The mill itself then becomes an instrument and figure of that extermination, one that hardly heralds progress. What finally inspires the Miller to throw John, the Indian, into the wheel pit? Visceral disgust because John dared to utter anything at all, dared to presume the right to be heard from:

> Some guttural exclamation of surprise
> The Red Man gave in poking about the mill
> Over the great big thumping shuffling mill-stone
> Disgusted the Miller physically as coming
> From one who had no right to be heard from.
> "Come, John," he said, "you want to see the wheel pit?"

Frost was depicting a brutal machinery of racial extermination while stripping the whole process of any rationalizations that could make it palatable. In light of the Miller showing John the "wheel pit," mention of the "meal sack" is as horrible a metaphor of the grinding waste of life and the separation of fruit and chaff as anything in Frost, including "the cider apple heap" of "After Apple-Picking."

Labor and beauty

Frost gives us a memorable dialogue of pastoral tension about the relationship of labor, contemplation, beauty, and equality, as well as one of his most memorable characters, Baptiste, in "The Ax-Helve." Critics often take the poem as an *ars poetica* because of comments Frost made in an interview and in prose about the pleasure he takes in the crooked straightness of things. In an interview in 1916, a year before publication of the poem, Frost discussed as a metaphor for true art the beauty and power of the way Canadian woodchoppers made their ax-handles, following the native grain of the wood:

> You know the Canadian woodchoppers whittle their ax-handles, following the curve of the grain, and they're strong and beautiful. Art should follow lines in nature, like the grain of an ax-handle. False art puts curves on things that haven't any curves.   (*I*, 19)

The poem itself presents a much more complex portrait of the woodchopper Baptiste and the implications of functional art well-made according to nature. We need to consider the narrator's attitude toward Baptiste and the relationship between him and Baptiste, who is French Canadian. The poem explores as much about human anxieties, about equality, race, and prowess, as it does about aesthetics. The narrator has been caught with a faulty machine ax but he feels both anxious about and superior to Baptiste, who seems motivated to "get his human rating" by showing what he knows about "ax-helves":

> Baptiste knew best why I was where I was.
> So long as he would leave enough unsaid,
> I shouldn't mind his being overjoyed
> (If overjoyed he was) at having got me
> Where I must judge if what he knew about an ax
> That not everybody else knew was to count
> For nothing in the measure of a neighbor.
> Hard if, though cast away for life with Yankees,
> A Frenchman couldn't get his human rating!

The narrator's accounting of Baptiste's motives seems at the least condescending, if not worse, and reveals some of his contempt for his French Canadian neighbor. But he knows, or thinks he knows, that his neighbor wants him to be recognized and treated as an equal. He, therefore, agrees to be shown how Baptiste makes his home-made ax-helves. The narrator appears aware that he knew very little about axes and was caught off-guard by a man of great prowess, and feels threatened by Baptiste's abilities.

Baptiste provides, and the narrator allows, his display of home-made ax-helves, which are most certainly displays of natural prowess and figures of ability that can neither be taught nor, perhaps, learned:

> He showed me that the lines of a good helve
> Were native to the grain before the knife
> Expressed them, and its curves were no false curves
> Put on it from without. And there its strength lay
> For the hard work. He chafed its long white body
> From end to end with its rough hand shut round it.
> He tried it at the eye-hole in the ax-head.
> "Hahn, hahn," he mused, "don't need much taking down."
> Baptiste know how to make a short job long
> For love of it, and yet not waste time either.

In crafting ax-helves, Baptiste displays sensuous, if not sensual pleasure, blending love and need, work and play, craft and power. And like a strong helve, Baptiste displays qualities "native to the grain" with "no false curves."

Indeed, the dialogue that ensues between the narrator and Baptiste, but is only reported to us indirectly, has very much to do with "what is native to the grain" among human beings and what truly counts for intelligence and knowledge. For the underlying dramatic tension of the poem is really about human equality and education:

> Do you know, what we talked about was knowledge?
> Baptiste on his defense about the children
> He kept from school, or did his best to keep –
> Whatever school and children and our doubts
> Of laid-on education had to do
> With the curves of his ax-helves and his having
> Used these unscrupulously to bring me
> To see for once the inside of his house.

Ax-helves are the tools, if not the weapons and the metaphors, for the drama of human equality. In the early part of the twentieth century, there was enormous controversy about the influx of French Canadians into New England and their

refusal to assimilate into American schools and speak English. French Canadians had protested violently in Canada about being forced to speak English in
schools. Questions were developing about the isolation and independence of
French Canadian immigrant communities in New England at the turn of the
twentieth century. An article in *The New York Times* in 1901 stated "A constant
increase of its French Canadian population is becoming a matter of vital interest
in New England. It is yet uncertain whether it should be regarded as a menace
or promise of good for the future." The author added, "This tendency [of the
French Canadians] to confine themselves to the society of their own country-
men very much retards the Americanization of the French. Neither business,
convenience, nor pleasure urges the emigrant to the difficult task of learning
the English language and he is usually content to leave that to his children."[13]
Surely Baptiste and the narrator recognize that the questions here are deeper
than the contemporary political controversy. The question of "false curves" on
ax-helves becomes a figure for "laid-on" education in schools. What, if anything, can be taught in schools? Are we, in fact, defined by our innate abilities
and nature? And by whose authority and to what knowledge must we submit
to become part of a culture?

The poem concludes with a dramatic focus on a "present" moment, as
Baptiste finishes an ax-helve. The difference in the way the two men regard
the image says much about how they regard each other and themselves. The
narrator imposes upon the helve an almost allegorical vision of Old Testament
evil. Perhaps, more insidiously, he regards the tool, or weapon, as analogous to
the man who made it. Baptiste, whose very name suggests both a martyr who
was beheaded and a French Canadian figure of courage – a "batiste" – sees the
helve as feminine and seductive:

> But now he brushed the shavings from his knee
> And stood the ax there on its horse's hoof,
> Erect, but not without its waves, as when
> The snake stood up for evil in the Garden,–
> Top-heavy with a heaviness his short,
> Thick hand made light of, steel-blue chin drawn down
> And in a little – a French touch in that.
> Baptiste drew back and squinted at it, pleased:
> "See how she's cock her head!"

Baptiste's love of the well-made helve or his anxiousness to earn his human
rating has produced an erotic creation that somehow brings men mysteriously
together. It becomes the focal point at which we become human, "stand up,"

become "erect," use tools, potentially as weapons as well as ways of creating order and, as Frost would say, "braving alien entanglements."

Baptiste takes pleasure in his workmanship. Utility and beauty, work and play unite in his craft. Yet within the drama of the poem, the helves take on different possibilities of meaning: a tool that could at any moment become a weapon, a metaphor about education, a figure of native intelligence, an instrument by which to lure and to communicate. Frost's dialogue and dramatic narratives demand serious questioning of the idea of pursuit of beauty for its own sake.

Several remarkable dramatic poems appear to put characters in severely challenged positions in their attempts to pursue visions of beauty or aesthetic perfection. In "The Self-Seeker" Frost presents us with one of the most complex of his characters. Biographers have long noted that Frost based him on his friend Carl Burrell, whose legs were severely injured in a box factory accident. Burrell also taught and discussed with Frost many aspects of contemporary botany, biology, and astronomy. A dialogue largely between the injured man, known as the "Broken One," and his friend Willis, the poem begins just before the arrival of a lawyer who will settle insurance claims with the broken one for his injuries. He's also going to sell his company and the surrounding land, with its beautiful flora, particularly its orchids:

> "I'm going to sell my soul, or rather, feet.
> Five hundred dollars for the pair, you know."
>
> "With you the feet have nearly been the soul;
> And if you're going to sell them to the devil,
> I want to see you do it. When's he coming?"

The pun that both the self-seeker and especially Willis make on soul and feet point in a half-joking, half-serious way to an underlying theme in the poem: the extent to which the demands of the material world ultimately entangle the will and the soul. We learn that the Broken One had loved to walk for miles pursuing many varieties of beautiful and rare wild orchids. What no doubt Carl Burrell and Frost knew about orchids was how their beauty in actuality was a type of machinery for procreation and survival.

When the Broken One describes his accident, he concedes to the power of the mill's machinery, particularly the wheel belt, which takes on the symbolic figure of the ourobouros, or the snake with its tail in its mouth, a symbol of the reconciliation of opposites and of eternity. For the Broken One, the mill's buzzing machinery means both life and death, something Willis cannot seem to accept:

"They say some time was wasted on the belt –
Old streak of leather – doesn't love me much
Because I make him spit fire at my knuckles,
The way Ben Franklin used to make the kite-string.
That must be it. Some days he won't stay on.
That day a woman couldn't coax him off.
He's on his rounds with his tail in his mouth
Snatched right and left across the silver pulleys.
Everything goes the same without me there.
You can hear the small buzz saws whine, the big saw
Caterwaul to the hills around the village
As they both bite the wood. It's all our music.
One ought to be a good villager to like it.
No doubt it has a prosperous sound,
And it's our life."

          "Yes, when it's not our death."

"You make it sound as if it wasn't so
With everything. What we live by we die by."

Willis's outrage at the Broken One's selling the mill is directed most at the loss of the wild flowers in the area: "'But your flowers, man, you're selling out your flowers.'" The Broken One insists that he's not selling them because unlike some fanciers of rare orchids, they meant much more to him than money: "Money can't pay me for the loss of them." He has great pride, though, in the book he was writing about "the flora of the valley" and the "friends it might bring me," such as the great naturalist John Burroughs, to whom he wrote about the discovery far north of the orchid *Cyprepedium regina.*

The Broken One had always been more obsessed with his orchids and the flora of the valley than with the mill. Before the accident he had enlisted a little girl, Anne, who may be Willis's daughter, to go searching for orchids on his behalf. She appears by his bed after the lawyer has arrived, having picked some orchids for him. But this produces some agitation between Anne and her mentor. She brought the Broken One a Ram's Horn orchid but when he asks her "'Were there no others,'" she replies "'There were four or five. / I knew you wouldn't let me pick them all.'" The Broken One points out that Anne had learned her lessons about plant ecology but seems to be more concerned that she may have picked something that was precious to him. When he asks her "'Where is it now, the Yellow Lady's Slipper?'" Anne's response reveals her contempt for his self-seeking obsession with rare beauty:

"Well, wait – it's common – it's too *common*."

"Common?
The Purple Lady's Slipper's commoner."

"I didn't bring a Purple Lady's Slipper.
To *You* – to you I mean – they're both too common."

The lawyer gave a laugh among his papers
As if with some idea that she had scored.

The Broken One tries to justify what he has done by reminding in an ironic comment on his own fate: "'I've broken Anne of gathering bouquets. / It's not fair to the child. It can't be helped though: / Pressed into service means pressed out of shape.'" The Broken One has himself broken a child of gathering orchids on a principle of service. He now wants her to serve as his legs to seek out orchids and leave them alone. She no doubt used to press flowers into a book. His interest is in making a book for the friends it will bring him. The machinery that broke his legs also presses people; it may be part of the machinery that produces ecological change, mutation, and survival in orchids. Self-seeking by nature, the Broken One has uncovered a terrible principle of mutability that makes his own pursuit of beauty nearly untenable.

The Broken One appears in every respect an impotent figure seeking to assert control where he has none. Obsessed with orchids, he appears to have no sense of how the world works, despite the wisdom of his utterances. Orchids, one of the most sexually successful forms in the botanic kingdom, will persist much better than this bipedal, whose feet are compared, ironically, to the regenerating points of starfish. He himself remains impotent (for which broken feet may be a metaphor) and only seems capable of controlling a young girl.

"The Housekeeper" presents another tragic drama of misplaced obsession with beauty at the expense of the demands of keeping the home and the more pressing needs of existence. The complexity of this dramatic narrative stems, in part, not only from the strange mother of the common-law wife housekeeper, who speaks most of it, but also from the mysterious role of the narrator. The mother tells us and the narrator that Estelle, her daughter, has run off from John, the man for whom she was housekeeper and common-law wife. The mother's story appears only partly humorous but becomes much more poignant and bitter near the end, when John appears. And his relationship to the narrator may be more questionable than one first assumed.

The mother paints a humorous but disturbing portrait of John as an incompetent farmer but she appears relatively forgiving. Somehow John has provided for her and her daughter fairly well, even though Estelle does both the housework and half of the outdoor work:

I guess Estelle and I have filled the purse.
'Twas we let him have money, not he us.
John's a bad farmer. I'm not blaming him.
Take it year in, and year out, he doesn't make much.
We came here for a home for me, you know,
Estelle to do the housework for the board
Of both of us. But look how it turns out:
She seems to have the housework, and besides
Half of the outdoor work, though as for that,
He'd say she does it more because she likes it.
You see our pretty things are all outdoors.
Our hens and cows and pigs are always better
Than folks like us have any business with.
Farmers around twice as well off as we
Haven't as good.

What turns out to be particularly good about John may also be particularly odd about him or at least different: as a hen farmer, he has a fascination with breeding beautiful birds for show. Frost, for a number of years a hen-man himself, was thoroughly familiar with hen-breeders and wrote stories about them for poultry magazines. But one senses that he was also aware of the peculiarity of people obsessed with prize-winning chickens, just as he must have been amused with the kind of self-obsession of the "Broken One" and his fascination with rare orchids. The way the mother describes John, there's something almost effeminate in his attention to the birds, even though Estelle shares the interest:

"One thing you can't help liking about John,
He's fond of nice things – too fond, some would say.
But Estelle don't complain: she's like him there.
She wants our hens to be the best there are.
You never saw this room before a show,
Full of lank, shivery, half-drowned birds
In separate coops, having their plumage done.
The smell of the wet feathers in the heat!
You spoke of John's not being safe to stay with.
You don't know what a gentle lot we are:
We wouldn't hurt a hen! You ought to see us
Moving a flock of hens from place to place.
We're not allowed to take them upside down,
All we can hold together by the legs.
Two at a time's the rule, one on each arm,
No matter how far and how many times
We have to go."

> "You mean that's John's idea."

> "And we live up to it; or I don't know
> What childishness he wouldn't give way to.
> He manages to keep the upper hand
> On his own farm. He's boss. But as to hens:
> We fence our flowers in and the hens range.
> Nothing's too good for them."

With his one interjection, the neighbor-narrator has enabled the mother to reveal that John drives both her and Estelle somewhat crazy over the hens, which are treated with the most precious care. Just a bit later, we learn that John paid fifty dollars (quite a sum for the time) for a specially bred cock. The mother cannot or, perhaps, will not answer the neighbor's question when he asks about Estelle:

> "What's the real trouble? What will satisfy her?"

> "It's as I say: she's turned from him, that's all."

The fascination with beauty in hens may have nothing to do with domestic science or what it takes to keep a house or satisfy sexually his common-law wife. The first decades of the twentieth century saw the rise of one of the most pernicious developments of nineteenth-century biology: eugenics. Some, including Darwin's cousin Francis Galton, thought that the principle of natural selection, based on an analogy of animal breeding, could be applied back to human society. Through principles of artificial breeding, one could, it was thought, produce an improved race. In "A Blue Ribbon at Amesbury," Frost satirizes both the ambitions of hen breeders and, by analogy, the insanity of eugenics. Both envision a kind of perfection and utopia, failing to take account of human and creaturely limitation:

> Such a fine pullet ought to go
> All coiffured to a winter show,
> And be exhibited, and win.
> The answer is this one has been –

> And come with all her honors home.
> Her golden leg, her coral comb,
> Her fluff of plumage, white as chalk,
> Her style, were all the fancy's talk.

Having been successful at the show, the bird must return to being ordinary or "common" with the rest of the flock, something that may make her a bit uncomfortable:

Here common with the flock again,
At home in her abiding pen,
She lingers feeding at the trough,
The last to let night drive her off.

Her breeder exhibits even more agitation, if not madness, since he desires something beyond the dusty life of caring for chickens in the pen. That breeds in him eugenic fantasies and "half a mind" to start a race:

The one who gave her ankle-band,
Her keeper, empty pail in hand,
He lingers too, averse to slight
His chores for all the wintry night . . .

He meditates the breeder's art.
He has half a mind to start,
With her for Mother Eve, a race
That shall all living things displace.

Frost's poultry stories reveal the successes and failures of breeding both for the beauty of the bird and also for egg productivity. In the second case, there were often grotesque catastrophes.

John's hen fascination made him a failure as a housekeeper. He drove his own housekeeper and common-law wife away. Though as the poem unfolds, the mother reveals that she too may well have been a pernicious presence in the relationship. She could barely move within the house and, in truth, did not seem to get along well with John at all. The mother appears to be the true housekeeper, controlling both John and her daughter. The final mystery of the poem remains unsettled. The mother reveals to the neighbor that Estelle did not just run off but married someone else. But there is some uncertainty about what the neighbor already does or does not know about Estelle, as well as the mother's true attitude toward what her daughter has done:

"I mean she's married – married someone else."

"Oho, oho!"

"You don't believe me."

"Yes, I do,
Only too well. I knew there must be something!
So that was what was back. She's bad, that's all!"

"Bad to get married when she had the chance?"

"Nonsense! See what she's done! But who, but who –"

"Who'd marry her straight out of such a mess?
Say it right out – no matter for her mother.
The man was found. I'd better name no names.
John himself won't imagine who he is."

"Then it's all up. I think I'll get away.
You'll be expecting John. I pity Estelle;
I suppose she deserves some pity, too.
You ought to have the kitchen to yourself
To break it to him. You may have the job."

This is a wonderfully crafted mutual fishing expedition: the mother tries to see what the neighbor knows and the neighbor tries to see what the mother knows. One wonders what's behind the neighbor's saying "Then it's all up. I think I'll get away." Has *he* run off with Estelle? Or been involved in the "mess," perhaps a pregnancy? All of these possibilities make the dialogue between the mother and the neighbor much more suggestive, particularly for what she has been trying to reveal about herself and her daughter's past. When John suddenly arrives he says perhaps joking but perhaps menacingly, to the narrator: "'How are you, neighbor? Just the man I'm after. / Isn't it Hell . . .'" "The Housekeeper" presents a complex study of several characters finding farm life and the pursuit of beautiful things anything but an harmonious existence.

Women, nature, and home

Some of Frost's most compelling narrative and lyric poems dramatize women on the border of nature and wildness, including "Paul's Wife," "Wild Grapes," "The Witch of Coos," "The Pauper Witch of Grafton," "Maple," "The Hill Wife," and "A Servant to Servants." No simple paradigm runs through all these poems, and it should be obvious from reading them that more often than not Frost gives women in his poetry enormous vocal presence and power: they speak for themselves. Few modern poets give women as much vocal prominence as Frost in lyrics, dramatic narratives, and dramatic monologues in which we find the speakers struggling against the entanglements of social and sexual domination for their own voice and sanity.

"Paul's Wife," one of the most spectacularly strange narratives of *New Hampshire*, adds a new dimension to the legend of Paul Bunyan. Despite his great prowess and skills, Frost's Paul is unusually susceptible to being teased by his fellow lumberjacks about his wife or his lack of one. Sexual competition and jealousy among the lumbermen proves to be a great driving force among them, and a far greater weakness in Paul than any popular legend about his strength would have indicated. Paul must have a wife suited to his greatness, and he creates one – Pygmalion-like – from the pith of a pine log that has been submerged in water. The woman that arises from the log astounds him, a full-blown goddess, to whom the great hero seems utterly beholden and enchanted. She becomes his unworldly spiritual possession, away from the lumbermen, who follow them and taunt them in "a brute tribute of respect to beauty." Their shouts destroy her as she "went out like a firefly, and that was all." Paul refused to let his spiritual and erotic world have anything to do with the world as we know it:

> Paul was what's called a terrible possessor.
> Owning a wife with him meant owning her.
> She wasn't anybody else's business,
> Either to praise her, or so much as name her,
> And he'd thank people not to think of her.
> Murphy's idea was that a man like Paul
> Wouldn't be spoken to about a wife
> In any way the world knew how to speak.

Paul "the terrible possessor" appears an idealist in the extreme in his idea of his wife, one who cannot possibly live in the world or live with someone in the world because of the terror and fear of his wife being anything other than his private dream. An heroic lumberjack, on the matter of his wife he won't be spoken to about a wife "in the way *the world*" knew. Frost once described Platonism in terms of marriage as

> one who believes what we have here is an imperfect copy of what is in heaven. The woman you have is an imperfect copy of some woman in heaven or in someone else's bed . . . I am philosophically opposed to having one Iseult for my vocation and another for my avocation . . . A truly gallant Platonist will remain a bachelor . . . from unwillingness to reduce any woman to the condition of being used without being idolized.   (*SL*, 462)

Paul has hopelessly divided his vocation and avocation. The wildness here may well be more on the part of Paul and the other lumbermen and less on the dreamlike wife who emerges from pine and lumber. In "Wild Grapes," a "little boyish girl" narrator becomes associated with wildness but in another sense she, like Paul, could also be said to be something of an uncompromising idealist.

"Wild Grapes" also presents a complex mythology of the feminine relationship with nature. In this lyric, which was a complement to "Birches," a girl recollects a traumatic childhood experience of nearly being carried away by a birch tree. Beginning with the title, the poem is replete with gnomic and suggestive references to biblical, classical (Bacchus, Dionysus, and Orpheus), and scientific literature, which all become stories whirling around her defiance and her desire for independence.[14] The title refers not only the wild grapes that were growing in an unexpected place but also the wayward children of God prophesied by Isaiah in his parable of the vineyard: "My well beloved hath planted a vineyard in a very fruitful hill: and he fenced it, and gathered out the stones thereof, and planted it with the choicest vine, and built a tower in the midst of it, and also made a winepress therein: and he looked that it should bring forth grapes, and it brought forth wild grapes." The narrator begins her story with a wry wink to a passage in Luke 6:44 that says only certain fruit can be gathered from certain trees: "For every tree is known by his own fruit. For of thorns men do not gather figs, nor of a bramble bush do they gather grapes." She, however, had become, like the grapes, a wild anomaly. She appears deliberately to chafe at the codes and expectations of those around her, including her brother. She tells us, as well, that she grew "to be a little boyish girl," and resistant to the control of her brother:

> What tree may not the fig be gathered from?
> The grape may not be gathered from the birch?
> It's all you know the grape, or know the birch.
> As a girl gathered from the birch myself
> Equally with my weight in grapes, one autumn,
> I ought to know what tree the grape is fruit of.
> I was born, I suppose, like anyone,
> And grew to be a little boyish girl
> My brother could not always leave at home.

But her experience that day would lead to a trauma and, yet, a new beginning. Her life would be in a positive sense "a waste," indifferent to the demands around her:

> But that beginning was wiped out in fear
> The day I swung suspended with the grapes,
> And was come after like Eurydice
> And brought down safely from the upper regions;
> And the life I live now's an extra life
> I can waste as I please on whom I please.
> So if you see me celebrate two birthdays,
> And give myself out as two different ages,
> One of them five years younger than I look –

She recounts the story, virtually a fable of temptation, of her brother leading her to a glade and offering her some grapes from a branch. But she becomes caught in the branch and cannot and will not let go. "The tree had me," she said. She refuses despite the imperatives of survival and of her brother to "let go." And she ignores her brother's literal demand that she be less of a girl and "weigh more." She insists, instead, on the heart before the mind:

> My brother had been nearer right before.
> I had not taken the first step in knowledge;
> I had not learned to let go with the hands,
> As still I have not learned to with the heart,
> And have no wish to with the heart – nor need,
> That I can see. The mind – is not the heart.
> I may yet live, as I know others live,
> To wish in vain to let go with the mind –
> Of cares, at night, to sleep; but nothing tells me
> That I need to let go with the heart.

We sense the same refusal "to let go with the heart" in the short lyric "The Rose Family," despite the encroachments of "theories" and complexities of taxonomies of naming on the mind. The narrator laments the fact that science has shown that the rose, associated with love and with femininity, is quite literally descended from the apple and related to other fruit. The ghostly figure of the tree life haunts the poem. Knowledge tends to undermine the poetic fictions we would like to hold eternally in our minds:

> The rose is a rose,
> And was always a rose.
> But the theory now goes
> That the apple's a rose,
> And the pear is, and so's
> The plum, I suppose.
> The dear only knows
> What will next prove a rose.
> You, of course, are a rose –
> But were always a rose.

The narrator lovingly bestows the essence of "rose" upon the one to whom he addresses the poem, even though he recognizes that the poets he has quoted on roses – Edmund Waller, Shakespeare, Gertrude Stein – no longer hold against the unruly facts about nature.

Frost allows the mystery of naming to govern the story of a girl's and then a woman's life in "Maple." Working against the traditional myth of the Adamic namer, we learn from her father that her mother, before her death soon after giving birth, bestowed the highly suggestive name upon her. Her father becomes dangerously suggestive and evasive in telling her the story of her naming and inspires his daughter's own search for self-understanding and self-revelation in her mother's intent:

> "I don't know what she wanted it to mean,
> But it seems like some word she left to bid you
> Be a good girl – be like a maple tree.
> How like a maple tree's for us to guess.
> Or for a little girl to guess sometime.
> Not now – at least I shouldn't try too hard now.
> By and by I will tell you all I know
> About the different trees, and something, too,
> About your mother that perhaps may help."
> Dangerous self-arousing words to sow.

The self-arousal here creates a life-determining drama: the search for the meaning of her name paradoxically governs her life's course. Strangely enough, it leads her away from the country to the city, where her strength and power become severely limited in the life as a secretary taking "shorthand" in an office:

> So she looked for herself, as everyone
> Looks for himself, more or less outwardly.
> And her self-seeking, fitful though it was,
> May still have been what led her on to read,
> And think a little, and get some city schooling.
> She learned shorthand, whatever shorthand may
> Have had to do with it – she sometimes wondered
> So, till she found herself in a strange place
> For the name Maple to have brought her to,
> Taking dictation on a paper pad,
> And in the pauses when she raised her eyes
> Watching out of a nineteenth story window
> An airship laboring with unship-like motion
> And a vague all-disturbing roar above the river
> Beyond the highest city built with hands.

Maple's "self-seeking" has ripped her as far as possible from her mystery and from nature, and imprisoned her in an alienated world of technology in which she is reduced to language and naming in a male world of dictation and shorthand. A man in her office oddly divines her mystery, saying to her that she reminds him of a maple tree, even though he thinks her true name is "Mabel" and not "Maple." Their marriage makes him part of the odyssey of her self-discovery.

Maple's husband suggests that her father may have held the key to the mystery of her name but may also not have told her *everything* about the story of her naming:

> "And then it may have been
> Something a father couldn't tell a daughter
> As well as could a mother. And again
> It may been their one lapse into fancy
> 'Twould be too bad to make him sorry for
> By bringing it up when he was too old."

Perhaps these are dangerous words for the husband to sow. Maple had remembered a maple leaf bookmark in the family Bible marking something about "wave offerings." Critics have noted that in the book of Numbers, wave offerings are associated with women discharging penalties for sexual infidelities. Has something gone on between the father and mother that only the mother could have told her daughter?

When at the end of the poem Maple contemplates maple trees at various seasons, we wonder what, figuratively, she may be seeing herself in:

> They kept their thoughts away from when the maples
> Stood uniform in buckets, and the steam
> Of sap and snow rolled off the sugar house.
> When they made her related to the maples,
> It was the tree the autumn fire ran through
> And swept of leathern leaves, but left the bark
> Unscorched, unblackened, even, by any smoke.
> They always took their holidays in autumn.
> Once they came on a maple in a glade,
> Standing alone with smooth arms lifted up,
> And every leaf of foliage she'd worn
> Laid scarlet and pale pink about her feet.
> But its age kept them from considering this one.
> Twenty-five years ago at Maple's naming
> It could hardly have been a two-leaved seedling
> The next cow might have licked up out at pasture.
> Could it have been another maple like it?
> They hovered for a moment near discovery,
> Figurative enough to see the symbol,
> But lacking faith in anything to mean
> The same at different times to different people.

The images of maples are, perhaps, suggestive of many different things, some of them erotic and others, perhaps, more disturbing. But Maple's ability to find symbolic significance between herself and nature has, somehow, been fractured by time and life's unruliness as well as a lack of mystical faith.

The dialogue of home

The uncertainty and sadness behind the domestic story of Maple's name underlies almost all of Frost's dramas of "home." Home remained one of Frost's most important figures: "All science is domestic science, our domestication on and our hold on the planet" (*N*, 656). Frost ripped open the home and allowed women and men not only to speak but allowed their words to *act* on each other's deeds. At his best, Frost allows us to see the psychological forces at work behind the sayings of his men and women as they struggle to maintain power and fragile domestic order. Elinor and Robert Frost were co-valedictorians at their Lawrence High School graduation, and Elinor's address was entitled "Conversation as a Force in Life." It might as well have been the keynote for much of Frost's most powerful poetry. "The Fear," "The Death of the Hired Man," "Home Burial," "A Servant to Servants," "West-Running Brook," and "In the Home Stretch" allow dialogue in general, and the dialogue between men and women in particular, to unfold without resolution of the question of what it means to be human. These poems show Frost at his dramatic best, allowing his characters to reveal themselves and each other. More important, the poems become ongoing philosophical dramas about the boundaries of home and what it means to be human.

"Home Burial" may be one of Frost's most intimate and disturbing poems. Rarely had anyone before explored the extremely delicate mood inside a marriage after the death of a child. Certainly Frost knew something of it, having lost his son Elliot to cholera at the age of three. As we enter the scene of this poem, which includes the dialogue of Amy and her unnamed husband as well as the narrator's commentary, we do not know for certain how long the child has been dead and how long the couple have argued. More uncertainties arise in the course of a poem that tends to arouse a reader's willingness to make ethical judgments about how to grieve and how to treat others in the face of tragedy.

One of the demands the poem makes upon us almost from line to line is a need to decide not only what Amy and her husband say to each other but what their words *do* to each other. One common strand of interpretation holds that the couple misunderstand each other. Others hold that they understand each other very well, and that the death of the child has only opened deeper fissures in the marriage and questions of power, which the dialogue exposes. The first encounter of the poem represents a complex dance of movements and words which can appear at various moments both caring and hurtful.

> He saw her from the bottom of the stairs
> Before she saw him. She was starting down,
> Looking back over her shoulder at some fear.
> She took a doubtful step and then undid it
> To raise herself and look again. He spoke
> Advancing toward her: "What is it you see
> From up there always – for I want to know."
> She turned and sank upon her skirts at that,
> And her face changed from terrified to dull.
> He said to gain time: "What is it you see,"
> Mounting until she cowered under him.
> "I will find out now – you must tell me, dear."
> She, in her place, refused him any help
> With the least stiffening of her neck and silence.
> She let him look, sure that he wouldn't see,
> Blind creature; and awhile he didn't see.
> But at last he murmured, "Oh," and again, "Oh."

The narrator makes it clear that Amy (we have not yet learned her name) fears something before she encounters her husband, from what she has been seeing. She also willfully refuses her husband any help in understanding what troubles her, what she *sees*. Her husband veers within a sentence between inquiring and demanding. We are given by the narrator to see that she regards him as contemptuously incapable, a "blind creature."

The challenge of Amy to her husband begins a drama about whether he knows how to speak. Amy wishes, if not demands to make him conform to her sense and sensibility of what it means to grieve. What he says in response remains open to considerable interpretation:

> "What is it – what?" she said.

> "Just that I see."

> "You don't," she challenged. "Tell me what it is."

> "The wonder is I didn't see at once.
> I never noticed it from here before.
> I must be wonted to it – that's the reason.
> The little graveyard where my people are!
> So small the window frames the whole of it.
> Not so much larger than a bedroom, is it?
> There are three stones of slate and one of marble,

Broad-shouldered little slabs there in the sunlight
On the sidehill. We haven't to mind *those*.
But I understand: it is not the stones,
But the child's mound –"

"Don't, don't, don't, don't," she cried.

Does Amy's pained interruption of her husband's description of the view from the window come precisely as a response to his speaking of "the child's mound," the way he speaks about it, or the accumulation of what he has already said about the graveyard? One might imagine that for Amy the reference to "my people," the analogy between the graveyard and the bedroom, the description of the slabs as "broad-shouldered," all might have had a chilling or disturbing effect on her before mention of "the child's mound." Later she will accuse him of not knowing how to speak. ("'A man can't speak of his own child that's dead.'/ 'You can't because you don't know how to speak.'") The poem's drama focuses around the great dramatic tension between words, deeds, and their interpretation. Does Amy misunderstand her husband? Does her husband misunderstand her or understand her all too well?

When Amy taunts her husband by asserting that he does not know how to speak, she recollects the moment when she saw him digging the child's grave. Her accusation of his insensitivity stems from the fact of the eagerness with which he went about the task and *her* recollection of his actions. The fact that he did dig his own child's grave and his "talk about everyday concerns" in themselves strike her, at least in this moment, as incomprehensibly insensitive behavior. One wonders whether there may be an essential divide here between masculine and feminine sensibilities or, perhaps, between country and city sensibilities. Another possibility may rest in the fact that Amy seeks any way to remind her husband of his inarticulateness and less than human sensibility:

"If you had any feelings, you that dug
With your own hand – how could you? – his little grave;
I saw you from that very window there,
Making the gravel leap and leap in air,
Leap up, like that, like that, and land so lightly
And roll back down the mound beside the hole.
I thought, Who is that man? I didn't know you.
And I crept down the stairs and up the stairs
To look again, and still your spade kept lifting.
Then you came in. I heard your rumbling voice
Out in the kitchen, and I don't know why,

But I went near to see with my own eyes.
You could sit there with the stains on your shoes
Of the fresh earth from your own baby's grave
And talk about your everyday concerns.
You had stood the spade up against the wall
Outside there in the entry, for I saw it."

"I shall laugh the worst laugh I ever laughed.
I'm cursed. God, if I don't believe I'm cursed."

Amy recounts her own dramatically astonished reaction to her husband's digging as well as the "stains on his shoes," which becomes almost miasma on his soul.

When Amy reports what her husband did say, we are left in an interesting interpretive quandary. She appears to take his words as no more than a country saying about the weather, and her husband says nothing to dispossess her of her interpretation or lack of it. But surely "Three foggy mornings and one rainy day / Will rot the best birch fence a man could build" may be his way of talking figuratively about his child but also about what the child meant in the marriage. Amy may or may not understand his way of talking about serious matters or just how articulate he can be:

"I can repeat the very words you were saying.
'Three foggy mornings and one rainy day
Will rot the best birch fence a man can build.'
Think of it, talk like that at such a time!
What had how long it takes a birch to rot
To do with what was in the darkened parlor."

The child helped create a barrier that enclosed the family and constituted home; it also provided a fence that brought husband and wife together but now does not exist.

Though her husband treats Amy with exasperation and condescension, she clearly refuses him any help in "how to speak." She insists not only that he does not care but that as a husband, a man, and also as another human being he must be incapable of caring and grieving sufficiently to qualify to her standards as human:

"You *couldn't* care! The nearest friends can go
With anyone to death, comes so far short
They might as well not try to go at all.
No, from the time one is sick to death,
One is alone, and he dies more alone.

> Friends make pretense of following to the grave,
> But before one is in it, their minds are turned
> And making the best of their way back to life
> And living people, and things they understand.
> But the world's evil. I won't have grief so
> If I can change it. Oh, I won't, I won't!"

Amy asserts a fundamental difference between herself and others, including her husband, in their approach to the dying and grief. Nothing is far enough, and all language suffers from being mere rhetoric in the worst sense – pretense. Uncertainty and potential violence erupts at the end when Amy threatens to leave the home and her husband threatens to bring her "back by force – I will –"

The mysterious forces that bind and threaten to destroy marriages in Frost's dramatic poems come from within the men and women, though other forces intrude sometimes as figures of projection, sometimes as direct threats. As early as "Love and a Question" from *A Boy's Will*, the question of what the presence of a stranger and poverty can do to a young fragile marriage emerges: "But whether or not a man was asked / To mar the love of two / By harboring woe in the bridal house, / The bridegroom wished he knew." Frost develops the idea of the extent of human sympathy within the home and beyond it in "The Death of the Hired Man."

"The Death of the Hired Man" gives us the indirect portrait of a homeless figure, Silas the hired man, as well as a married couple, Mary and Warren, whose discussion over his return and impending death becomes a philosophical dialogue about the nature of home and the extent of human relations. Frost's own comments about the poem in his 1960 *Paris Review* interview tend to simplify the poem by turning the gendered voices into political allegory:

> They think I'm no New Dealer. But really and truly I'm not, you know, all that clear on it. In "The Death of the Hired Man" that I wrote long, long ago, long before the New Deal, I put it two ways about home. One would be the manly way: "Home is the place where, when you have to go there, They have to take you in." That's the man's feeling about it. And then the wife says, "I should have called it / Something you somehow hadn't to deserve." That's the New Deal, the feminine way of it, the mother way. You don't have to deserve your mother's love. You have to deserve your father's. He's more particular. One's a Republican, one's a Democrat. The father is always a Republican toward his son, and his mother's always a Democrat. Very few have noticed the second thing; they've always noticed the sarcasm, the hardness of the male one.   (*CPPP*, 885)

It may be that Frost is constructing an overlay of political allegory on one of his most widely anthologized poems to combat the reputation that haunted him then and continues to trouble his legacy: his questioning of the New Deal and his perceived skepticism of egalitarianism. For this reason, he may be overemphasizing (as well as oversimplifying) the complexity of voices in this and many of the other domestic poems.

In "The Death of the Hired Man," Mary and Warren may complement each other as much as critics have found them vocal and ethical opposites. Mary reports to Warren that since returning to the farm, Silas has been rambling on about Harold Wilson, the young boy he once worked with at the farm. As she describes this, it could be said that Mary sees some of herself in Silas – an underdog finding the right arguments too late. Embedded within the story is Harold Wilson himself and his interest in Latin and the violin for its own sake. Mary appears mocking this form of sophistication and knowledge for its own sake, even though Silas himself appears little better in accomplishment. Warren may only be concerned that his hired man will simply wander off again. One of the most powerful moments in the poem comes in the way Mary and Warren complement each other in dialogue, as Mary speaks openly that Silas has come to them to die, and that he regards them as family and home:

> "Warren," she said, "he has come home to die:
> You needn't be afraid he'll leave you this time."
>
> "Home," he mocked gently.
>
>   "Yes, what else but home?
> It all depends on what you mean by home.
> Of course he's nothing to us, any more
> Than was the hound that came a stranger to us
> Out of the woods, worn out upon the trail."
>
> "Home is the place where, when you have to go there,
> They have to take you in."
>
>   "I should have called it
> Something you somehow haven't to deserve."

In describing Silas as coming home and then in conceding somewhat to her husband's gentle mocking, Mary generates a dialogue about home that does not reconcile opposites but keeps them within viable tension.

Intrusion, isolation, and eventual madness all contribute to the fragility of home and the tensions between men and women within the home. It may be impossible to determine what precisely lies at the root of the struggle for power and the fear of loss and change generated within poems such as "The

Hill Wife," "The Witch of Coos," or "The Fear." In "The Fear," Frost creates
a stunning dramatic narrative of uncertainty; the precise nature of "the fear"
never becomes definite. Joel and his wife, if she is his wife, throw shadows
outside the farmhouse. She intimates, if not insists that she saw someone and
there is yet further suggestion that it is someone with whom she had some kind
of history:

> "It's not so very late – it's only dark.
> There's more in it than you're inclined to say.
> Did he look like–?"
>
>   "He looked like anyone.
> "I'll never rest tonight unless I know.
> Give me the lantern."
>
>   "You don't want the lantern."
>
> She pushed past him and got it for herself.
>
> "You're not to come," she said. "This is my business.
> If the time's come to face it, I'm the one
> To put it the right way. He'd never dare –
> Listen! He kicked a stone. Hear that, hear that!
> He's coming towards us. Joel, *go* in – please.
> Hark! – I don't hear him now. But please go in."
>
> "In the first place you can't make me believe it's –"
>
> "It is – or someone else he's sent to watch.
> And now's the time to have it out with him
> While we know definitely where he is."

Frost creates an intricate dance of dramatic escalation; both Joel and his wife
contribute to elevating the tension; Joel by denying any possibility of its being
the man his wife thinks it is and she both insisting that he would never dare
confront them and that *she alone* must handle the confrontation.

When the encounter comes it leaves many questions unresolved and brilliantly heightens the tension. She approaches the voice, and then he emerges.
It remains uncertain both what she sees and who, if anyone, she recognizes:

> And then the voice again: "You seem afraid.
> I saw by the way you whipped up the horse.
> I'll just come forward in the lantern light
> And let you see."
>
>   "Yes, do. – Joel, go back!"

> She stood her ground againt the noisy steps
> That came on, but her body rocked a little.
>
> "You see," the voice said.
>
> > "Oh." She looked and looked.
>
> "You don't see – I've a child here by the hand.
> A robber wouldn't have his family with him."
>
> "What's a child doing at this time of night?"
>
> "Out walking. Every child should have the memory
> Of at least one long-after-bedtime walk.
> What, son?"

We still cannot be sure from the man's cryptic comments of his relationship to the woman. The narrative observations about her looking followed by his statement that she does not see echoes Amy's criticism of her husband's "blindness" in "Home Burial." The conclusion of the poem demands that we remain unassuming, for we cannot be sure why she is calling out to Joel or what has happened to him or what is or may be about to happen in her encounter with this mysterious man:

> "But if that's all – Joel – you realize –
> You won't think anything. You understand?
> You understand that we have to be careful.
> This is a very, very lonely place.
> Joel!" She spoke as if she couldn't turn.
> The swinging lantern lengthened to the ground,
> It touched, it struck, it clattered and went out.

Did Joel's wife intensify fear as a form of psychological manipulation? Or did the man from the road turn out to be either someone she expected from her past or, if not, someone equally, if not more menacing? Frost's drama cultivates the terror of the uncertainty.

It would be wrong to view Frost's women, as a few critics have, as neurotics or purely wild. Their suffering in no way diminishes their capacity either to control, to be playful, or to perceive a reality which the poetry suggests is elusive but still there, palpable, and often menacing. Without question that reality must be judged from the perspective of the speakers, who prove to be enormously seductive, if often baffling and sad. "A Servant to Servants" shows Frost working in another poetic form – the dramatic monologue – giving particular poignancy to the speaker's domestic and emotional predicament. A recurring phrase of the speaker's "But I don't know" becomes the resonant assertion of uncertainty of a self caught between the isolation and demands of domestic labor and the fear and hopelessness of inherited madness. The title echoes a phrase from Genesis 9: 25, the curse given to Ham, the son of Noah, for seeing his father naked: "a servant of servants shall he be unto his brethren." Why would Frost be echoing such a thing in this instance? One reason may have to do with the speaker's audience. This is a woman speaking *to* women, a servant to servants. In that sense, she is telling women something about the condition of women, and the title becomes a subtle extra-poetic commentary on the subject matter of the poem:

> I didn't make you know how glad I was
> To have you come and camp here on our land.
> I promised myself to get down some day
> And see the way you lived, but I don't know!
> With a houseful of hungry men to feed
> I guess you'd find . . . It seems to me
> I can't express my feelings any more
> Than I can raise my voice or want to lift
> My hand (oh, I can lift it when I have to).
> Did you ever feel so? I hope you never.
> It's got so I don't even know for sure
> Whether I *am* glad, sorry, or anything.
> There's nothing but a voice-like left inside
> That seems to tell me how I ought to feel,
> And would feel if I wasn't all gone wrong.

We are stunned by the eloquence of this woman but can well imagine how stunned her audience must be within the dramatic context of the poem. They are likely botanizers, as we learn later when she asks them how they learned of Lake Willoughby, "In a book about ferns?" At the turn of the twentieth century, botanizing trips were often for women, though not exclusively. Frost, himself, was, of course, an amateur botanist and would take his family on trips to the Lake Willoughby area to escape hay fever. The audience that hears her must have been surprised to come upon this woman who begins to tell them about her broken life, with nothing but a "voice-like left inside." It changes the mood and context, if we imagine that these temporary campers, perhaps young women, have not as yet suffered any of the experiences of married life which she will be unfolding to them in the course of her monologue.

We cannot debate her truthfulness but the quality of her storytelling remains overwhelmingly compelling. Rather than complain or seem bitter, she gives wrenching glimpses of the cruelty of her husband, Len. As her story builds, we hear the possibility of madness running in the family, the horrifying story of an uncle kept in a cage in her parents' house and making music from it as a form of solace, and her fear that she is merely following the cycle:

> They tried to keep him clothed, but he paraded
> With his clothes on his arm – all of his clothes.
> Cruel – it sounds. I s'pose they did the best
> They knew. And just when he was at the height,
> Father and mother married, and mother came,
> A bride, to help take care of such a creature,
> And accommodate her young life to his.
> That was what marrying father meant to her.
> She had to lie and hear love things made dreadful
> By his shouts in the night. He'd shout and shout
> Until the strength was shouted out of him,
> And his voice died down slowly from exhaustion.
> He'd pull his bars apart like bow and bowstring,
> And let them go and make them twang until
> His hands had worn them smooth as any oxbow.
> And then he'd crow as if he thought that child's play –
> The only fun he had. I've heard them say, though,
> They found a way to put a stop to it.
> He was before my time – I never saw him;
> But the pen stayed exactly as it was
> There in the upper chamber in the ell,
> A sort of catch-all full of attic clutter.
> I often think of the smooth hickory bars.
> It got so I would say – you know, half-fooling –
> "It's time I took my turn upstairs in jail" –
> Just as you will till it becomes a habit.
> No wonder I was glad to get away.
> Mind you, I waited till Len said the word.
> I didn't want the blame if things went wrong.
> I was glad though, no end, when we moved out,
> And I looked to be happy, and I was,
> As I said, for a while – but I don't know!
> Somehow the change wore out like a prescription.

We cannot be certain whether the description of the uncle she never knew is purely fictive, a form of her own imaginative play against the labor and isolation she now faces. The trajectory of the story takes a painful downward turn, an escape from one "asylum" into another, but her storytelling subtly saves her for some moments and provides the voice-like order against the chaos of her life. She may be cursed with madness of a kind but she, like Ham, also exposes the nakedness of Len, who appears blind and deaf to the lonely existence as a servant he has created for his fragile partner.

When the narrator of "A Servant to Servants" says "the place is the asylum," she resigns herself grimly to state care for the mentally ill. The irony of the colloquial phrase also suggests that her home too has become an asylum in both senses of the word, a refuge and something of a place of madness. In Frost's narrative domestic poems, "home" becomes a metaphor for locating and grounding the self, for finding origins, and for establishing, ultimately, what it means to be human. More often than not, that drama takes place as an unresolved sexual conflict, in which a hierarchy of human values appears continually in debate and in flux. Frost's concern almost always appears to be with those voices in resistance to authority or, rather, with not allowing one single voice to become authoritative. What can be regarded as authoritative is continually thrown into question as the drama of each poem develops.

Both "The Witch of Coos" and "The Generations of Men" present the stories of home from the standpoint of what can be imagined from the lost past. The "witch" or old woman of Coos lives with her somewhat demented older son, concocting for the narrator of the poem a story about a ghost that rose, bones and all, to threaten her and husband. The old woman, a French Canadian, also happens to be a spiritualist. But what we find behind the story is one of marital treachery and power. She may have concocted the story of the ghost to inspire fear or at least some kind of passion in her husband or to rekindle in her imagination the power she once held over the man to whom the bones belonged. The bones figure in her mind as guilt over her infidelity. The bones, now allegedly nailed in the attic, she tells the narrator, were of a man with whom she had an affair and whom her husband, Toffile Lajway, killed instead of her.

Home in Frost's world always borders on becoming a fragile dream, something nearly lost that must be constantly brought into being and maintained in the minds of the men and women who live there. In the "Generations of Men," two distantly related members of the Stark family, a young man and woman, meet at a cellar hole that has been proclaimed to have been the original Stark home of years past. In setting the poem, Frost plays on the tourist events held in early twentieth-century Vermont and New Hampshire to try to rekindle interest in the vanishing rural past of New England. This event, a calling together of all members of the Stark family, has been cancelled because of rain. Only the boy and girl show, and their dialogue both projects an imagined past upon an obliterated history and reveals the sexual dynamics that would make a future history possible. But all of their concern about pride of ancestry and attempt to prove priority in "Starkness" reveals the possibility of a kind of madness and degeneracy:

"D'you know a person so related to herself
Is supposed to be mad."

       "I may be mad."

"You look so, sitting out here in the rain
Studying genealogy with me
You never saw before. What will we come to
With all this pride of ancestry, we Yankees?
I think we're all mad. Tell me why we're here
Drawn into town about this cellar hole
Like wild geese on a lake before a storm?
What do we see in such a hole, I wonder."

While she encourages him to imagine vividly their ancestors, and he claims to hear vividly the "purer oracle" of the nearby brook in its "wild descent," she reminds him skeptically: "'It's as you throw a picture on a screen: / The meaning of it all is out of you; / The voices give you what you wish to hear.'" In a flirtatious tale, the boy imagines himself as Odysseus and the girl as Nausicaa, and then turns ventriloquist again as Granny and Grandsir Stark ordering him to build a new home out of the ruined timbers of the past. Yet for all his imaginative projections onto the wasteland of the cellar hole, he admits to the girl, "Don't you think we sometimes make too much / Of the old stock? What counts is the ideals, / And those will bear some keeping still about." This mysterious admission comes as a surprise because neither he nor the girl ever quite states what the ideals are or have been. We find that same intimation of stasis in the midst of constant change in the dialogue between Joe and his wife "In the Home Stretch." Having moved from the city to the country and feeling that they have also moved closer to the end of their lives, they debate what in life may be truly new. Joe's wife provides a vision of two tracks of time: "'It would take me forever to recite / All that's not new in where we find ourselves.'" The dialogue itself on the verge of the ruins of a former home and an obliterated past has become the essential life force that may bring this boy and girl back together for another day, "sometime in rain," because it was the moody force that brought them together, "[b]ut if we must, in sunshine."

Frost and the poetry of nature

Because of the landscape of Frost's poetry, some find it easy to characterize him as a "nature poet." Frost, aware of this epithet, was quick to challenge it. "Some have called me a nature poet, because of the background, but I'm not a nature poet. There's always something else in my poetry" (*I*, 114). In a letter to

Untermeyer, Frost underscored the importance of the human in any landscape: "Not even in the most natural of nature poetry was nature ever anything but the background to the portrait of a lunatic, a lover, or a farmer" (*LU*, 243). In the pastoral dramas Frost will depict a close ecological relationship between man and nature.

Plant and human ecology become inextricable parts of pastoral drama in "Blueberries." The poem takes the form of a narrative dialogue between two companions who seek to pick the blueberries growing in the pasture of an absentee landlord named Patterson. (Frost changed the name, after the first publication of the poem in *North of Boston*, from Mortenson, which means "son of death.") The anapestic meter and rhymed couplets of their dialogue adds to our sense of their playfulness; yet the apparent innocence may mask more complications in the ecology of pastoral life. In the beginning, we learn that blueberries are growing where there had been a fire, as though by magic. The fire itself was the result of deforestation to make way for pasture:

> "You know where they cut off the woods – let me see –
> It was two years ago – or no! – can it be
> No longer than that? – and the following fall
> The fire ran and burned it all up but the wall."

> "Why, there hasn't been time for the bushes to grow.
> That's always the way with the blueberries, though;
> There may not have been the ghost of a sign
> Of them anywhere under the shade of the pine,
> But get the pine out of the way, you may burn
> The pasture all over until not a fern
> Or a grass-blade is left, not to mention a stick,
> And presto, they're up all around you as thick
> And hard to explain as a conjuror's trick."

The speakers may be rather innocent but they describe a well-known ecological phenomenon. The predominately anapestic meter of the passage underscores the playfulness and delight that the speaker takes in finding the blueberries growing there, inexplicable as "a conjuror's trick." The destruction of stronger, taller growths such as pines, allows for the possibility of certain plants, including more palatable ones, to grow that otherwise could not survive in their shade. Further, fire enables the seeds of certain types of ground fruit to burst, particularly blueberries. What may be destructive to fern and grass actually gives life to other plants. The "conjuror's trick" turns out to be no trick at all but a type of ecological subversion of hierarchy or sudden reversal of fortune: one form of life's loss becomes another's gain.

This ecological principle sets the figurative background for the tensions between the speakers and the Lorens, the family that lives in the pasture. The blueberries take their color and taste from the soil, their "'blue's but a mist from the breath of the wind, / A tarnish that goes at a touch of the hand, / And less than the tan with which pickers are tanned.'" One senses, at this point, that blueberries are metaphors for whatever manages to thrive or struggle unexpectedly, up from the "soot." Differences in skin color – perhaps among blueberries or humans – may be only superficial.

The speakers wonder whether they have the right to these berries in Patterson's pasture. Patterson walled in the pasture two years ago. One of the narrators hopes that Patterson doesn't care as much for gathering the valuable berries in his pasture as a ground robin might: "'He may and not care and so leave the chewink / To gather them for him – you know what he is. / He won't make the fact that they're rightfully his / An excuse for keeping us other folk out.'" But Patterson may be less of a problem than the Lorens. We learn when they encounter Loren and his children that they store up on wild berries, and that the berries have become an important source of food and income:

> "He seems to be thrifty; and hasn't he need,
> With the mouths of all those young Lorens to feed?
> He has brought them all up on wild berries, they say,
> Like birds. They store a great many away.
> They eat them the year round, and those they don't eat
> They sell in the store and buy shoes for their feet."

It certainly sounds as if the Lorens have made much of the economy of wild berries. So much so, that one wonders about how the fire got started. One of the speakers reflects pleasantly, if somewhat naively about this seemingly life of leisure "'. . . It's a nice way to live, / Just taking what nature is willing to give, / Not forcing her hand with harrow and plow.'"

This lovely vision of country life appears as naïve about human relations as it is about the struggle among species of flora and fauna for survival. The Lorens appear to know where all kinds of wild berries grow. When one of the speakers approaches Mr. Loren about where to find berries, he receives a polite but clearly sardonic pun about "*berrying*" by way of warning:

> "There *had* been some berries – but those were all gone.
> He didn't say where they had been. He went on:
> 'I'm sure – I'm sure' – as polite as could be.
> He spoke to his wife in the door, 'Let me see,
> Mame, *we* don't know any good berrying place?'
> It was all he could do to keep a straight face."

Who really possesses what grows wild? The Lorens have an interest in keeping the berries to themselves. But the narrators have other ideas:

> "If he thinks all the fruit that grows wild is for him,
> He'll find he's mistaken. See here, for a whim,
> We'll pick in the Pattersons' pasture this year.
> We'll go in the morning, that is, if it's clear,
> And the sun shines out warm: the vines must be wet."

In their adventure in the pasture, they also drive a bird from its nest. In "Blueberries," many indeed appeared threatened within the "walled" pasture of the Pattersons, alternately attracted by the ineluctable beauty of fruit and the need to survive. The poem concludes with one of the narrators describing the fruit in both sensuous and pernicious terms: "'You ought to have seen how it looked in the rain, / The fruit mixed with water in layers of leaves, / Like two kind of jewels, a vision for thieves.'" The old meaning of "paradise" comes to mind, a "walled-in" garden or pasture and the idea of unavoidable strife within paradise may come to mind as well.

In the "Letter to the *Amherst Student*," Frost described the background as "hugeness and confusion." In his notebooks, as we have seen, he describes nature as "chaos." In the poetry Frost creates a drama between human and non-human nature. In other words, there is always the question of the perception of non-human nature, whether of other creatures or of the landscape and matter. We see that sense of "hugeness" as a temptation of the thrush's music and the "pillared dark" for the speaker in "Come in," for example, a temptation from which he retreats and for which he recognizes he has not been called. It should be very clear from what Frost said about his empirical tendencies, allying him with Aristotle more than Plato, that he had a natural scientist's interest for noticing things in specific detail and in the way they interact with one another. When Wallace Stevens wrote in "The Snow Man" that "to have a mind of winter" one should write of "[n]othing that is not there and the nothing that is," he asserts *the* nothingness as an essential basis of reality. Frost's poetry may often express skepticism about what we project onto nature and about the centrality of the human mind in the world. But there always seems to be some apprehension or attempt to apprehend *something* as the basis for the way the world operates, sometimes consonant with what we think and sometimes beyond what we think. That *something* in Frost, however elusive, always amounts to more than nothing. Frost's "For Once, Then, Something" exemplifies the precariousness of the problem. He wrote the poem in a classical meter, phalaecean, named after a Greek epigrammatic poet, hendecasyllables (a trochee, a dactyl, followed by three more trochees) as if to emphasize the firm cultural framing of the well into which he peers. At first, the speaker seems mocked for finding himself reflected, Narcissus-like, in the well; the surface "Gives me back in a shining surface picture / Me myself in the summer heaven godlike / Looking out of a wreath of fern and cloud-puffs." But "*[o]nce]*" he thought he penetrated "the picture" and saw something "white," evoking perhaps the ungraspable phantom in Melville's reinterpretation of Ovid in the first chapter of *Moby-Dick*, "something more of the depths." That turned out to be fleeting because:

> Water came to rebuke the too clear water.
> One drop fell from a fern, and lo, a ripple
> Shook whatever it was lay there at the bottom,
> Blurred it, blotted it out. What was that whiteness?
> Truth? A pebble of quartz? For once, then, something.

There may be considerable self-mockery in the notion that the whiteness may be "Truth" (even though Frost echoes an old Greek saying that truth can be found at the bottom of a well). The "then" in the title and final phrase could suggest both time past and also an emphatic sense that "something," not "nothing," exists beyond our limited perceptions. As we have seen and will see in other poems, "Mending Wall," "Design," "The Oven Bird," "The Need of Being Versed in Country Things," the word "something," or "thing" in Frost becomes a signifier for irreducible yet still not quite graspable *pragma* or fact. The flux and fluidity of the natural world, for which the water and the simple are metaphors, indicate the difficulty of perceiving phenomena in anything but a momentary way. The ferns, probably of the *polyploidy* variety, grow on rocks and threaten the integrity of the well-curb or human order itself. The very concepts of surface and depth, which have long been important in distinguishing aspects of human thought, may themselves be only metaphoric constructs or the metaphors may aptly describe, within limits, the pursuit of the real.

Frost's poetry does draw analogies between the mind of man and the rest of the creaturely world and animate world. What do our emotions and our perceptions have to do with those of the rest of the animal and insect kingdom? Do we have a tendency to project or humanize where the rest of the creaturely world is somehow indifferent? What place, if any, does "mind" have in nature? These were not new philosophical questions when Frost began writing. In "A Considerable Speck," the narrator observes of the nearly microscopic mite that crosses his paper, "Plainly with an intelligence I dealt. / It seemed too tiny to have room for feet, / Yet must have had a set of them complete / To express how much it didn't want to die." The extended downward sympathy toward this one small creature stands in contrast to the "tenderer-than-thou / Collectivistic regimenting love / With which the modern world is being swept." The poems become subtle meditations on the relationship between man and the rest of the creaturely world, and tend to challenge the romantic tendency to use nature in purely symbolic and emblematic ways. But they also have additional philosophical, if not political, edge to them. Several of Frost's later animal poems do become parabolic in their strategies: "The Bear," "The Egg and the Machine" (from *West-Running Brook)*, "A Drumlin Woodchuck," "Departmental," "At Woodward's Gardens," and, as we shall see, "The White-Tailed Hornet" (from a *Further Range)*. All of these poems tend to satirize through "downward comparisons" between man and other creatures the presumptions, regimentations, and dissatisfactions of the human intellect while also emphasizing the fluid line between man and the rest of the creaturely world. These poems raise challenging questions about the line between our instincts and our intellects.

Fluidity, transience, and metamorphosis in nature haunt some of Frost's most memorable poems. "Hyla Brook," an unorthodox sonnet of fifteen lines, follows a brook named for the small peeper frogs that inhabit its banks. (Frost also evokes Virgil's account in "Eclogue VI" of the spring where Hylas was left, as well as Darwin's discussion of Hyla frogs in chapter 2 of *The Voyage of the Beagle*, one of Frost's favorite books). By summer both the brook and the peepers for which it was named have disappeared. Yet the speaker invokes, parenthetically, the memory of their sound in winter and in human terms: "Like ghost of sleigh-bells in a ghost of snow." The brook's metamorphosis has occurred in a seed-producing plant. In the final analogies of the poem, leaves and paper sheets, the speaker suggests that the brook may survive only as a palimpsest of human memories, a brook only in memory, faded in natural history:

> By June our brook's run out of song and speed.
> Sought for much after that, it will be found
> Either to have gone groping underground
> (And taken with it all the Hyla breed
> That shouted in the mist a month ago,
> Like ghost of sleigh-bells in a ghost of snow) –
> Or flourished and come up in jewel-weed,
> Weak foliage that is blown upon and bent
> Even against the way its waters went.
> Its bed is left a faded paper sheet
> Of dead leaves stuck together by the heat –
> A brook to none but who remember long.

This as it will be seen is other far
Than with brooks taken otherwhere in song.
We love the things we love for what they are.

The final fifteenth line, with its striking monosyllables and simplicity of diction, seems to save what has been transformed from loss. What, though, "are" the "things" to which it refers? What kind of existence or being do they have once they exist only in memory? What other brooks "taken otherwhere in song" does the speaker mean?

"Hyla Brook" appeared in *Mountain Interval* (1916). He began the book *West-Running Brook* (1928), the title poem of which will be discussed in more detail later, with another powerful meditation on fluidity and transformation in nature, "Spring Pools." The pools themselves become a figure for that reflective consciousness which comes into being temporarily in nature only to vanish again. The pools seem like eyes which "still reflect," in the sense of being both persistent and contemplative, but are fragile as "flowers beside them, chill and shiver" (with a superb internal rhyme). One of the striking points of the poem is the recognition of what threatens the existence of the pools and the flowers: the trees' need of water and light:

These pools that, though in forests, still reflect
The total sky almost without defect,
And like the flowers beside them, chill and shiver,
Will like the flowers beside them soon be gone,
And yet not out by any brook or river,
But up by roots to bring dark foliage on.

The fact of competition in nature's annual cycles destroys small and often lovely things. They are lovely to the speaker who threatens the trees and imputes near demonic drives to their "pent-up buds" and "powers" against doing what they cannot help doing to survive. Perhaps he feels the threatening fluidity, ephemeral, and reflexive quality of all forms of life, "flowery waters" and "watery flowers" transformed "snows that melted only yesterday."

"Spring Pools" brings the basic fact not only of transformation but of competition into the image of nature. Our consciousness tries to resist the erosion of that competition. We would like to hold ourselves above what appears to be the cruelty of nature. (Perhaps only we call natural processes cruel.) Frost recognized in certain respects our apartness from everything but also enjoys poking fun at our pride in believing ourselves unique and morally superior to the rest of nature. Frost considered the question of whether nature was non-moral and whether we were merely projecting our consciousness onto nature in evaluating its morality. In one interview, he takes delight in deflating the views that nature is any way benign or that man is any way exempt from its cruelty:

> I know [nature] isn't kind. As Matthew Arnold said: "Nature is cruel. It's man that's sick of blood." And it doesn't seem very sick of it. Nature is always more or less cruel. Shall I tell you what happened on the porch of a professor – minister he was, too? The war was going on, a beautiful moonlit night. He was there with some boys, talking about the horrors of war – how cruel men were to each other and how kind nature was, what a beautiful country this was spread beneath us, you know – moonlight on it. And just as he talked that way, in the woods – something had got into its nest. Nature was being cruel. The woods are killing each other anyway. That's where the expression came from "a place in the sun." A tree wanting a place in the sun it can't get. The other trees won't give it to it.[15]

Frost had a keen sense of the subtlety and universality of ecological warfare. Perhaps because of this fundamental sense of struggle in the nature of things, he had little sense of sentimentality about history. In fact, as he wrote in his "Letter to *The Amherst Student*," he viewed it as "immodest" to regard one's own time as worse than any other:

> We have no way of knowing that this age is one of the worst in the world's history. Arnold claimed the honor for the age before this. Wordsworth claimed it for the last but one. And so on back through literature. I say they claimed the honor for their ages. They claimed it rather for themselves. It is immodest of a man to think of himself as going down before the worst forces ever mobilized by God.   (*CP*, 114)

Frost deplored the humanist stance that distanced itself from science and the kind of penetration into matter that science championed. This positive attitude toward empirical observation of the world, as he said, "developed from the ground up," led him to embrace not only Thoreau's *Walden* but Darwin's *The Voyage of the Beagle*. In a letter to his Amherst colleague Theodore Beard, who had written an essay on metaphor in Darwin, Frost discussed Darwin's work and science in general as one of the humanities because of its reliance on metaphor, its building of a larger picture of the world from smaller details:

> Others who have known my predilection for The Voyage have given me the first editions of it, British and American. I find it hard to decide which to put your essay into. Even the deserving seldom get such right (and pretty things) said of them – even after the lapse of so long a time. Why read Carlyle for something to do when there is always The Voyage

to read again. I must look up the spelling of Yammerscooner and Lampalagua. We are considering one of the three best books of prose of the nineteenth century, though I doubt if it is on Hutchins list at St. Johns. The other two were written in America. I am away over on the side of Darwin as you depict him. My accusation that he was only adding to our metaphorical heritage falls to the ground when you make me realize that he said so first himself. My accusation becomes a citation for bravery. You make him even more what I like to think he was. These straight-laced humanists had better be careful about whom they read out of the party. I got a dose of them in Cincinnati last week – bush leaguers. It takes too long to dawn on them that science is merely one of the Humanities.[16]

Frost's interest in Darwin went beyond the epistemology of observing small natural details from which to infer a larger picture. The tension between the meaning of the small event and its larger implications and the place of the human mind in interpreting "the facts" of the scene forms the background of Frost's sonnet "Design." The argument from design had long been used to prove the existence of divinity by analogy; Paul in Romans had talked of God's two books – scripture and his creation. By the seventeenth century, there grew to be much more of an acrimonious split between those who held that one could find divinity either in one, the book of nature, or in scripture, but not in both, and that the two could not be harmonized. In the nineteenth century, medieval arguments from design had continued to be refined. William Paley put forward the argument based on the analogy to a watch. If we find a watch, looking at its intricate mechanism implies a watchmaker. If we look at wonders of creation, it implies a creator and, one would like to think, a benevolent creator. Darwin's way of looking at the world did extraordinary damage to the argument from design because in the small ranges of observation it showed more chance, blunder, and change than order.

"Design," one of Frost's most memorable sonnets, invokes a little drama of someone observing a little scene in nature and trying to find some design in it, perhaps some indication of a larger meaning. The title, too, carries with it the suggestion of the history of the "argument from design," namely that the things of the earth reveal by analogy the plan of a creator. The poem, playful and sly, appears to undermine that kind of reasoning. The first stanza has the quality of a song of innocence, particularly with its grace analogies of "dimpled," "dew drop," "kite," and "snow-white" even though the spider and moth are "characters of death and blight" in some kind of ritual of death. The rhyming of "moth," "froth," and "broth" also suggest a grim blurring of the scene and impending meal into a white whole:

> I found a dimpled spider, fat and white,
> On a white heal-all, holding up a moth
> Like a white piece of rigid satin cloth –
> Assorted characters of death and blight
> Mixed ready to begin the morning right,
> Like ingredients of a witches' broth –
> A snow-drop spider, a flower like a froth,
> And dead wings carried like a paper kite.

The finely crafted octave leads to a sestet in which we might expect to find a resolution, a design or, more important, evidence of a designer. Instead, we are left with a series of questions. The observer-speaker may wonder whether all this concatenation of whiteness means something or happens to be nothing more than a chance occurrence in a very small, isolated moment. First, what does the mutation of the "heal-all" mean? Second, what brought all the various white characters together for the somewhat grisly ceremony:

> What had that flower to do with being white,
> The wayside blue and innocent heal-all?
> What brought the kindred spider to that height,
> Then steered the white moth thither in the night?
> What but design of darkness to appall? –
> If design govern in a thing so small.

The penultimate question sounds large and apocalyptic. But "appall" has no object, and there is something slightly amusing about the fact that the etymology of the word means "to make white." Is the horrific "design of darkness," then, nothing more than a tautology, deflating the implication that some evil demiurge is at work in the world? The final line of the poem deflates the horror and suggests that whole scene may be, "a thing," indeterminate, and too "small" from which to draw grand emblematic or symbolic inferences.[17]

The concluding questions of the poem echo the questions of William Blake's "The Tyger": "Tyger Tyger, burning bright, / In the forests of the night; / What immortal hand or eye, / Could frame thy fearful symmetry?" The basic problems of theodicy lurk behind both poems: if a good God's creation is good and beautiful, why should there be evidence of such suffering in it? If God is all powerful, perhaps he is not good. If he is good, then he is not all powerful. These questions become related to the design argument, if we look at nature as in any way providing evidence for the presence of divinity or for man to find a connection between himself and divinity.

What kind of "design" would Frost let himself see in nature? The poem itself, as many have said, may be a "design," "a momentary stay against confusion imposed upon a chaotic scene. Nature might allow a moth a certain color to protect itself from predators, yet here it has been caught by a spider. Mutations, whether by a "heal-all" or a moth, may not always work and produce waste in a process of trial and error as species struggle to leave progeny. The sense of "waste" haunted Frost in human and non-human nature. His poems often explored the limits of both sympathy and empathy about the fact of waste.

Frost dramatizes the extent and limit of human sympathy to the creaturely world poignantly in "To a Moth Seen in Winter." Though it would be unlikely that this was a winter moth, it has made the flight, "the venture of eternity," between the wood where it was hatched and the wood where presumably it will mate or lay its eggs. Yet, here is a moth, replete with colorings to lure a mate and to camouflage and protect it from predators hopelessly seeking a mate in the wrong season. Its entire evolutionary structure has become meaningless yet it has somehow driven itself out of season. A "gloveless" human hand, not protected itself except for a few moments from the cold, offers a warm, momentary haven for the moth:

> Here's first a gloveless hand warm from my pocket,
> A perch and resting place 'twixt wood and wood,
> Bright-black-eyed silvery creature, brushed with brown,
> The wings not folded in repose, but spread.
> (Who would you be, I wonder, by those marks
> If I had moths to friend as I have flowers?)

The moth takes flight to "seek the love of kind," and "eternity," "spending" its energy in flight, though that very movement warms it in winter. Some impulse or instinct drives the moth despite the hostility and impossibility of the situation. The speaker recognizes, however, that though what he pities in the moth is something human, "untimeliness," his pity cannot reach, nor save the moth. He has much to do to save his own life. We sense this not only in the immediate, literal sense of how much he can withstand being out in the cold but also in some larger, unspecified sense in the world where others are dying:

> And what I pity in you is something human,
> The old incurable untimeliness,
> Only begetter of all ills that are.
> But go. You are right. My pity cannot help.
> Go till you wet your pinions and are quenched.
> You must be made more simply wise than I
> To know the hand I stretched impulsively
> Across the gulf of well nigh everything
> May reach to you, but cannot touch your fate.
> I cannot touch your fate, much less can save,
> Who am tasked to save my own a little while.

It may be worth noting that Frost dated the poem "circa 1900," the year his son Elliot died of cholera. The feeling of being unable to save his own three-year-old son may have, in part, inspired this meditation on the fragility of all life and the limits of what one can do for the sick and dying, through its ascription of human "untimeliness" in the moth, and the recognition of the futility of pity. Frost finally published the poem in *A Witness Tree* (1942), giving the poem added historical freshness by the context of the war.

What can one, then, learn from a poetical education in nature? That may be partly the suggestion of the title "The Need of Being Versed in Country Things," a poem as much about unlearning our assumptions about nature as confirming them. What, after all, are "country things"? The title subtly evokes Hamlet's rejoinder to Ophelia about "country matters," a euphemism for sex or fornication. What would that have to do with a poem about a burned-out farm now inhabited by small birds?

The poem begins with language suggestive of purpose and design. Yet the very idea that a burning house had brought sunset color to the sky seems a parody of the idea of design. The irony deepens with the fact that only the chimney remains after the fire:

> The house had gone to bring again
> To the midnight sky a summer glow.
> Now the chimney was all of the house that stood,
> Like a pistil after the petals go.

The analogy of the chimney to a pistil without its petals also indicates the position of the human in the biological scheme: bereft of a home or nest, humans are incapable of attracting and keeping family and, therefore, breeding as any other members of the biological world (the feminine reproductive part of the flower remains without the parts necessary for attracting pollinators). "Again" at the end of the first line indicates that this kind of frightening accident has happened before.

Humans are completely absent from this poem except as memories or elegies to what they used to control. In this case, the barn only remains left "to bear forsaken the place's name." The barn opened for the horses, once the domesticated creatures of farm labor, and now only a memory:

> No more it opened with all one end
> For teams that came by the stony road
> To drum on the floor with scurrying hoofs
> And brush the mow with the summer load.

Birds now occupy the barn and the property. The narrator allows himself to project for a moment human sadness into their murmurs. He puns on "dwelling"; what the birds do literally in the old barn, we do in emotional futile attachment, as we once did in the home itself:

> The birds that came to it through the air
> At broken windows flew out and in,
> Their murmur more like the sigh we sigh
> From too much dwelling on what has been.

The next stanza allows some retreat from that emotional investment in the birds' putative sadness. Nature goes on in renewal. The pump, which once had the function of extracting water for human beings, now serves a different function for the birds. The fence wire, once used as a barrier, ironically, does little other than give the birds a place to perch:

> Yet for them the lilac renewed its leaf,
> And the aged elm, though touched with fire;
> And the dry pump flung up an awkward arm;
> And the fence post carried a strand of wire.

The final stanza finally denies the projection of human pathos onto non-human nature while at the same time suggesting another projection to the birds' song, if a projection at all "rejoicing." At this final moment, a powerful syntactic twist holds back the final punch – how much one needs to be "versed in country things" *not* to believe that nature shares our sadness:

> For them there was really nothing sad.
> But though they rejoiced in the nest they kept,
> One had to be versed in country things
> Not to believe the phoebes wept.

The choice of "versed" still indicates that "country things" may never be quite certain and always the matter of interpretation and of lore. Be that as may be, the speaker has saved the specific name of these birds for the final line. Phoebes are voracious ant and insect hunters. They engage in remarkable acrobatic feats in their pursuit of their prey. Moreover, they are staunchly territorial birds. Indeed, the observation that they have staked out a new nest which they seem to keep and that they seem to rejoice much more than weep would be the conclusion of a good ornithologist and observer of nature. This is a poem about the indifference of nature to human sentiment, in fact to sentiment in general in the pursuit of survival.

Frost always thought that "waste" presented itself as an essential fact of natural process. Not only did he not lament it, he appeared as time went on both to accept and even to insist on its virtues. In "Pod of the Milkweed," the drab flower attracts pollinating butterflies. In true Darwinian fashion, the beautiful butterflies turn into pugnacious fighters, struggling with each other:

> Its flowers' distilled honey is so sweet
> It makes the butterflies intemperate.
> There is no slumber in its juice for them.
> One knocks another off from where he clings.
> They knock the dyestuff off each others' wings –
> With thirst on hunger to the point of lust.
> They raise in their intemperance a cloud
> Of mingled butterfly and flower dust
> That hangs perceptibly above the scene.

The sustenance provided by the flower to the butterflies and the fight of the butterflies have no purpose other than reproduction, presumably both for the butterflies and for the milkweed. The process, however, comes at terrible expense. The speaker acknowledges this near the conclusion of the poem:

> But waste was of the essence of the scheme.
> And all the good they did for man or god
> To all those flowers they passionately trod
> Was leave as their posterity one pod
> With an inheritance of restless dream.

We might wonder at this point whether the pod will be of the milkweed or of the butterflies, which may be no more than instruments of the milkweed's purposes. It may be strange to consider "waste" as the "essence of [a] scheme"; the line suggests both cruelty and randomness as well as the possibility of some kind of vaguely discernable design.

Frost became more vocal about waste as a principle of life in the years after World War I. He wrote to Untermeyer in 1931: "We were brought up on principles of saving everything, ourselves included. The war taught us a new gospel. My next book is to be called The Right to Waste. The Right? The duty, the obligation, to waste everything, time, material, *and* the man . . ." (*LU*, 209). In his notebooks, Frost could sound even more poignant and illiberal about the necessity of waste:

> The philosopher says dismiss the idea of purpose. And in the same breath he speaks as if the purpose of everything was our purpose to come out on a mountain top level of peace and equality. He thinks we have something in us that won't be gotten the better of by our needs and greeds. He assumes we have no need of strengthening ourselves in human rivalry to hold our own against nature. Our dissatisfaction with

we know not what enemy be the evolutionary thing in our bones – a
strain – blind

He who stays out of waste and lives to save
His home his money or his very life
Who does not join in the unselfish waste
Of everything who pays not daily tribute
To the eternal rubbish refuse heap of God
Better beware he will be held a cheat

(*N*, 280)

"The Bonfire," becomes a metaphor of the great refuse heap, a ruck of brush
that a laborer-father tells his children they should set on fire to scare themselves
in preparation for war. When Frost published "The Bonfire" in 1916, the United
States had not entered the Great War, but the Zeppelin bombing of England and
the sinking of the Lusitania had occurred. So when the children assert "'Oh,
war's not for children – it's for men,'" the father's demonic response, derived
in part from his memory of the power of a bonfire of his own making that had
nearly gone out of control, grimly asserts the need for the ritual preparation,
which includes children:

> " . . . Haven't you heard, though,
> About the ships where war has found them out
> At sea, about the towns where war has come
> Through opening clouds at night with droning speed
> Further o'erhead than all but stars and angels,–
> And children in the ships and in the towns?
> Haven't you heard what we have lived to learn?
> Nothing so new – something we had forgotten:
> *War is for everyone, for children too.*
> I wasn't going to tell you and I mustn't.
> The best way is to come up the hill with me
> And have our fire and laugh and be afraid."

"For" in the phrase has the force of meaning both "to preserve" and "appropri-
ate" for the participation of children. War and its waste become more encom-
passing and universal.

Frost's sense of the universality of "wanton waste in peace and war," as he
called it in "Pod of the Milkweed," in knowledge of the ways of both human
and non-human nature, inspired Frost to write as complex a sonnet as "Range-
Finding," one of a number of war poems written and published around the
time of World War I. The human world of battle recedes into the background
and becomes part of the general ecology of nature. Remarkably, Frost rather

unselfconsciously invests the non-human world with a sense of life and emotional struggle. We see "a stricken flower" and the "dispossessed" butterfly:

> The battle rent a cobweb diamond-strung
> And cut a flower beside a ground bird's nest
> Before it stained a single human breast.
> The stricken flower bent double and so hung.
> And still the bird revisited her young.
> A butterfly its fall had dispossessed
> A moment sought in air his flower of rest,
> Then lightly stooped to it and fluttering clung.

The poem concludes with a beautiful description and strange trick of perspective. A spider had restrung its web, its "cables" or technology, of death and entrapment. Yet another bullet merely touching it, fools the spider into thinking it had caught a fly. Perhaps the bullet was "range-finding," too, but the shooters do not recognize the smaller range of life. But the poem acknowledges a strange interconnectedness of life, sometimes struggling to reproduce, sometimes predatory. From the spider's range of perspective, not finding a fly signifies "nothing." He allows the spider, who "sullenly withdrew," the emotion of disappointment:

> On the bare upland pasture there had spread
> O'ernight 'twixt mullein stalks a wheel of thread
> And straining cables wet with silver dew.
> A sudden passing bullet shook it dry.
> The indwelling spider ran to greet the fly,
> But finding nothing, sullenly withdrew.

It would be difficult to put a name on what motivates the spider, and the speaker writes about it, the way Darwin wrote about insects, without any self-conscious sense of anthropomorphic emotional projection.

Frost could also write poems in which scientific theories, conjectures, or other intellectual presumptions had gone too far, leaving man, ironically, in a hopeless skeptical position. Perhaps the most challenging and intriguing of these, "The White-Tailed Hornet," subtitled "or the revision of theories," reveals a narrator melding an ideal divine perfection with animal or insect instinct, a process of "downward comparison" that does not hold in observation and reveals his own folly. The speaker, who should not be too hastily identified with Frost himself, readily assumes that a hornet ("White-Tailed Hornets" do not actually exist – like a white whale, it may be a mythic phantom) has perfect control of his behavior based on instinct. The opening lines reveal the speaker's striking and somewhat repetitious analogies for the hornet ("like a bullet," "like the pupil of a pointed gun," "more unerring than a bullet"), all of which are decidedly anthropomorphic:

> The white-tailed hornet lives in a balloon
> That floats against the ceiling of the woodshed.
> The exit he comes out at like a bullet
> Is like the pupil of a pointed gun.
> And having power to change his aim in flight,
> He comes out more unerring than a bullet.
> Verse could be written on the certainty
> With which he penetrates my best defense
> Of whirling hands and arms about the head
> To stab me in the sneeze-nerve of a nostril.
> Such is the instinct of it I allow.

The power of instinct here appears to be everything we would ordinarily ascribe to a creature that does not err, whether from "power to change" or inherited "certainty." What is amusing, if not ironic, is the way the narrator states that "verse could be written" about this certainty, almost as if he would write a paean to nature. He seems not to realize that the "verse" is his own analogy-making, the ascription of his ideals of perfection, associated with the elusive concept of instinct, to the insect hornet. In this little comic moment, we learn that the hornet may be interested in those "sneeze-nerves" because hornets look to such openings as places to lay eggs.

The speaker, though, doesn't understand this fact about hornets. Instead, he sees or rather tries to deny that he was attempting to steal the hornet's nest. These nests were often taken and used as decorations in people's homes. At this moment, the speaker may be finding himself more dangerously close to being comprehended by the hornet and wishes to retract the allowance of perfection *he* had granted to the insect. As a human, he insists that the hornet "recognize in me the exception / I like to think I am in everything":

> Yet how about the insect certainty
> That in the neighborhood of home and children
> Is such an execrable judge of motives
> As not to recognize in me the exception
> I like to think I am in everything –
> One who would never hang above a bookcase
> His Japanese crepe-paper globe for trophy?
> He stung me first and stung me afterward.
> He rolled me off the field head over heels,
> And would not listen to my explanations.

The comedy continues as the speaker hopes to find the hornet's instincts, whatever that may mean, working infallibly at his house. There the hornet will not recognize him as an enemy, and focus with unerring precision, "hawking for flies." (In an interesting essay on this poem, B. J. Sokol has pointed out that this phrase betrays a joke at the heart of the poem. There is no white-tailed hornet in North America but there is a white-tailed hawk and a white-headed hornet. Sokol suggests that Frost is deliberately mixing the terms. Perhaps this is part of a Frost fable of the phantom-elusiveness of "instinct" and the totality of "nature.")[18] Soon enough, our speaker finds the hornet, again, less than instinctively perfect when it comes to hunting.

> I watched him where he swooped, he pounced, he struck;
> But what he found he had was just a nailhead.
> He struck a second time. Another nailhead.
> "Those are just nailheads. Those are fastened down."
> Then disconcerted and not unannoyed,
> He swooped and struck a little huckleberry
> The way a player curls around a football.
> "Wrong shape, wrong color, and wrong scent," I said.
> The huckleberry rolled him on his head.

When the hornet actually misses a fly instead of something that just looked like a fly, then the speaker becomes "dangerously skeptic." But this is at the same time almost amusing because he was willing to see the hornet figuratively as a poet, and a poet who makes faulty analogies and seems to have ultimately a poor grasp of the real:

> At last it was a fly. He shot and missed;
> And the fly circled round him in derision.
> But for the fly he might have made me think
> He had been at his poetry, comparing
> Nailhead with fly and fly with huckleberry:
> How like a fly, how very like a fly.
> But the real fly he missed would never do;
> The missed fly made me dangerously skeptic.

The poem concludes with a remarkable meditation on the effect of "downward comparisons," something that had been going on in poetry for several hundred years, even before the Romantic revolution. We project our analogies onto the natural world whose creatures we imbue with an ideal of perfection that is all our own:

Won't this whole instinct matter bear revision?
Won't almost any theory bear revision?
To err is human, not to, animal.
Or so we pay the compliment to instinct,
Only too liberal of our compliment
That really takes away instead of gives.
Our worship, humor, conscientiousness
Went long since to the dogs under the table.
And served us right for having instituted
Downward comparisons . . .

Emerson and Thoreau had both been willing to see divine qualities in nature. Emerson regarded nature as "a symbol of the spirit." In *Walden*, we find Thoreau seeking to obtain a new, unmediated Adamic language rooted in the facts of nature. There can be little question that Darwin made analogy literal and homologous by suggesting that we were similar to but actually the same as other creatures, different in degree only. The grounding, then, for our ideals of perfection becomes as shifting as the phenomenon we choose to observe:

. . . As long on earth
As our comparisons were stoutly upward
With gods and angels, we were men at least,
But little lower than the gods and angels.
But once comparisons were yielded downward,
Once we began to see our images
Reflected in the mud and even dust,
'Twas disillusion upon disillusion.
We were lost piecemeal to the animals,
Like people thrown out to delay the wolves.
Nothing but fallibility was left us,
And this day's work made even that seem doubtful.

The final twenty-one lines may be simply the disillusioned torrent of the somewhat foolish narrator. They also encapsulate a particular problem in intellectual and poetic history about taking the comparison between man and other creatures too far. It becomes both a moral problem, for what, if anything, should insect societies tell us about how we ought to live, as well as an epistemological problem. We cannot help but make *downward comparisons* but there must be some judgment about how to make them. The final line of the poem can be taken as a reversal of the assertion in the previous line that "Nothing but fallibility was left us." As a thorough skeptic, the narrator must doubt even that assertion, as he does in the final line.

Frost's view that the tones of speech existed before words makes several of his other poems about birds, in addition to "The Need of Being Versed in Country Things," particularly poignant. "On a Bird Singing in Its Sleep," "The Oven Bird," and "Never Again Would Birds' Song Be the Same," all explore the proximity of meaning of creaturely sound to the meanings we wish or hope to hear. Frost paired "On a Bird Singing in Its Sleep" with "Design" in *A Further Range* (1936). The octave of this sonnet makes observations about a bird singing at night but saves for the sixth, seventh, and eighth lines the reason for concern: its singing could put it in danger of predators:

> A bird half wakened in the lunar noon
> Sang halfway through its little inborn tune.
> Partly because it sang but once all night
> And that from no especial bush's height;
> Partly because it sang ventriloquist
> And had the inspiration to desist
> Almost before the prick of hostile ears,
> It ventured less in peril than appears.

The sense of the bird's unconscious behavior suggested by "half wakened" and "inborn" stand in contrast to its strategic and willful behavior suggested by "ventriloquist" and "inspiration to desist." Nevertheless, hostile ears have been alerted to its presence. In the concluding sestet the poet-speaker, feeling kinship to the bird, seems to believe that the behavior of the bird "singing out of sleep and dream" must not threaten its survival or it would not already have survived so long on earth:

> It could not have come down to us so far
> Through the interstices of things ajar
> On the long bead chain of repeated birth
> To be a bird while we are men on earth
> If singing out of sleep and dream that way
> Had made it much more easily a prey.

The phrases, "interstices of things ajar," "bead chain of repeated birth," as well as "while we are men on earth," suggest a mystical way of looking at the problem of ecological niches, evolutionary descent, and the interconnectedness of life.

Both "The Oven Bird" and "Never Again Would Birds' Song Be the Same" dramatize Frost's fascination with the primordial relationship of sound to meaning. Both sonnets are also remarkable studies of origins and attempts to recover loss. Both "indoor" and "outdoor" schooling come into play in Frost's choice of the oven bird as a symbolic warbler.[19] The North American oven bird sings at dusk, and its remarkable tune – "teacher, teacher, teacher"– must have struck Frost for its suggestiveness. This is a different species from the South American oven bird that Frost noted in one of his favorite books, Darwin's *The Voyage of the Beagle*. This oven bird builds its nest, which looks very much like a large oven with a door, on the ground. The nest also has a front and inner chamber, very much like a human house. Darwin thought the bird might provide some clue about the relationship of all creatures.[20] As in the case of "the White-Tailed Hornet," Frost was quite willing to conflate species for poetic purposes. He probably does so here as he fashions a sonnet about a universal singer, announced boldly in the sestet:

> There is a singer everyone has heard,
> Loud, a mid-summer and mid-wood bird,
> Who makes the solid tree trunks sound again.
> He says that leaves are old and that for flowers
> Mid-summer is to spring as one to ten.
> He says the early petal-fall is past
> When pear and cherry bloom went down in showers
> On sunny days a moment overcast;

This bird has much to say, and speaks to and through the poet unselfconsciously. There is a strong insistence that the tone of the birds' song speaks perfectly to this midsummer moment that dissolves into fall. With the season, the sonnet turns at the sestet, and we learn that the bird has a gnomic adjustment to the situation:

> And comes that other fall we name the fall.
> He says the highway dust is over all.
> The bird would cease and be as other birds
> But that he knows in singing not to sing.
> The question that he frames in all but words
> Is what to make of a diminished thing.

The first line stresses that the "other fall" happens to be one that "we name." All other seasons could be noted for something falling. This midsummer bird has a way of coping with the difficult situation of dust and heat. The bird has a consciousness and knowledge similar in kind to ours. The bird frames the question "in *all but words*," indicating that words are but a minor addition to the power of sound that comes from deep in nature but to which we feel a clear bond.

Yet that bond seems connected to a mutual understanding of sadness and diminishment.[21] Diminishment, one might ask, of what? The expectations of love appear to be high in "Never Again Would Birds' Song Be the Same," so the feelings of loss are of equal magnitude. What has happened in this poem appears to be a great change in expectations about what nature means or, at least, how we experience and hear it. In this sonnet, the speaker describes a character, an Adamic figure, who has dramatic expectations of the meaning of the birds' song:

> He would declare and could himself believe
> That the birds there in all the garden round
> From having heard the daylong voice of Eve
> Had added to their own an oversound,
> Her tone of meaning but without the words.

So great is this Adam's love for Eve that he attributes what he hears in nature to the very influence of her tone of voice. Mankind here influences the creaturely world rather than the creaturely world influencing man. As the sonnet continues, however, qualifications arise:

> Admittedly an eloquence so soft
> Could only have had an influence on birds
> When call or laughter carried it aloft.
> Be that as may be, she was in their song.
> Moreover her voice upon their voices crossed
> Had now persisted in the woods so long
> That probably it never would be lost.

"Call or laughter" may have something to do with sexual play, and perhaps that may account for some sense of why the scene of the poem has moved from the "garden" to the "woods," where human and other creatures persist in a world in which all voices upon each other are "crossed."

There has been something of a temptation (a loaded word in this case) to interpret both sonnets theologically, as allegories of one kind or another about the Fall. While one cannot exclude that interpretation, another way to look at them is in terms of psychological recognition that the world has not changed but that our particularly human perceptions of it do. Consciousness may alter, affected by breakthroughs and contact unexpectedly from otherness. The world may change but so may our recognition of it, perhaps as a result of our experiences, including being wounded in love. The sonnet concludes with two of the most memorable lines in Frost: "Never again would birds' song be the same. / And to do that to birds was why she came." The penultimate line has the sense and weight of loss. The final line may be harder to interpret.

Does "to do that" have the force of a something done deliberately, perhaps even maliciously? Is there a sexual pun in the conclusion?

"The Most of It" may be one of Frost's most powerful sonic utterances in addition to being a baffling study of the human relationship to nature. No reader should forget that its speaker describes a character, a "he," who makes a supposition about his relationship to the universe. His agony is depicted in two dramatic sentences broken evenly into four lines each. This mysterious Narcissus-Adamic figure desires something that seems paradoxical, both "counter-love" as well as "original-response":

> He thought he kept the universe alone;
> For all the voice in answer he could wake
> Was but the mocking echo of his own
> From some tree-hidden cliff across the lake.
> Some morning from the boulder-broken beach
> He would cry out on life, that what it wants
> Is not its own love back in copy speech,
> But counter-love, original response.

At this moment in the lyric, "it" appears to be life but becomes more mysterious as it finds "embodiment" in the stunning one-sentence torrent that comes, just perhaps, in response:

> And nothing ever came of what he cried
> Unless it was the embodiment that crashed
> In the cliff's talus on the other side,
> And then in the far distant water splashed,
> But after a time allowed for it to swim,
> Instead of proving human when it neared
> And someone else additional to him,
> As a great buck it powerfully appeared,
> Pushing the crumpled water up ahead,
> And landed pouring like a waterfall,
> And stumbled through the rocks with horny tread,
> And forced the underbrush – and that was all.

This "nothing" turns out to be quite a something, even though whatever "it" is, it is not human and mysteriously an "embodiment" that appeared "*as* a great buck." The force of this single sentence dwarfs and humiliates the grandiosity of the character who thought he kept the universe alone. It has much of the effect of God's revelation to Job out of the whirlwind; God reveals absolutely nothing human in creation and his theophany culminates in images of behemoth and leviathan, all powerful and suggestively sexual and masculine. The anaphora with which the last three lines build comes to a crashing conclusion with the final phrase in which "all" could be taken to mean everything or very little.

"The Most of It" deserves to be read in the context of the poems that follow it in *A Witness Tree*: "Never Again Would Birds' Song Be the Same" and "The Subverted Flower." There is some suggestion here of a narrative, however dark, of what happens when love's cries are answered. But from the standpoint of man's relationship to the natural world, "The Most of It" gives the impression of man belittled and bewildered in any search for recognizable response in nature. It would be wrong, however, to view "The Most of It" as being Frost's final word on the subject. "Two Look at Two," published earlier in *New Hampshire*, would give at least a somewhat different impression of Frost's vision of man's relationship to the rest of the creaturely world. The word "love" begins and ends this short, blank-verse narrative. A couple have been wandering at dusk up a mountainside path but there is both some trepidation and lack of impulse in their ability to carry further on. As the couple think, in language similar to "The Most of It," that they have reached an end, they encounter a doe. The language allows a remarkable proximity of both fields of perception, "across the wall" or boundaries of otherness, underscored in the intricately crossed line "She saw them in their field, they her in hers":

> " . . . This is all," they sighed,
> "Good-night to woods." But not so; there was more.
> A doe from round a spruce stood looking at them
> Across the wall, as near the wall as they.
> She saw them in their field, they her in hers.
> The difficulty of seeing what stood still,
> Like some up-ended boulder split in two,
> Was in her clouded eyes: they saw no fear there.
> She seemed to think that two thus they were safe.
> Then, as if they were something that, though strange,
> She could not trouble her mind with too long,
> She sighed and passed unscared along the wall.
> "*This*, then, is all. What more is there to ask?"

Of course, there is more. After the doe, "an antlered buck of lusty nostril" appears and seems in gesture to ask the couple "'Why don't you make some motion? / Or give some sign of life? Because you can't. / I doubt if you're as living as you look.'" The buck then passes "unscared," a word repeated, as if to emphasize that the couple must be just that. In this poem there has been a rather powerful level of communication between the doe and buck and the couple, relatively untroubled by problems of analogy, perhaps because the vision was "unlooked for":

> "This *must* be all." It was all. Still they stood,
> A great wave from it going over them,
> As if the earth in one unlooked-for favor
> Had made them certain earth returned their love.

Whatever the strength of the couple's "love," the word that frames the poem, the experience enabled them to feel some mutual, if very momentary creaturely bond with earth – even if slightly threatening – not in the least present in "The Most of It."

Frost and believing-in

It may be inevitable to want to talk about religion in Frost's poetry since the figures of traditional and mostly western faith – "God," "spirit," "heaven" – appear with more than just passing mention in a number of the poems. Did Frost hold any known religious convictions or adhere to any definable religion? No. He once spoke of his religious convictions as something to be inferred from his words and deeds:

> If you would have out the way a man feels about God, watch his life, hear his words. Place a coin, with its denomination unknown, under paper and you can tell its mark by rubbing a pencil over the paper. From all the individual rises and valleys your answer will come out.   (*I*, 149)

It may be a great deal to ask of a reader and biographer to follow Frost's metaphor in order to grasp how he felt about God and the nature of his belief. The complexity and contradictory nature of the poetry, as well as his talks and other comments, make it more than a little difficult to make simple, comprehensive, or satisfying statements. Certain kinds of contradictions, metaphors, and mythologies do recur in his work and suggest a mind in which poetry is ceaselessly in pursuit of ultimate mysteries on the edge of faith, science, and philosophy.

In the same 1955 interview in which Frost made the analogy about tracing the coin, the interviewer asked him specifically about the pointed reference to God at the conclusion to his poem "Bereft." Frost has told biographers that the poem originated as early as the summer of 1893, after he was left alone by Elinor and some other women with whom he was staying. He did not publish the poem until the 1920s but the enormity of the speaker's loneliness and the terrifying imagery suggests great loss and portends worse things to come:

> Where had I heard this wind before
> Change like this to a deeper roar?
> What would it take my standing there for,
> Holding open a restive door,
> Looking down hill to a frothy shore?
> Summer was past and day was past.
> Somber clouds in the west were massed.
> Out in the porch's sagging floor,
> Leaves got up in a coil and hissed,
> Blindly struck at my knee and missed.
> Something sinister in the tone
> Told me my secret must be known:
> Word I was in the house alone
> Somehow must have gotten abroad,
> Word I was in my life alone,
> Word I had no one left but God.

The final lines "Word I was in my life alone / Word I had no one left but God" may strike less as statements of faith than as utterances of loneliness and slightly chilling expressions of fear of that being the case. The figure of the great wind in the context of total loss may also evoke the specter of Job and the showing of God from the whirlwind. This would not be a mere random association given, as we shall see, *The Masque of Reason*. If Frost might tend to be drawn to *that* particular book of the Bible, what does it say about him and his poetry?

Poetry should not be viewed as encapsulated religion or, more specifically, packaged theology. However many commentators have examined Dante's debt to Aquinas, Dante still remains true to his own way, his own symbolic vision for attaining the stars (and each part of *The Divine Comedy* ends with that word), and one that cannot simply be translated back into a theology. Unlike Frost, however, Dante wrote at a time in which while there was, of course, great political strife, a Christian and largely Catholic worldview dominated religion and theology. After Dante, Milton's poetic rendering of the fall in *Paradise Lost* deeply influenced and also threatened "to ruin the sacred truths" "to fable and old song."

In the transition from the nineteenth to the twentieth century, it has been the challenges to traditions of faith, including almost all forms of Christianity, that has often preoccupied poets as they have drawn upon religious themes. From the late Victorians to the early moderns – Tennyson, Arnold, Browning,

Melville, Hardy – the redemptive power of art in the face of diminished or unsatisfying religious faith has been a persistent theme. More important, poetry may provide a language for contradictions and tensions made too simple by the answers of theologians. The twentieth-century Polish poet Czeslaw Milosz put the predicament very succinctly:

> What is deepest and most deeply felt in life, the transitoriness of human beings, illness, death, the vanity of opinions, convictions, cannot be expressed in the language of theology, which for centuries has responded by turning out perfectly rounded balls, easy to roll but impenetrable. Twentieth century poetry, or what is most essential in it, gathers data on the ultimate in the human condition and elaborates, to handle the data, a language which may or may not be used by theology.[22]

Frost, as has been discussed, developed a particular sense of metaphor for his poetry, and it appears to have been developed in response less to politics than to both faith and science, in our time both deeply related to each other. He was born after the American Civil War, had his education, and published his two greatest books before World War I. What Frost witnessed and what both inspired and seemed somewhat to threaten him as a human being and as a poet was science, which he sometimes called "the great event of history" (*I*, 189). If Frost explored and welcomed spiritual tensions as part of poetry, "Where Poetry is Poised – on the brink of spiritual disaster," he wrote in his "notebooks" (*N*, 654).

A great deal, though certainly not quite all, of Frost's poetry, including those poems that seem to have apparently religious themes, might make more sense if read in light of his lifelong preoccupation with the relationship, though some might regard it as a conflict, between science and faith in the modern world. Frost critics are generally now in agreement that science was an enormous preoccupation of Frost's, even if they disagree ultimately on how he saw poetry's cultural relationship to it.[23] Without question, science has enjoyed the prestige in our culture once accorded to religion and theology in the middle ages (science, of course, meant something different at that time from what it does now). Unlike almost all of his modernist counterparts, Frost sought rather to engage science directly in poetry and poetics, and he manifested his admiration for science in almost every aspect of his work. When one says "science," there is always the question of precisely what one means by the word: Science as empirical investigation and then speculative theory; science as technology in peace and war; science as the pursuit of understanding independent from dogma. Frost was pleased to embrace with qualification all these aspects of science:

> [Science] is not all. But it is much. It comes into our lives as domestic science for our hold on the planet, into our deaths with its deadly weapons, bombs and airplanes, for war, and into our souls as pure science for nothing but glory; in which last respect it may be likened unto pure poetry and mysticism. It is man's greatest enterprise. It is the charge of the ethereal into the material. It is our Substantiation of our meaning. It can't go too far or too deep for me. Still it is not a law unto itself. (*CP*, 209)

Frost held an early fascination with the literature of exploration. Among his favorite books, as I mentioned earlier, were works about scientific exploration, botany, and astronomy ("About one-tenth of my poems are astronomical; and I've had a glass a good deal of the time" *I*, 189). More to the point were the figures he used to talk about poetry: "Every poem is a voyage of discovery. I go in to see if I can get out, like you go to the North Pole" (*I*, 188). That sense of discovery and exploration, along with other aspects of science – the making of hypotheses, the creation and use of technology, the willingness to abandon idols of the mind and religious dogma, the fascination with the material world – are all very much a positive part of Frost's imaginative métier.

A fundamental mythology appears to govern Frost's poetry from his earliest work in *A Boy's Will* through his last *In the Clearing* (and even his last published poem, "The Prophets Really Prophesy as Mystics, the Commentators Merely by Statistics"): it is what he called "plunge of mind, the spirit in the material universe." For Frost, this was the governing story not only of science but also of poetry and western religion. As a *story*, it was for the poet to describe, not the scientist. However, it was a vision that Frost had developed not in opposition to science but with poetry in a relation closer to what Whitman had called "the tuft and final applause of science." Frost avoided the nineteenth-century division of poetry into a form of mysticism or a form of pure aestheticism.

Journeys into matter

It would be too easy to say that Frost had found a simple reconciliation between science, religion, and poetry. Science had become deeply troubling to many in Frost's youth because it shattered cherished notions of divine human origins. Social Darwinist claims for the possibility of human progress aside, for those, like Frost, who had grown up reading Emerson or Thoreau and having some mystical sense in the power of nature to reveal spiritual mysteries or to affirm the divine in man, Darwin did much to undermine such a view. Nevertheless, the material world had a great fascination for Frost and at various points in his youth he may have been more or less troubled by his own seeking of divinity within it. Frost subtitled "The Demiurge's Laugh," from *A Boy's Will*, "About Science." In antiquity and then in some forms of heretical Christianity, the demiurge was the sublunary god who created the world. In Gnosticism, the "true" Christian was completely elsewhere than earth. Some, including for example Herman Melville, saw the condition of modern science as a rebirth of the Gnostic predicament. Science had created a world of material knowledge devoid of divinity; God was elsewhere:

> It was far in the sameness of the wood:
>   I was running with joy on the Demon's trail,
> Though I knew what I hunted was no true god.
>   It was just as the light was beginning to fail
> That I suddenly heard – all I needed to hear:
> It has lasted me many and many a year.
>
> The sound was behind me instead of before,
>   A sleepy sound, but mocking half,
> As of one who utterly couldn't care.
>   The Demon arose from his wallow to laugh,
> Brushing the dirt from his eye as he went;
> And well I knew what the Demon meant.

We do not know for certain whether the speaker in being "on the Demon's trail" pursues the Demon or is on the trail created by the Demon. In either case, he soon learns that he has been fooled, because whatever he has been pursuing in the "sameness" does not lie in front of him but really "behind" him, as though figuratively indifferent to his goals, "mocking half." If this seeker has been pursuing some ultimate, transcendent knowledge *through* nature, the Demon sitting in a wallow, with dirt in his eyes, would be indifferent to that obscure goal. The initial wild joy turns into a more contemplative awareness of limitations, as the speaker sits, suggestively, under a tree after hearing the laugh:

> I shall not forget how his laugh rang out.
>   I felt as a fool to have been so caught,
> And checked my steps to make pretense
>   It was something among the leaves I sought
> (Though doubtful whether he stayed to see).
> Thereafter I sat me under a tree.

A powerful sense of irony arrests the consciousness that seeks ultimate truth in matter. Consider what he said years later: "I'm lost in my admiration for science . . . It can't go too far or too deep for me." But he added, "If it penetrates straight to hell, then that's all right, too" (*I*, 266).

While Frost never quite shed faith in spirit, he always envisioned it incarnated in matter. From "The Trial by Existence," "Sitting by a Bush in Broad Sunlight," "The Aim Was Song," to "Kitty Hawk," his three-beat, semi-autobiographical poem from *In the Clearing*, Frost admires penetration of mind and spirit into matter as a virtue. In fact, he links matter and spirit, science and faith, without any certainty about their eventual separation. Frost plays with the phrase "that fall / From the apple tree," because "from" could mean "because of" or "out of," suggesting the debate about human origins:

> Pulpiteers will censure
> Our instinctive venture
> Into what they call
> The material
> When we took that fall
> From the apple tree.
> But God's own descent
> Into flesh was meant
> As a demonstration
> That the supreme merit
> Lay in risking spirit
> In substantiation.
> Westerners inherit
> A design for living
> Deeper into matter –
> Not without due patter
> Of a great misgiving.
> All the science zest
> To materialize
> By on-penetration
> Into earth and skies
> (Don't forget the latter
> Is but further matter)
> Has been West Northwest.

Science had in a number of ways penetrated dangerously into the material. The study of the Book of Nature in addition to the Bible had been given in scripture itself. Not until the Renaissance did the study of nature come into conflict with what was given in scripture. Francis Bacon compromised by suggesting in *The Advancement of Learning* that in both "books" God's hand could be found. The question of whether the compromise could be held at all became particularly strained in the late nineteenth and early twentieth century as the world of Genesis and evolutionary geology drew farther and farther apart. Frost himself appeared deeply concerned about the question of the relationship of science and faith, though his thinking about the two sometimes changed and was contradictory. Rather than deny, distance himself, or despair over Darwinism, for example, he appeared to embrace its challenges and uncertainties. Writing in his notebooks, Frost emphasized a refusal to despair over the end of special creation, even suggesting a form of immanent teleology. He goes on to suggest that what appears in nature to be waste is really only nature's form of sacrifice:

> When the fact of Evolution came up to shake the church's certainties about creation and the date of it 4004 BC, I bade myself be not discouraged. The old idea we were asked to give up was God made man out of mud at one stroke. I saw that the new idea would have to be that God made man out of prepared mud that he had taken his time about working up gradation. I was not much put out or off my own thinking. There was as much of a God in it as ever.
>
> When the waste of codfish eggs to produce one codfish seem too disillusioning for young Bostonians to bear and stay even Unitarians, I would have come to their rescue, if they would have listened to me, with the suggestion that the death of all those eggs was necessary to make the ocean a froth fit for the one codfish to live in. But I would go further today in standing my ground. There is no waste, and all that looks like waste is some form of sacrifice, like tithes to the Lord, absolute Sabbath. Keeping (throwing the day away entirely), and flowing out a libation on the ground or fire. It is once wasted on the ground. It is twice wasted down the gullet of the worshipper. Then it not only washes the liquor but it also wastes the man.   (*N*, 522–523)

Frost could sound much less optimistic about the relationship of waste to sacrifice in other published prose and poems. Consider, for example, this essay on "The Future of Man," presented by Frost at a panel in 1959, celebrating the centenary of Darwin's *On the Origin of Species*. He speaks of Darwin's tree of life and the human tree of life as the Norse tree Yggdrasil with roots above and below the ground. Frost considers our consciousness as "terminal," and the god of waste as indifferent to us:

> I take it that evolution comes under the head of growth. Only it has a strange illusory way of making you think it goes on forever. But all growth is limited – the tree of life is limited like a maple tree or an oak tree – they all have a certain height, and they all have a certain life-length. And our tree, the tree Yggdrasil, has reached its growth. It

doesn't have to fall down because it's stopped growing. It will go on blossoming and having its seasons – I'd give it another hundred or two hundred million years. Make that anything you please . . .

. . . There's nothing coming beyond us. The tree Yggdrasil has reached its growth.

Then I want to say another thing about the god who provides the great issues. He's a god of waste, magnificent waste. And waste is another name for generosity of not always being intent on our own advantage, nor too importunate even for a better world. We pour out libation to him as a symbol of the waste we share in – participate in. Pour it on the ground and you've wasted it; pour it into yourself and you've doubly wasted it. But all in the cause of generosity and relaxation of self interest.   (*CP*, 207)

This version of waste as sacrifice and its vision of the god of waste seems far less humane than the one offered previously. It does not suggest a finality to human consciousness without a final destiny for humanity or individual human lives.

In his comments on "The Future of Man," Frost was particularly attentive to other scientists and with social scientists who entertained strong hopes for human progress. He had in mind the early discussions about genetics and the possibilities of improvements in genetics, precursors of what we now call the human genome project. He still had a strong memory of the eugenics movement as it had developed in turn-of-the-century Vermont but also the horror it had become in mid-century Germany. His satiric tone was also aimed at Marxism, whose utopianism he also found inhuman, because it failed to allow for individual responsibility even in failure.

The heroic sense of pilgrimage and risk is a crucial part of the mythology of Frost's poetry and has extended to the idea readers have of his life. "Stopping by Woods on a Snowy Evening" and "The Road Not Taken" have an indelible place among the pantheon of those lyrics of heroic endurance, even if their subtlety and ironies are, more often than not, completely glossed over. One of the less known but important early poems in which Frost explores the soul's descent into matter and the ultimate questions of human responsibility, choice and destiny is "The Trial by Existence." Helen Bacon has shown the extent to which Frost based the poem on Plato's myth of "Er," a man who comes back to life after having died in battle. Er reports to the living of the souls who, after rewards and punishments in the next world, gather for rebirth where they will select the life they will live in their transmigration to another body. Frost's recasting of this story turns the classical heaven into a version of the Judeo-Christian God. But there is no final resting of the soul in heaven, only the choice of life, which yet "admits no memory of choice." Somehow, we are responsible for our fate:

> But always God speaks at the end:
> "One thought in agony of strife
> The bravest would have by for friend,
>   The memory that he chose the life;
> But the pure fate to which you go
>   Admits no memory of choice,
> Or the woe were not earthly woe
>   To which you give the assenting voice."

Frost's God emphasizes "earthly woe," and with it the elimination of certainty and pride but not, perhaps, of responsibility. The next and, penultimate stanza, builds on the idea that all choices are the same and, perhaps, more important, an ongoing mystic link between spirit and matter "until death come" (though nothing is promised of what may come after):

> And so the choice must be again,
>   But the last choice is still the same;
> And the awe passes wonder then,
>   And a hush falls for all acclaim.
> And God has taken a flower of gold
>   And broken it, and used therefrom
> The mystic link to bind and hold
>   Spirit and matter till death come.

What, then, does the poem conclude about the soul's destiny? It ends leaving it "crushed and mystified":

> 'Tis of the essence of life here,
>   Though we choose greatly, still to lack
> The lasting memory at all clear,
>   That life has for us on the wrack
> Nothing but what we somehow chose;
>   Thus are we wholly stripped of pride
> In the pain that has but one close,
>   Bearing it crushed and mystified.

This may be a painful conclusion for a poem that began by echoing an ancient myth about heroic souls. Frost's conception of the heroic remained rather tough, demanding an almost unbearable degree of uncertainty about the fate of the spirit and a willingness to accept material existence and suffering, and a sense of responsibility for one's own predicament no matter how fated.

"The Road Not Taken" remains the most famous and most quoted of Frost's poems that present his complex and subtle mythology of apparently heroic choice in the midst of uncertainty and doubt. After all, the title could refer to the road not taken by most individuals as well as the speaker's regrets for the road he, after all, did not take. The final lines of the poem are frequently quoted in affirmation without recognition of their temporal relation to the rest of the poem – from an imagined future looking back into the past and not the present. It evokes, though does not rely, upon older mythologies of heroic figures at moments of terrible decision, including Oedipus at the crossroads and Dante entering an obscure wood before entering hell:

> Two roads diverged in a yellow wood,
> And sorry I could not travel both
> And be one traveler, long I stood
> And looked down one as far as I could
> To where it bent in the undergrowth;
>
> Then took the other, as just as fair,
> And having perhaps the better claim,
> Because it was grassy and wanted wear;
> Though as for that the passing there
> Had worn them really about the same, . . .

In attempting to make his decision, his "choice," the speaker finds little difference and very little in the way of originality – both had been worn well before him. He possesses really little in the way of *a priori* judgment or knowledge. He uses the verb "take" to assess the roads, and it is the same verb used colloquially for the road actually chosen; "take" suggests less of a "choice" as rational decision than something seized upon. Later Frost would vary the title of a poem "Choose Something Like a Star" to "Take Something Like a Star," so the difference between the two verbs meant something to him. What appeared to be choice or selection turned out to be less rational than we would like it to be, stripping the outcome of some of the bravado we would arrogate to ourselves.

The irony about that bounded sense of choice contributes much to the strangeness of the conclusion of the poem, a strangeness often overlooked in the way the poem has been quoted as a statement of unqualified triumph. The penultimate stanza expresses the regret that haunts the whole poem, particularly the title, for what might have been, and the way each change irrevocably alters the traveler and what came before. The ultimate stanza may cause the reader to wonder why "a sigh"? Where would one be "ages and ages hence"? The stanza begins with the speaker stating that he "*shall* be telling this"; it is a projection, not a certainty in the present. There may be much, too, in the pause after the third line:

> And both that morning equally lay
> In leaves no step had trodden black.
> Oh, I kept the first for another day!
> Yet knowing how way leads on to way,
> I doubted if I should ever come back.
>
> I shall be telling this with a sigh
> Somewhere ages and ages hence:
> Two roads diverged in a wood, and I –
> I took the one less traveled by,
> And that has made all the difference.

We might ask from the perspective of the present, "what difference" or, from the perspective of the future, what does the speaker really know of the difference? Has his "difference" really something to do with his foresight, insight, and has it made him somehow better than others?

The idea of an itinerant, spiritual pilgrimage has it roots in Bunyan. An important American antecedent for Frost would have been Thoreau's essay "Walking," in which the very idea of movement west in the wilderness guided by nature became a new form of salvation. In Thoreau's words, "in wildness is the salvation of the world." Yet Thoreau believed that nature somehow could become an adequate guide to our choices:

> What is it that makes it so hard sometimes to determine whither we will walk? I believe there is a subtle magnetism in Nature, which if we unconsciously yield to it, will direct us aright. It is not indifferent to us which way we walk. There is a right way, but we are very liable from heedlessness and stupidity to take the wrong one. We would fain take that walk, never yet taken by us through the actual world, which is perfectly symbolical of the path which we love to travel in the interior and ideal world, and sometimes, no doubt, we find it difficult to choose our direction, because it does not yet distinctly exist in our idea.[24]

From where do we derive this "subtle magnetism of Nature"? Frost admired greatly Thoreau's writing, and *Walden*, especially. He could, however, be a bit wry when considering the implications of Thoreau's emphasis on the particularity of nature and upon finding an Adamic language of nature by which to recover a perfect and perhaps divine reality.

Great Frost poems, "Into My Own," "The Demiurge's Laugh," "The Wood Pile," and "Directive," play on the myth of the "itinerant" errand into the wilderness, risking getting lost in the material world, perhaps in search of the wildness that Thoreau viewed as salvation. One can readily think of the terrifying "Desert Places," whose speaker appears threatened by the imminent annihilation and loneliness of winter around him. The whole poem may be a reaction to Pascal's meditation that "The eternal silence of those infinite places fills me with dread." But whereas Pascal's fear inspired him with faith, Frost's moves him differently:

> Snow falling and night falling fast, oh, fast
> In a field I looked into going past,
> And the ground almost covered smooth in snow,
> But a few weeds and stubble showing last.
>
> The woods around it have it – it is theirs.
> All animals are smothered in their lairs.
> I am too absent-spirited to count;
> The loneliness includes me unawares.

The speaker intensifies the loneliness so much that he seems to own it as a prophet would. The first lines of the final stanza form a defiant refusal to succumb to the fear of the vastness of interstellar space, a refusal affirmed – and oddly undercut – in the final two lines. Instead the speaker presents us with a deeper ability to scare himself "nearer home," in himself and from unspecified threats of isolation and extinction. The woods "have it – it is theirs," whatever "it" may be, possession or self-possession. The other animals, like the woodchuck in "After Apple-Picking," have gone to safety, while this human creature suffers an exposed isolation. The feminine rhyme of "spaces" and "race is," by suggesting the pun "races," underscores the uncertainty of human life in the universe and the fragility of its survival on this planet:

> And lonely as it is that loneliness
> Will be more lonely ere it will be less –
> A blanker whiteness of benighted snow
> With no expression, nothing to express.
>
> They cannot scare me with their empty spaces
> Between stars – on stars where no human race is.
> I have it in me so much nearer home
> To scare myself with my own desert places.

Being lost, annihilated, and far from home are notorious threats in Frost as we know in so many poems, including some of his dramatic pastorals, "Snow," "The Death of the Hired Man," as well as best-known lyrics, including "Acquainted with the Night," and "Stopping by Woods on a Snowy Evening."

These last two have an interesting resonance with Dante's infernal journey; "Acquainted with the Night" is written in *terza rima*, a rare verse form in English but the verse form of Dante's *Commedia*. Unlike Dante's poem, the speaker does not journey in one direction but walks "out and back," with no final goal. The speaker of "Stopping by Woods on a Snowy Evening" expresses some fear because he knows the woods do not belong to him, "he will not mind me stopping here to watch his woods fill up with snow." We also learn, though, that he is "between the woods and frozen lake," the zone where Dante's journey in *Inferno* started and finished.

Metaphor or simply form becomes the instrument by which the soul approaches and saves itself from becoming lost in matter. "There is nothing quite so composing as composition. Putting anything in order a house a business a poem gives a sense of sharing the mastery of the universe" (*N*, 281). He defends himself against materiality, if not materialism, by extolling the shaping power of metaphor in "Education by Poetry," where he talks about the precarious balance between spirit and matter. "Greatest of all attempts to say one thing in terms of another is the philosophical attempt to say matter in terms of spirit, or spirit in terms of matter, to make the final unity. That is the greatest attempt that ever failed. We stop just short there" (*CP*, 107).

What does Frost mean by "spirit"? An eternal emanation from heaven? Or simply what the word means from its root, "breath"? Frost appears to take different positions in different poems. We can remember the early poem "Pan with Us," in which magical pipes of the Greek god "kept less of power to stir" "[t]han the merest aimless breath of air." "The Aim Was Song" appears to present man as the physical force that gives order to the aimless wind. The repetition of wind in the last stanza – "The wind the wind had meant to be –" raises the question of whether man is merely an instrument of a prior aim, if not a higher aim – if the wind could possibly "see" such a thing:

> Before man came to blow it right
>   The wind once blew itself untaught,
> And did its loudest day and night
>   In any rough place where it caught.
>
> Man came to tell it what was wrong:
>   It hadn't found the place to blow;
> It blew too hard – the aim was song.
>   And listen – how it ought to go!
>
> He took a little in his mouth,
>   And held it long enough for north

> To be converted into south,
>   And then by measure blew it forth.
>
> By measure. It was word and note,
>   The wind the wind had meant to be –
> A little through the lips and throat.
>   The aim was song – the wind could see.

This poem tends to deflate the idea of inspiration, spirit as some kind of mysterious force coming from within. Instead, the man as human body serves as vessel for literal wind coming from without.

"Sitting by a Bush in Broad Sunlight" measures the crisis in faith created by modern empiricism and science. The speaker sits unmoved by light:

> When I spread out my hand here today,
> I catch no more than a ray
> To feel of between thumb and fingers;
> No lasting effect of it lingers.

Light in the modern view would be viewed in the scientific sense as a ray, something "physical," to be "caught" with the opposable "thumb" by which we are defined as hominids.

The account of God speaking to Moses from the burning bush as well as the evolutionary accounts of life's beginnings both seem too distant to be believed and too disparate to be reconciled with our contemporary yearnings for divinity. Yet the speaker attempts to do that, insisting that the divine speaking to us persists in our "breath":

> God once declared he was true
> And then took the veil and withdrew,
> And remember how final a hush
> Then descended of old on the bush.
>
> God once spoke to people by name.
> The sun once imparted its flame.
> One impulse persists as our breath;
> The other persists as our faith.

The intertwined impulse of spirit and matter persist inextricably bound in us at this moment. Both tales of origins remain unrecoverable and subject to belief. In a moment of surprise, Frost concludes the poem by linking our "breath" with God's original impulse but our "faith" with the sun's flame.

Frost concluded his "meditative monologue" on metaphor with a statement about the four beliefs he found bound to his experience in poetry:

the personal belief, which is a knowledge that you don't want to tell other people about because you cannot prove that you know. You are saying nothing about it till you see. The love belief, just the same, has that same shyness . . . And the national belief we enter into socially with each other, all together, party of the first part, party of the second part, we enter into that to bring the future of the country . . . And then the literary one in every work of art, not of cunning and craft, mind you, but of real art; that believing the thing into existence . . . And then finally the relationship we enter into with God to believe the future in – to believe the hereafter in. (*CP*, 110–111)

Frost's use of "in" in relation to belief places the emphasis on the act of belief as a creative covenant and bridge rather than on the existence of the thing believed, whether it be "the future" or "the hereafter." He underscored this sense of belief in a 1961 interview:

You believe yourself into existence. You believe your marriage into existence, you believe in each other, you believe that it's worthwhile going on, or you'd commit suicide, wouldn't you? And the ultimate one is the belief in the future of the world. I believe the future *in*. It's coming in by my believing it. You might as well call that a belief in God. This word *God* is not an often-used word with me, but once in a while it arrives there. (*I*, 271)

Frost defers the sense of finality or arrival in many of his itinerant journey poems by putting himself or us on the verge of becoming lost. Such a journey could describe a number of Frost's most remarkable poems, not only "The Road Not Taken," but also "The Wood Pile," and, late among his poems, "Directive," in which the narrator seems to direct or order us "back out" of the present confusion and then "back in a time made simple." The goal of this "directive" would seem for us to become so lost as to restore our belief. Yet the simplicity of past time derives oddly from "loss" and from ruins and destruction:

Back out of all this now too much for us,
Back in a time made simple by the loss
Of detail, burned, dissolved, and broken off
Like graveyard marble sculpture in the weather,
There is a house that is no more a house
Upon a farm that is no more a farm
And in a town that is no more a town.
The road there, if you'll let a guide direct you
Who only has at heart your getting lost,
May seem as if it should have been a quarry –

Going back in time imaginatively to a time made simple may seem a pastoral gesture of retreat. In Frost, however, it often signals a history of loss and decay, as it did in "Ghost House," "The Generations of Men," and most acutely "The Census Taker," in which the narrator's finding "This house in one year fallen to decay / Filled me with no less sorrow than the houses / Fallen to ruin in ten thousand years / Where Asia wedges Africa from Europe." All the "melancholy of having to count souls" where they have grown, ironically, "to none at all" drives him to a skeptical utterance of survival: "It must be I want to go on living."

"Directive" leads us in "the height of adventure" where "two village cultures faded / Into each other. Both of them are lost." Looking deep into the past for simplicity, one finds divergence, competition, and destruction. The poem guides us backward through a natural history of the entire region until we are left with nothing but what might be a "belilaced cellar hole, / Now slowly closing like a dent in dough." Here, the shaman-like narrator has left, near the source of brook "too lofty and original to rage":

> A broken drinking goblet like the Grail
> Under a spell so the wrong ones can't find it,
> So can't get saved, as Saint Mark says they musn't.
> (I stole the goblet from the children's playhouse.)
> Here are your waters and your watering place.
> Drink and be whole again beyond confusion.

The "broken goblet like the Grail" as well as the reference to waters has rightly seemed a send-up of the archaic yearnings of Ezra Pound and T. S. Eliot, and particularly a parody of the final section of Eliot's "The Waste Land" where the grail quest ends in a place with no water. Readers debate how to take the thrust and conclusion of this rich combination of lyric, narration, and meditation, a work that enfolds within it so much of Frost's earlier work. The tone of the poem in part and whole may be hard to comprehend. How should one take the attitude of the line "Weep for what little things would make them glad," referring to the children's playhouse of make-believe? As slightly satiric comment on Yeats's "foul rag and bone shop of the heart" of "The Circus Animals' Desertion"? At this moment, we may wonder whether time past can be the source, the well of belief or only of make-believe; a revision of child-like faith or childishness. Frost knew that Saint Mark's version of Jesus's parable of the sower (Mark 4: 1–20), a parable of why Jesus spoke in parables, seemed to argue that it was necessary to speak in parables to exclude certain people from understanding and, therefore, from being saved. Was Frost poking fun at the obscurity of Eliot's Christian modernism? Or was he making more of a suggestion that one need become "as little children" in order to understand? With what tone do we take "Here are your waters and your watering place"? With the thrill of revelation or contempt at belief in childish romanticism?

"The Fear of God," also in *Steeple Bush*, presents a baldly unpleasant view taking one's success too personally and as the act of a merciful God:

> If you should rise from Nowhere up to Somewhere,
> From being No one up to being Someone,
> Be sure to keep repeating to yourself
> You owe it to an arbitrary god
> Whose mercy to you rather than to others
> Won't bear too critical examination.

This arbitrariness, lack of mercy, and lack of oversight in human affairs has much of the quality of divinity to which Frost gave expression in the early poem "Stars":

> And yet with neither love nor hate,
>   Those stars like some snow-white
> Minerva's snow-white marble eyes
>   Without the gift of sight.

Frost, even more hauntingly, personifies the stars as the material manifestation of divinity in "A Question":

> A voice said, Look me in the stars
> And tell me truly, men of earth,
> If all the soul-and-body-scars
> Were not too much to pay for birth.

The question turns immediately into an answer about suffering and sacrifice.

Sacrifice

Frost knew that both suffering and the desire to make a worthy sacrifice could turn individuals to wild acts, some beautiful and others dangerous. "The Star-Splitter" becomes exciting because of the risk taken by farmer Brad McLaughlin to answer the indifferent stars. McLaughlin has had enough with "hugger-mugger farming" and feels just slightly unhinged at being looked in upon by the starry heavens. So, he burns down his farm. With the insurance money, he buys a telescope to look back at the stars, "To satisfy a life-long curiosity / About our place among the infinities." At first the narrator, one of his neighbors from the town, does not understand his motives. McLaughlin has been laboring in the near impossible rock-strewn farmland of New England, with little opportunity in the future to sell it. He recognizes that the telescope becomes an instrument but "less a weapon in our human fight." Perhaps equally remarkable, the narrator comes around to seeing that everyone in the town should have one:

> "What do you want with one of those blame things?"
> I asked him well beforehand. "Don't you get one!"
> "Don't call it blamed; there isn't anything
> More blameless in the sense of being less
> A weapon in our human fight," he said.
> "I'll have one if I sell my farm to buy it."
> There where he moved the rocks to plow the ground
> And plowed between the rocks he couldn't move,
> Few farms changed hands; so rather than spend years
> Trying to sell his farm and then not selling,
> He burned the house down for the fire insurance
> And bought the telescope with what it came to.
> He had been heard to say by several:
> "The best thing that we're put here for's to see;
> The strongest thing that's given us to see with's
> A telescope. Someone in every town
> Seems to me owes it to the town to keep one.
> In Littleton it may as well be me."
> After such loose talk it was no surprise
> When he did what he did and burned his housed down.

Both we and the narrator have been let in on this crime and this "wastefully lonely" little madness. How mad is it? The town does forgive him, as the narrator says later, somewhat ironically, "For to be social is to be forgiving." What Brad McLaughlin did had the quality of something holy: "Why not regard it as a sacrifice, / And an old-fashioned sacrifice by fire, / Instead of a new-fashioned one at auction?" The narrator has some recognition that labor has been given up for contemplation, and some risk taken in the process of doing so. McLaughlin wants to find out deeper, more penetrating things than plowing furrows hopelessly between rocks.

What, though, of "our place among the infinities"? The phrase itself Frost acknowledged came from a book that he cherished as a young man – *Our Place Among the Infinities* by the distinguished nineteenth-century English astronomer Richard A. Proctor. "One of the earliest books I hovered over, hung around, was called *Our Place Among the Infinities*," Frost recalled in his *Paris Review* interview (*I*, 231). Proctor described in evolutionary terms the material origins of the planet and the galaxies. The earth itself and all plants and animals had been formed from gases and matter from other parts of the universe (Pierre Laplace's nebular theory) formed over millions and millions of years. The universe was not a closed system but infinitely open to change, waste, and dissolution according to fixed laws:

> Let it suffice that we recognise as one of the earliest stages of our earth's history, her condition as a rotating mass of glowing vapour, capturing then as now, but far more actively then than now, masses of matter which approached near enough, and *growing* by these continual indraughts from without. From the very beginning, as it would seem, the earth grew in this way. The firm earth on which we live represents an aggregation of matter not from one portion of space, but from all space. All that is upon and within the earth, all vegetable forms and all animal forms, our bodies, our brains, are formed of materials which have been drawn in from those depths of space surrounding us on all sides. This hand that I am now raising contains particles . . . drawn in towards the earth by processes continuing millions of millions of ages, until after multitudinous changes the chapter of accidents has so combined them, and so distributed them in plants and animals, that after coming to form portions of my food they are here present before you . . . is not the thought itself striking and suggestive, that not only the earth on which we now move, but everything we see and touch, and every particle in body and brain, has sped during countless ages through the immensity of space?[25]

This would appear to be an absolutely material description of the world, one in which every form would have had a prior existence not as a soul but in the indestructible transformations of matter over vast periods of time. The passage helps in providing a context for what happens to both Brad McLaughlin and the narrator of "The Star-Splitter" as they look through the telescope, bought for six hundred dollars with the insurance money from the burning of Brad's farm. What is "our place among the infinities"? The telescope is christened the "star-splitter" because it sees binary stars, or twin-stars, perhaps a metaphor for the way matter does not exist in isolation but constantly changes and transforms itself. The analogies the narrator uses about "quicksilver" and "mud," as well as their leisure talk instead of "splitting wood," all suggest a pleasure in the transformation in matter and a delight in "waste":

> He got a good glass for six hundred dollars.
> His new job gave him leisure for star-gazing.
> Often he bid me come and have a look
> Up the brass barrel, velvet black inside,
> At a star quaking up the other end.
> I recollect a night of broken clouds
> And underfoot snow melted down to ice,
> And melting further in the wind to mud.

> Bradford and I had out the telescope.
> We spread our two legs as we spread its three,
> Pointing our thoughts the way we pointed it,
> And standing at our leisure till the day broke,
> Said some of the best things we ever said.
> That telescope was christened the Star-splitter,
> Because it didn't do a thing but split
> A star in two or three the way you split
> A globule of quicksilver in your hand
> With one stroke of your finger in the middle.
> It's a star-splitter if there ever was one
> And ought to do some good if splitting stars
> 'Sa thing to be compared with splitting wood.

Whatever they see or don't see, binary stars or parallax, the community activity, the binding activity of Brad and his neighbor, becomes more important than ascertaining what we can or cannot know about the infinite. The final questions appear to confirm nothing more than the uncertain:

> We've looked and looked, but after all where are we?
> Do we know any better where we are,
> And how it stands between the night tonight
> And a man with a smoky lantern chimney?
> How different from the way it ever stood?

Despite our desire to be relieved from hopeless labor long enough to reflect, what in the end do we learn about our place? Proctor suggests that we were not in a position to know much about the very beginning of things in the universe; when we look in a telescope the question of where we are becomes inextricably bound to when we came to be. The limits of our knowledge of the evolution of the universe are analogous to the limits of our knowledge of the evolution of life on the planet:

> I think we arrive here at a point where speculation helps us as little as it does in attempting to trace the evolution of living creatures across the gap which separates the earliest forms of life from the beginning itself of life upon the earth. Since we cannot hope to determine the real beginning of the earth's history, we need not at present attempt to pass back beyond the earliest stage of which we have any clear information.[26]

This shows a scientist who believes in science also showing the limits of science. Frost understood well that the best scientists did not claim that science explained everything. Nor, for that matter, did all versions of religion. Proctor defended the possibility that the vast, seemingly impersonal universe uncovered by science could also be governed by a deity. He did so not by appealing to intelligent design or any form of special creation by simply invoking the language of the Book of Job, and the idea that God is always just beyond what human consciousness can possibly comprehend:

> The wave of life which is now passing over our earth is but a ripple in the sea of life within the solar system; this sea of life is itself but as a wavelet on the ocean of eternal life throughout the universe. Inconceivable, doubtless, are these infinities of time and space, of matter, of motion, and of life. Inconceivable that the whole universe can be for all time the scene of the operation of infinite personal power, omnipresent, all-knowing. Utterly incomprehensible how Infinite Purpose can be associated with endless material evolution. But it is no new thought, no modern discovery, that we are thus utterly powerless to conceive or comprehend the idea of an Infinite Being, Almighty, All-Knowing, Omnipresent, and Eternal, of whose inscrutable purpose the material universe is the unexplained manifestation. Science is in the presence of the old, old mystery; the old, old questions are asked of her, "Canst thou by searching find out God? canst thou find out the almighty unto perfection? It is as high as heaven; what canst thou do? deeper than hell; what canst thou know?" And science answers these questions, as they were answered of old, – "As touching the Almighty, we cannot find Him out."[27]

Proctor's thoughts on the limits of science in the realm of religion may indeed shed some light on the final question of "The Star-Splitter," "how different from the way it ever stood"?

Frost distinguished himself from most modernist poets in not taking the view that the world was somehow worse at the dawn of the twentieth century than it ever had been. If anything, the discoveries of science had humiliated mankind like religion had done in centuries before, in reminding him of his mortality and his relatively small, uncertain position in the scheme of things. As he wrote in "The Lesson for Today," speaking to an imagined scholastic of the Middle Ages:

> Space ails us moderns: we are sick with space.
> Its contemplation makes us out as small
> As a brief epidemic of microbes
> That in a good glass may be seen to crawl
> The patina of this the least of globes.
> But have we there the advantage after all?
> You were belittled into vilest worms
> God hardly tolerated with his feet;
> Which comes to the same thing in different terms.
> We both are the belittled human race,

One as compared with God and one with space.
I had thought ours the more profound disgrace;
But doubtless this was only my conceit.
The cloister and the observatory saint
Take comfort in about the same complaint.
So science and religion really meet.

But this may not have always been his position. Frost appeared to wrestle with aspects of science as an arbiter of reality since he began writing. Brought up in a tradition of reading Emerson, Swedenborg, and Wordsworth, he was inclined to view the natural world empathetically. The sense of mutability, destruction, and flux, however, both haunted and, strangely, inspired him from the beginning.

Belief and truth

One senses early in Frost a tension between belief and truth. There is an effort to believe that may coincide with what James called "the will to believe," the force of the will to create order or seek like response from the world around it. A great dramatic tension exists when this will to believe and when beliefs do not find themselves reciprocated or answered – perhaps not at all or perhaps not in precisely the way that we expected to conform to our human expectations. The conclusion of the complex narrative "The Black Cottage" has a minister describing to a narrator, half a century after the Civil War, why he did not change the Creed during sermons, even though he does not seem to hold it to be true. He claims that he maintained the Creed out of sentiment for the old woman, who also believed in Jefferson's claim that "all men are created free and equal." Despite his doubt about the truths of Christianity, he imagines an arid, if not infertile, landscape where such truths might be preserved. Such a landscape might include the Lord's nativity but would be free of conquest and change, and he argues, in part, that change may be merely truths going "in and out of favor":

I'm just as glad she made me keep hands off,
For, dear me, why abandon a belief
Merely because it ceases to be true.
Cling to it long enough, and not a doubt
It will turn true again, for so it goes.
Most of the change we think we see in life
Is due to truths being in and out of favor.
As I sit here, and oftentimes, I wish
I could be the monarch of a desert land
I could devote and dedicate forever

To the truths we keep coming back and back to.
So desert it would have to be, so walled
By mountain ranges half in summer snow,
No one would covet it or think it worth
The pain of conquering to force change on.
Scattered oases where men dwelt, but mostly
Sand dunes held loosely in tamarisk
Blown over and over themselves in idleness.
Sand grains should sugar in the natal dew
The babe born to the desert, the sand storm
Retard mid-waste my cowering caravans –
"There are bees in this wall." He struck the clapboards,
Fierce heads looked out; small bodies pivoted.
We rose to go. Sunset blazed on the windows.

The bees in the walls of the decaying cottage come as an interruption to the pre-serve of truth envisioned by the minister. They represent a "fierce" monarchy of their own, different and indifferent to the human world, highly organized, and a truth about power that disrupts and undermines any unchanging idealized world or one without hierarchy and struggle.[28]

"Birches" provides a rich metaphor of play but also of striving toward an ureachable ideal, separated from belief by truth. At first the speaker envisions the birch trees as personified dead souls, bent low and beaten from ice storms. Ice storms become an irreducible truth that prevents his imagining the trees and the playful process of bending and mastering nature to his will:

But I was going to say when Truth broke in
With all her matter-of-fact about the ice-storm
I should prefer to have some boy bend them
As he went out and in to fetch the cows –
Some boy too far from town to learn baseball,
Whose only play was what he found himself,
Summer or winter, and could play alone.

He would only like to go "[t]toward heaven" because "earth's the right place for love," or, perhaps, the only place for love, some truth about the immensity of the universe having the ultimate say in belief.

This immense tension between belief and truth is everywhere in Frost's work. It does not mean that he insists that he knows what truth is but it does make one cautious about calling Frost a nihilist – if, by nihilist, one would mean that there is nothing beyond what the mind projects and nothing is either true or false. "The Most of It" provides a typically surprising instance of Frost presenting a character in search of love and response beyond himself. The "he" of the poem has been described as both Adamic and Narcissus-like. In some ways, he may be both and something more. His desire for what seems the paradoxical idea of "counter-love, original response," is met with an "embodiment" that appears "*as* a great buck."

In Frostian terms, that may indeed not be so bad. In a remarkable passage in his notebooks that seems to echo both "The Most of It" and the language of Thoreau's *The Maine Woods*, and its call for "contact, contact," Frost envisions life as a continual flux of sorrows. Those sorrows and the flux give a sense of certainty, however terrible, *outside the self:*

> Here where we are life wells up as a strong spring perpetually piling water on water with the dancing high lights from upon it. But it flows away on all sides as into a marsh of its own making. It flows away into poverty into insanity into crime . . .
> . . . Dark darker darkest
> Dark as it is that there are these sorrows and darker still that we can do so little to get rid of them the darkest is still to come. The darkest is that perhaps we ought not to want to get rid of them. They be the fulfillment of exertion. What life craves most is signs of life. A cat can entertain itself only briefly with a block of wood. It can deceive itself longer with a spool or ball. But give it a mouse for consummation. Response response. The certainty of a source outside of self – whether love or hate fierceness or fear.   (*N*, 327–328)

The importance of a certainty of a source outside the self helps us, then, to understand why Frost's dialogues remain some of his most powerful works. "West-Running Brook" not only provides the figure of life as water flowing away but, more important, it provides the figure of a man and a woman responding to each other and defining between them who and where they are. Fred views the wave from the standpoint of eternity, a Platonic stance "ever since rivers were made in heaven." His wife or lover views the wave personally and mystically as "an annunciation." Their dialogue about origins proceeds by contraries from and to the source; but the parenthetical intrusion of the narrator provides yet a third plane of regard on the brook.

> "Why, my dear,
> That wave's been standing off this jut of shore –"
> (The black stream, catching on a sunken rock,
> Flung backward on itself in one white wave,
> And the white water rode the black forever,
> Not gaining but not losing, like a bird

> White feathers from the struggle of whose breast
> Flecked the dark stream and flecked the darker pool
> In a white scarf against the far shore alders.)
> "That wave's been standing off this jut of shore
> Ever since rivers, I was going to say,
> Were made in heaven. It wasn't waved to us."
>
> "It wasn't, yet it was. If not to you,
> It was to me – in an annunciation."
>
> "Oh, if you take it off to lady-land,
> As't were the country of the Amazons
> We men must see you to the confines of
> And leave you there, ourselves forbid to enter,–
> It is your brook! I have no more to say."
>
> "Yes, you have, too. Go on. You thought of something."

The sexual and erotic dialogue drives the philosophical drama of creation in the poem. Truth stands external to the beliefs expressed by the two players.

Perhaps the ultimate demand for response comes in *A Masque of Reason*, Frost's addendum to the Book of Job. Job demands of God a reason ultimately for the suffering he was once put through in the original story. Job still insists on a reason in order to maintain belief:

> You'd be the last to want me to believe
> All Your effects were lucky blunders.
> That would be unbelief and atheism.
> The artist in me cries out for design.
> Such devilish ingenuity of torture
> Did seem unlike You, and I tried to think
> The reason might have been some other person's.
> But there is nothing You are not behind.

Almost comically, God does what he did in the Hebrew Bible – refuse to give Job a reason. But it is Job's wife, named significantly Thyatira for one of the wayward cities in the Book of Revelation, who helps push the dialogue and God to something of dark revelation. She quotes Job as asking whether there can really be any form of spiritual salvation on earth:

> For instance, is there such a thing as Progress?
> Job says there's no such thing as Earth's becoming
> An easier place for man to save his soul in.
> Except as a hard place to save his soul in,
> A trial ground where he can try himself

> And find out whether he is any good,
> It would be meaningless. It might as well
> Be Heaven at once and have it over with.

As though ventriloquist, this seems to be one of the most Frostian comments
in the poem, quite similar to the outlook in the notebook entry "Dark, Darker,
Darkest": difficulty from a definite source outside the self gives life definition
and meaning. She also expresses the strong anti-utopian psychology, the wel-
coming of difficulty and challenge that came to mark Frost's sense of poetic
vocation from "The Trial by Existence." At this moment, we learn the most
human and, also, terrible admission from God: That he tortured Job because
he was simply "showing off to the devil." The revelation produces a resignation
in Job that knowledge of the reasons he sought was not more "but less than he
can understand."

  If Frost could not ultimately reconcile truth with belief, he may have been left
with what he called "phrases of salvation," as he called them in his notebooks:
"So I have found that for my own survival I had to have phrases of salvation if I
was to keep anything worth keeping" (*N*, 523). Yet, alluding to Pilate's question
before Jesus (and Bacon's echo of it), Frost allowed himself the possibility of
pursuing and uttering truth, however elusive:

> Truth, what is truth? said Pilate; and we know not and no search can
> make us know, said someone else. But I said can't we know? We can
> know well enough to go on with being tried every day in our courage to
> tell it. What is truth? Truth is that that takes fresh courage to tell it. It
> takes all our best skill too.   (*N*, 523)

This does quite seem to mean that for Frost the challenge of difficulty or skill
in language had become the only indicator of reality or of truth. In an early
notebook Frost wrote "metaphor is our furthest forth." Much of the later poetry
and, indeed, both masques try to embrace the contradictions in his thought in
terse, dark sayings.

Justice, mercy, and passionate preference

A Masque of Mercy identifies the contradiction between justice and mercy,
though it ultimately seems to hover around the idea that courage in action,
without any certainty of salvation, is the only possible ethical standard. Frost
has been called and was said to call himself "an Old Testament Christian." This,
again, is one of those tricky contradictions. In his discussions in the 1940s with
Rabbi Victor Reichert, Frost asserted that there was no teaching in the New
Testament that was not also in the Old Testament. We can see just how tricky

Frost was about the matter in a recounting he gave of his conversation with
Reichert in the essay "On Extravagance." He refers to the fact that the moral
command "You shall love your neighbor as yourself" is both in the Hebrew Bible
(Leviticus) and the New Testament. Frost adds his own dark spin, though, on
its full meaning in the context of his understanding of human nature:

> For instance, somebody says to me – a great friend – says, "Everything's
> in the Old testament that you find the New." You can tell who he was
> probably by his saying that.
>   And I said, "What *is* the height of it?"
>   "Well," he said, "love your neighbor as yourself."
>   I said, "Yeah, that's in both of them." Then, just to tease him, I said,
> "But it isn't good enough."
>   He said, "What's the matter with it?"
>   "And *hate* your neighbor as you hate yourself."
>   He said, "You hate yourself?"
>   "I wouldn't be religious unless I did." You see, we had an argument –
> of that kind.   (*CPPP*, 910)

Reichert and Frost were essentially right. From the golden rule to the shema
to the circumcision of the heart, all of the essential moral teachings of the
New Testament could be found in the Old Testament. As much as those teachings could be founded on love, much of the religious experience could also
be said to be based on human limitation, doubt, and failure. Frost based both
of his masques on Old Testament works – the books of Job and Jonah. The
fact that he did so raises some very significant questions about Frost's religious
thinking. First, both masques in form recall Milton's masque *Comus*, a work
about Puritan thought that Frost loved to have his students at the Pinkerton
Academy perform. For Frost, Milton's work tests the limits of theodicy and the
ability of the mind and spirit to consider maintaining unworldly standards.
Both of Frost's masques appear to be in considerable argument with Milton,
particularly about the ability to justify evil, much less stand above it. Second,
both of Frost's masques challenge the idea that there are any appreciable revelations to be had in the New Testament. Since both masques are about revealing
answers to final questions and apocalyptic subjects, they demur from the Book
of Revelation as well as poke fun at such apocalyptic modernist writers as
Yeats. Instead, there he presents a view consonant with one stated elsewhere
that "Life is punishment. All we can contribute to it is gracefulness in taking
the punishment" (*N*, 663).

Frost saw the Book of Jonah as the first book in the Bible in which the
question of God being merciful appeared. Jonah's demand for God to confirm

human expectations of justice appears as comical as Job's demands for an explanation for his suffering. As Frost's Jonah says "I've lost my faith in God to carry out / The threats He makes against the city evil. / I can't trust God to be unmerciful." Frost introduces a bookstore owner named "Keeper," Paul (the author of Christian theology), and Jesse Bel, Keeper's wife. Jesse Bel's name is particularly interesting because it links her to the city of Thyatira, one of the seven cities mentioned in the Book of Revelation of the New Testament. She is among the faithless in that city and her name is supposed to remind us of Jezebel, the idolatrous wife of Ahab in Kings. Thyatira was the name Frost gave to Job's wife in *A Masque of Reason*. Yet, both these women play important ethical roles in challenging God and Paul. Frost appears to turn the New Testament against itself, pointing to the women not as traitors but to the Bible as a unified document or one that transcends the bifurcation of new and old wisdom. This is significant given that the masques were published in 1945 and 1946 respectively, after the revelations of the Holocaust, when apocalyptic visions of human history were particularly potent, when demands for explanations of suffering and justice were widespread and exigent, and when relations between Jews and Christians were horribly strained.

Frost places one of the key thematic phrases of *A Masque of Mercy*, that of courage, with its original emphasis on the heart, in the mouth of Jesse Bel. She tells Jonah: "Your courage failed. The saddest thing in life / Is that the best thing in it should be courage." Keeper says near the end of the drama "Courage is of the heart by derivation, / And great it is. But fear is of the soul. / And I'm afraid." Both Paul and Keeper agree that fear and courage go together in uncertain sacrifice.

> We have to stay afraid deep in our souls
> Our sacrifice, the best we have to offer,
> And not our worst nor second best, our best,
> Our very best, our lives laid down like Jonah's,
> Our lives laid down in war and peace, may not
> Be found acceptable in Heaven's sight.

Keeper's response to Paul also admits of failure in courage:

> My failure is no different from Jonah's.
> We both have lacked the courage in the heart
> To overcome the fear within the soul
> And go ahead to any accomplishment.
> Courage is what it takes and takes the more of
> Because the deeper fear is so eternal.

Fear here, as elsewhere in Frost, expresses the terror of uncertainty. In emphasizing courage and playing on its derivation from "the heart," Frost seems to leave as impossible the merciful love of the sacred heart of later Christianity. "The courage in the heart" does, however, encompass and echo the circumcision of the heart that one finds expressed at the core of the teachings of both Old and New Testaments.

When Frost expresses himself in poetic prayer in the "Cluster of Faith" section of *In the Clearing*, his last book, he leaves clearly stated but nevertheless baffling tensions. "Accidentally on Purpose" pokes fun at cartoon-like notions of evolution, giving the impression that he is dismissive altogether of the notion of descent with modification. When he comes to the question of who or what may have been steering "the Omnibus," he leaves that to rationality and limits himself to prayer and belief:

> Whose purpose was it? His or Her or Its?
> Let's leave that to the scientific wits.
> Grant me intention, purpose, and design –
> That's near enough for me to the Divine.

He prays to be granted "intention, purpose, and design" and that would be "near enough" to the "Divine." But the final stanza admits a more modest sense of human motive, placing our "passionate preference" in line with the simple heliotropism of a plant:

> And yet for all this help of head and brain
> How happily instinctive we remain,
> Our best guide upward further to the light,
> Passionate preference, such as love at sight.

The couplet that concludes "Cluster of Faith" may be at once more amusing and more disturbing in its brilliantly paradoxical embodiment both of the childish motives of prayer to the child-like and bumbling creator to whom they may be directed:

> Forgive, O Lord, my little jokes on Thee
> And I'll forgive Thy great big one on me.

In a letter he wrote to Wallace Stevens in 1935, Frost repeated a phrase he liked to say in one form or another in both correspondence and talks, claiming he was "never so serious as when playful."

Chapter 4

Reception

Robert Frost's recognition as a poet came relatively late but grew into a spectacular crescendo that has never stopped, even if critical appreciation has been divided among poets, literary critics, and general readers. He had tried and most often failed to publish his poems in magazines in the United States. The only collections of his poetry that he had assembled before 1912 were the privately printed *Twilight,* just two copies of three poems for Elinor, and a small collection for Susan Hayes Ward, editor of the *Independent.* After arriving in England, Frost assembled *A Boy's Will,* and the first English publisher to whom Frost presented it, David Nutt, agreed to publish it. Frost was thirty-nine when it appeared. A year later, Nutt published *North of Boston,* a book consisting of poems far different in form from the first book.

Frost received remarkable praise on both sides of the Atlantic, expressing different perceptions on how he had become an American poet. Of *A Boy's Will,* Norman Douglas wrote in *The English Review:*

> Nowhere on earth, we fancy, is there more outrageous nonsense printed
> under the name of poetry than in America; the author, we are told, is an
> American. All the more credit to him for breaking away from this
> tradition – for such it can be called – and giving us not derivative,
> hypersensuous drivel, but an image of things really heard and seen.
> There is a wild, racy flavour in his poems; they sound that *inevitable*
> response to nature which is the hallmark of true lyric feeling.[1]

F. S. Flint, in another strong review in *Poetry and Drama,* similarly emphasizes Frost's breaking away from America and the merits of his simplicity of diction:

> Be it said, however, that Mr. Frost has escaped America, and that his first
> book, *A Boy's Will,* has found an English publisher. So much
> information, extrinsic to the poems, is necessary. Their intrinsic merits
> are great, despite faults of diction here and there, occasional inversions,
> and lapses, where he has not been strong enough to bear his own

simplicity of utterance. It is this simplicity which is the great charm of the book; and it is a simplicity that proceeds from a candid heart.[2]

Though he had nothing to do with getting either book published, Ezra Pound reviewed both books and later took credit for discovering Frost. "This man has the good sense to speak naturally and to paint the thing, the thing as he sees it. And to do this is a very different matter from gunning about for the circumplectious polysyllable," Pound wrote of *A Boy's Will* in *Poetry*,[3] casting Frost in a positive light with a range of literary camps including the Imagists, and other such writers as H. D. and William Carlos Williams. In the same review, Pound also erroneously described Frost as having been "scorned by the 'great American editors.'" The image troubled Frost, who wrote to Sidney Cox, "It was not in anger that I came to England" (*SL*, 148). Pound wrote an even stronger review of *North of Boston*, praising both the fresh depiction of New England life and the naturalness of its speech.

> Mr. Frost is an honest writer, writing from himself, from his own knowledge and emotion; not simply picking up the manner which magazines are accepting at the moment, and applying it to the topics in vogue. He is quite consciously and definitely putting New England rural life into verse. He is not using themes cribbed out of Ovid . . . Mr. Frost has dared to write for the most part with success, in the natural speech of New England; in natural spoken speech, which is very different from the "natural" speech of the newspapers.[4]

Whatever irritations and resentments Frost may have harbored toward Pound's pressures and condescension, his praise and patronage were extremely important at the early moment in his publishing career. The remarkable fact was the range of praise Frost received for his first two books from influential critics, including Pound, Flint, Ford Madox Ford, William Dean Howells, and Amy Lowell. The praise he had won in England did not in the least bit hurt him with reviewers in the United States. When Amy Lowell reviewed *North of Boston* for *The New Republic* in 1914, she was struck by the flexibility of his blank verse "which does not hesitate to leave out a syllable or put one in," and she said regarding Frost's poetics, "he goes his own way, regardless of anyone else's rules, and the result is a book of unusual power and sincerity." Perhaps the most remarkable aspect of Lowell's review included her observation of the darker aspects of Frost's New England:

> Mr. Frost has produced both people and scenery with a vividness which is extraordinary. Here are huge hills, undraped by any sympathetic legend, felt as things hard and unyielding, almost sinister, not exactly

feared, but regarded as in some sort influences nonetheless. Here are great stretches of blueberry pasture lying in the sun; and again, autumn orchards cracking with fruit which is almost too much trouble to gather. Heavy thunderstorms drench the lonely roads and spatter on the walls of farm-houses rotting in abandonment; and the modern New-England town, with narrow frame houses, visited by drummers alone, is painted in all its ugliness. For Mr. Frost is not the kindly New England of Whittier, nor the humorous and sensible one of Lowell; it is the latter-day New England, where a civilization is decaying to give place to another and very different one.[5]

Frost experienced simultaneous waves of accolades and severe criticism, sometimes both severely misguided, during his own lifetime and since. Nevertheless, his appeal to a wide audience and a great variety of readers, with strong and sometimes merely passing interests in poetry, philosophers, historians, both in the United States and abroad, has diminished little since his death in 1963. Unlike most of his contemporaries, Frost has a readership that extends to school children and adults with no formal education in poetry. Those readers look to him as an icon of meaning and order in a chaotic world. For the same reasons and others, he is often regarded within academia as of little interest because, on superficial reading, he raises no obvious questions or radical eccentricities about language, gender, race, or politics. Given the very powerful and complex dramatic presence of women in the poetry, the economic, social, and ethnic tensions in the pastoral narratives, and the intensity of Frost's intellectual preoccupations, such assumptions can only be the result of what Walter Pater called "the roughness of the eye." It may also be true that however complex or subtle he may be, he can never be the attraction for some that Whitman or Dickinson may be. However complex his politics, he will never satisfy those who demand that he should have been a Marxist or Stalinist. Critics will appear to forgive or at least turn Eliot's anti-Semitism into a subject of theoretical interest; Frost's skepticism about the New Deal and socialism has become some form of unforgivable conservatism akin to proto-fascism. Critics will dance circles to forgive or to explain as psychological eccentricity Pound's fascist radio rants but regard evidence of Frost's personal ambition or his family tragedies as either indecency or cruelty. Though Frost wrote strange and sometimes wildly innovative poems, his resistance to modernist mantras of the need for a radically new poetics on the grounds of his perception of the world has rarely merited serious attention – until recently. Nevertheless, anthologists, poets, and readers appear to recognize what academics have failed to see – that Frost gives a powerful and compelling vision of the world, with insight into nature and human nature that stirs thought and recognition and brings one continually back to the poems. They are rich in ways that take years to mine. The freshness and strangeness of both *A Boy's Will* and especially the dramatic poetry of *North of Boston, Mountain Interval*, and *New Hampshire* established a new boundary and new audiences for American poetry while exploring the range of human existence with concision and depth.

1920s–1940s

With the exception of the title poem, *West-Running Brook* (1928) has none of the dramatic pastorals of his earlier books. The title poem is a departure in its philosophical texture, and a number of the poems have a similar, perhaps more austere quality than readers had previously encountered in Frost's work.

The 1930s saw the first harsh wave of criticism directed against Frost. It came, as one might expect, at the height of praise. Frost had already received two Pulitzer Prizes, the first for *New Hampshire* and the second for *Collected Poems*. "The Road Not Taken" and "Stopping by Woods on a Snowy Evening" had already achieved iconic status, even if fewer people read the remarkable formal breakthroughs of the pastoral dramatic poems of the first three books. *West-Running Brook* (1928) had baffled some readers with its more austere, philosophical poems. There is little question that both reviewers had some impatience with Frost's reputation as a popular poet but one who failed to hold deeper views or whose views remained either elusive or uncongenial to those who expected of him a more explicitly political and especially sympathetic response to a leftist agenda. When Frost's *Collected Poems* appeared in 1930, Granville Hicks, a Marxist, reviewed it in *The New Republic*, and found the poetry lacking completely in the subjects of industrialism, the disruptive effects of scientific effects of scientific hypotheses, and nothing about Freudianism. He concluded that Frost could not "contribute to the unification, in imaginative terms, of our culture. He cannot give us the sense of belonging in the industrial, scientific, Freudian world in which we find ourselves." The *Collected Poems* received a Pulitzer Prize, and more recent critics have pointed out the extent to which Frost engaged in ways that must have escaped Hicks's radar the very subjects he seemed to believe were completely absent from Frost's work. Though Frost was unlikely Freudian, few recent critics would deny his acute and nuanced engagement with psychology.

But the Depression had exacerbated political lines in all areas of American politics including literary politics. A third Pulitzer Prize had been awarded for *A Further Range* in 1936. R. P. Blackmur attacked not only the book but

Frost, regarding him a technical virtuouso, "at heart, an easy-going versifier of all that comes to hand, and hence never lacks either a subject or the sense of its mastery."[6] Showing his political hand, Blackmur condemned "Build Soil." Showing his ignorance, he condemned "Desert Places" as an inferior lyric. The translator and poet Rolfe Humphries was even more severe with what he saw as Frost's weak, reactionary political posturings: "The further range to which Frost invited himself is an excursion into the field of the political didactic, and his address is unbecoming." Humphries concluded bluntly "*A Further Range? A further shrinking.*"[7]

Leftist attacks on Frost would continue into the 1940s, the most notable coming in 1944 from literary editor and champion of Faulkner Malcolm Cowley in a essay entitled unambiguously "The Case Against Mr. Frost." There are several interesting aspects of Cowley's essay, including the fact that it is as much a case against advocates of Frost as it is against Frost himself. In his leveling criticism against what he takes to be the anti-New Deal poetry of *A Further Range*, Cowley also concedes:

> a poet has the right to be judged by his best work, and Frost has added to our never sufficient store of authentic poetry. If in spite of this I still say that there is room for a dissenting opinion, perhaps I chiefly mean that there is a case against the zealous admirers who are not content to take the poet for what he is, with his integrity and limitations, but insist on regarding him as a national sage. Still worse, they try to use him as a national banner for their own moral or political crusades.[8]

Cowley characterized these supporters of Frost as those who "demand, however, that American writing be affirmative, optimistic, and, not too critical" and also as those who do not like poetry, especially modern poetry. This would seem a slightly ironic turn, given the kind of characterizations and support that came early on from Pound and Amy Lowell. When Cowley criticizes the poetry directly, he claims Frost was dismissive of scientific matters (a poignantly ironic claim in light of recent scholarship), and for not following in the politically revolutionary paths of his New England predecessors, particularly Thoreau and Emerson, or at least Cowley's version of the latter.

Yvor Winters also joined those who felt that Frost's reputation exceeded his achievement but for reasons that would seem somewhat opposite to those put forward by Cowley, at least on the question of Frost's alignment with the New England romantic tradition. In his 1948 essay "Robert Frost, Or, the Spiritual Drifter as Poet," Winters criticized Frost not so much for his politics but for what he perceived to be his lack of intelligence. Winters took issue with Frost's subject matter and style as fit for great poetry; he regarded Frost as working within a tradition of romantic sentiment and nostalgic attitudes toward rural life (Winters did not seem to recognize the deeper ironies inherent in the concept of the pastoral). He also objected to Frost's interest in ordinary speech:

> Frost early began his endeavor to make his style approximate as closely
> as possible to the style of conversation, and this has added to his
> reputation: it has helped him to seem "natural." But poetry is not
> conversation, and I see no reason why poetry should be called upon to
> imitate conversation. Conversation is the most careless and formless of
> human utterance; it is spontaneous and unrevised, and its vocabulary is
> commonly limited. Poetry is the most difficult form of utterance; we
> revise poems carefully in order to make them nearly perfect.[9]

Aside from these assumptions, Winters objected to Frost's uncertainties, which he saw inherited uncritically from the romanticism of Emerson and Thoreau. The only valuable aspects of Frost, Winters believed, were "principles of Greek and Christian thought . . . of which the implications are understood by relatively few of our contemporaries, by Frost least of all; they operate upon Frost at a distance, through social inheritance, and he has done his best to adopt principles which are opposed to them."[10]

1947–1963

Reviews of Frost's last books varied from sharp to polite but reviews did not in the least diminish serious appreciation of his work, which continued to grow. Writing in *The New York Times*, Randall Jarrell said of *Steeple Bush*, "that most of the poems remind you, by their persistence in their mannerisms of what was genius, that they are the productions of somebody who once, somewhere else, was a great poet," though Jarrell acknowledged the brilliance of "Directive," a poem that almost all critics find not only one of Frost's best but one of the great meditative lyrics of the twentieth century.[11] A reviewer for *Time* acknowledged the vigor and craftsmanship but bristled at what he regarded as Frost's "uninspired Tory social commentary," referring specifically to the dozen concluding poems grouped under the heading "Editorials."

Such opposites as Jarrell and W. H. Auden as well as Robert Lowell in the last decade of Frost's life wrote some of the most powerful, perceptive, and lasting appreciations of his work. Jarrell wrote two essays, "To the Laodecians" and "The Other Robert Frost," which he published in his collection *Poetry and the Age* (1953). Those essays along with a lengthy, detailed study of his favorite Frost poem, "Home Burial," emphasized greatly the psychological and largely tragic vision in Frost's work which no one had really done before. Jarrell emphasized such poems as "Provide, Provide," "Neither Out Far Nor In Deep," "Design," and "The Most of It," to counter the misimpression some may have, however, misguided, of a somewhat sentimental Frost. At Frost's eighty-fifth birthday dinner, Lionel Trilling had created something of a scandal by asserting this poet was "anything but" a writer "who assures us by his affirmation of old values, simplicities, pieties, and ways of feeling." Also pointing to "Design," and "Neither out Far Nor in Deep," Trilling called Frost a "terrifying poet."[12]

An émigré to the United States since just before World War II, W. H. Auden was keenly aware of both the American and English literary landscapes. In an essay from the late 1940s, published in *The Dyer's Hand*, Auden characterized Frost as "a Prospero poet," mature and controlled. He writes appreciatively of Frost's pastoral poems, such as "The Generations of Men" and "The Ax-Helve," as well as the shorter lyrics. Rather than characterizing Frost as tragic or terrifying, Auden saw him as wise, as he explained by comparing him to both Yeats and Hardy by their self-epitaphs:

> Hardy, Yeats, and Frost have all written epitaphs for themselves.
>
> *Hardy*
>
> I never cared for life, life cared for me.
> And hence I owe it some fidelity. . . .
>
> *Yeats*
>
> Cast a cold eye
> On life and death
> Horseman pass by.
>
> *Frost*
>
> I would have it written of me on my stone
> I had a lover's quarrel with the world.
>
> Of the three, Frost surely comes off the best. Hardy seems to be stating the Pessimist's Case rather than his real feelings. "I never cared . . ." *Never?* Now, Mr. Hardy, really. Yeats's horseman is a stage prop; the passer-by is much more likely to be a motorist. But Frost convinces me that he is telling neither more nor less than the truth about himself. And when it comes to wisdom, is not having a lover's quarrel with life more worthy of Prospero than not caring or looking coldly?[13]

The young Robert Lowell and Elizabeth Bishop were strong admirers of the skill of Frost's work, though Bishop found Frost's attitude toward life hard to take. In his *Paris Review* interview of 1961, Lowell pointed to the strength of Frost's narrative poems:

> nobody except Frost can do a sort of Chaucerian narrative poem that's organized and clear. Well, a lot of people do them, but the texture of their verse is so limp and uninspired. Frost does them with great power. Most of them were done early, in that *North of Boston* period. That was a miracle, because except for Robinson – and I think Frost is a greater poet than Robinson – no one was doing that in England or America. His "Witch of Coos" is absolutely there. I've gathered from talking to him that most of the *North of Boston* poems came from actual people he knew shuffled and put together. But then it's all important that Frost's plots are so extraordinary, so carefully worked out though it seems that they're not there. Like some things in Chekhov, the art is very well hidden.

The three-volume Thompson biography, a work that Robert Lowell aptly called "tone-deaf" and "poisonous," fed a prurient interest in knocking down an image of Frost as a wholesome man but maintaining a naïve view of him as a triumphant post-Emersonian poet of American individualism. After the first wave and controversy of the Thompson biography had subsided, a new wave of scholarly assessment rode on the crest of the centennial of Frost's birth. Three substantial volumes entitled *Robert Frost: Centennial Essays* (1974–1978) circled a wide range of subjects from biography and religion to modernist contexts to focused scholarship on individual poems. Frank Lentricchia, one of the contributors to that project, would publish an expansion on his argument as *Robert Frost and the Landscapes of Self* (1975). Lentricchia took issue with both George Nitchie's (explored in *Human Values in the Poetry of Robert Frost*, 1960) and Winters's view that Frost had no guiding approach to nature, and with Reuben Brower's Emersonian interpretation of Frost's imagination constituting the world. Instead, Lentricchia pointed to the importance of Frost's early engagement with the work of William James and James's post-Kantian, skeptical thinking, which allowed for a transformative engagement with an already accepted environment, "social and natural"; Lentricchia's sophisticated advocacy grew larger with the publication of Richard Poirier's *Robert Frost: The Work of Knowing* (1977). Poirier, a new critic and a student of Brower's, underscored the need for viewing Frost in a pragmatist tradition extending from Emerson through James. Poirier also caught the interest of a growing number of academic readers concerned with language theory and hermeneutics who had turned their attention to Stevens by asserting:

Frost seems to me of vital interest and consequence because his ultimate subject is the interpretive process itself. He "plays" with possibilities for interpretation in a poetry that seems "obvious" only because it is all the while also concerned with the interpretations of what, in the most ordinary sense, are the "signs" of life itself, particular and mundane signs which nonetheless hint at possibilities that continually elude us.

Poirier focused especially on Frost's domestic poems as figurative sites or boundaries for "extravagance," the title of his late essay on Emerson. Poirier dismissed as unimpressive such Frost poems as "Death of the Hired Man," "Directive," and "West-Running Brook," and focused attention on others he regarded as psychologically more perceptive, such as "Home Burial" and "The Fear," as well as shorter lyrics, such as "Design," that put Frost, as Poirier argued, in direct line with James, or other, neglected poems, such as "A Star in a Stone-Boat," which were regarded as daring or extravagant.

An important tradition of understanding Frost's relationship to New England literary culture had been growing since the publication of Reuben Brower's landmark *The Poetry of Robert Frost: Constellations of Intention* (1963). John Lynen's *The Pastoral Art of Robert Frost* (1964) took a significant step in the direction of interpreting the symbolic mode of Frost's landscapes. Both John C. Kemp's *Robert Frost and New England* (1979) and George Monteiro's *Robert Frost and the New England Renaissance* (1988) took deeper looks at the question of Frost's regionalism and his debt to the nineteenth-century American poetic traditions.

Frost criticism developed greatly in the late 1990s from a variety of scholars working independently and then, some, collaboratively. Judith Oster's *Toward Robert Frost: The Reader and the Poet* (1991) combined close readings and reader criticism to highlight the tensions and ambiguities of many of Frost's works. Katherine Kearns's *Robert Frost and a Poetics of Appetite* (1994) was a groundbreaking reading of Frost in terms of antinomies of gender: "For Frost, anything that expends itself in generation necessarily winds down acceleratively to death, but unlike nature and unlike women, men are possessed of the (potential) rationality by which they may hold this process in abeyance."[14] Karen Kilcup's *Robert Frost and Feminine Literary Tradition* (1998) described the complex ways Frost's poetry participated in complex and culturally resonant literary traditions which appealed to the voices of women and men. Mark Richardson's *The Ordeal of Robert Frost* (1997) portrayed Frost working within the tension of "formity" and "conformity," a heroic desire to build his imagination within the context of the public realm. Richardson also paid close attention to Frost's concepts of fate and freedom as portrayed in such poems as "The Trial by Existence." In the same year, Robert Faggen published *Robert*

Frost and the Challenge of Darwin (1947), arguing that Frost's engagement with science in general and Darwin in particular was a defining question for his poetic mythology and his relationship with modernism in general. Faggen placed Frost's interest in pragmatism within the general problem of evolution and natural selection and read his pastoral themes in terms of technology, animal analogies, gender relations, and problems of theodicy. Frost, in Faggen's view, uncovered not a new world but a world of ancient struggle and skeptical, uneasy knowledge. Robert Bernard Hass's study *Going by Contraries* (2002) also argued that Frost's engagement with science was crucial to his poetic vision. In contrast to Faggen, Hass argued that Frost saw the findings of science as less threatening, more ultimately part of the play of metaphor and, therefore, one of the humanities. In Hass's view, Frost was clearly able to make an extremely strong apology for poetry's cultural ascendancy.

Several volumes of focused essays also added considerably to the understanding of Frost's work. *Roads Not Taken* (2001), edited by Earl Wilcox and Jonathan Barron, collected fresh approaches to Frost's poetry including highly insightful takes on "The Black Cottage" as well as groundbreaking work on Frost's politics and some of the first really insightful looks at the cold war poems. *The Cambridge Companion to Frost* (2001) brought to full focus Frost's complex relationship to ancient traditions, the extreme difficulty of biographical approaches to his work, and Timothy Steele's study, probably the finest in print to date, of Frost's metrical practice and its relationship to what he meant by "the sound of sense."

The new Harvard edition of Frost's complete works marks a new stage in Frost scholarship. For the first time in more than forty years, significant unpublished material is being made available that is beginning to inspire reevaluation of Frost's reputation. *The Notebooks of Robert Frost* (2007), edited by Robert Faggen and published unexpurgated, provides few drafts of Frost's published poems but offers extensive insight into Frost the thinker as he ranged over such diverse subjects as politics, science, prosody, history, and religion for more than half a century. The notebooks revealed Frost's aphoristic style, apparent also in the "dark sayings" that permeate the poetry. Their appearance has dispelled almost any notion that Frost did not push the boundaries of poetic thought. Writing about the *Notebooks*, critic Adam Kirsch observed:

> Lionel Trilling insisted on calling Frost, to his face, "a terrifying poet." Really, he had less in common with Longfellow than with Sophocles, "who made plain . . . the terrible things of human life." Trilling's remarks came in for what seems now like a surprising amount of criticism . . . If

Trilling had read *The Notebooks of Robert Frost* . . . he would have smiled to see how they completely vindicate his view of Frost . . . without warning, Frost will suddenly jot down a phrase that seems to open onto an abyss, showing how truly "terrifying" his wasteful, inhuman universe can be. Frost is known as a master of metaphor, and many of his poems take the form of extended metaphors. Yet when he writes, "I doubt if any thing is more related to another thing than it is to any third thing except as we make it," he shows how the power of metaphor can turn on the poet, plunging him into a world of sheer perspectivism where there is no essence, only likeness. If we can make anything resemble anything else, then we are doomed to perish from the very excess of significations. This is the terror that has always loomed behind the willful optimism of the Emersonian tradition, and which Frost, very much like Nietzsche, was able to exhume from the corpse of Emerson's gentility. Perhaps not even Nietzsche ever captured the terror in an image as striking and bottomless as Frost's: "We get truth like a man trying to drink at a hydrant." At such moments, Frost's *Notebooks*, like his best poems, remind us that there has never been a more genuinely mystical American writer.[15]

Some of the most powerful advocacy for Frost's work has come from English-language poets and from European exiles living in the United States. Seamus Heaney, one of Ireland's most acclaimed contemporary poets, writes in a pastoral tradition that acknowledges the inheritance of Wordsworth and Frost. Heaney himself grew up on a farm in County Derry and the accuracy and hardness of Frost's evocations of farm life attracted him. Ultimately, Heaney found, referring specifically to the conclusion of "Home Burial," "the rising note out of the fallen condition is the essential one which Frost achieves in his greatest work."[16] The pressure of intellect in Frost releases, according to Heaney, the powerful, deep wellsprings of sound and language. Heaney's younger contemporary, Paul Muldoon, who also grew up in Northern Ireland and now lives and teaches in the United States, admires Frost greatly for the adventurousness and playfulness of his language and drama. Muldoon alludes to such trickster figures in his own work as the farmer of "The Mountain" or the narrator of "Directive."[17] Derek Walcott, while acknowledging some of the politically backward or at least temporally defined aspects of Frost's social perspectives, credits him immensely with a revolution in the pentameter line: "He wrote free or syllabic verse within the deceptive margins of the pentameter." Pointing to the first lines of "Mending Wall" as an example, Walcott saw "as monumental a breakthrough for American verse as anything in Williams or Cummings . . ." He added "This happened with equal force with Yeats, but with Frost it is more alarming, since Yeats contracted the pentameter to octosyllabics for propulsion's sake, for 'that quarrel which we call rhetoric,' for the purposes we call political passion, but Frost achieved this upheaval within the pentameter. He accomplished it, that is, without making his meter as wry and sarcastic as Williams's, or as pyrotechnic as Cummings's, or as solemn and portentous as Stevens."[18]

The most influential of the three essays in the volume has been Brodsky's "On Grief and Reason," for several reasons: it first appeared in *The New Yorker*, with a relatively wide circulation and then as the title essay in his final collection of prose. But more to the point, the essay focused almost entirely on one poem, "Home Burial" (although he gives "Come in" close devotion also). Set against Jarrell's detailed reading of the same poem several decades earlier, it made a strong case for Frost's power in writing dramatic dialogue, in creating "a tragedy of communication," and in his evocation of the "terror of uncertainty," by which Brodsky meant to distinguish him from the sense of tragedy suggested when Trilling called him a terrifying poet. Brodsky's reaction to Frost seemed all the more remarkable because he first encountered him while serving time on a work farm in the Soviet Union.

Czeslaw Milosz, another Nobel Laureate émigré, a friend and admirer of Brodsky's, recognized Frost's "superb ear," "powerful intellect, unusual intelligence," and that he was "well-read in philosophy." He saw Frost's strategy as one of "such enormous deceptiveness that he was capable of hiding his skepticism behind his constant ambivalence, so that his poems deceived with their supposedly wise affability."[19] For Milosz, Frost's poetry ultimately concealed "a grim, hopeless vision of man's fate." Milosz, who wrestled more often with the work of Robinson Jeffers, tended to resist what he considered the aesthetics of indirection and concealment as well as a tragic and nihilistic vision of human history.

Frost and the postmodern

The story of Frost's reception in the past and future can, in a limited way, be captured in an interview with literary critic Charles Bernstein, published in *The Antioch Review*. Bernstein has written primarily on avant garde and modernist writers. When in the interview he started discussing modernist writers who use the vernacular and "nonstandard and decentered Englishes," the interviewer assumed he was not talking about Robert Frost. Bernstein gave a rather lengthy reply about the pleasures of teaching Frost and how much a poem such as "Mending Wall" was misunderstood by readers. Bernstein points to a recurrent theme in Frost's reception: the way the poetry continues to speak in its complexity beneath or against what it appears to be doing at first. Frost seemed to have a genius for being misunderstood:

> A funny thing happens when you become a professor of poetry as I am: you end up teaching Frost with great pleasure. You also realize that there is a Robert Frost who is no more assimilable than his more overtly radical contemporaries to a nonpoetry culture, that is to say a group of people who don't read poetry. Appearances to the contrary, whose woods these are we really have no idea but in closer listening. Two prosodies diverged in a striated field, and I – I took the hired man, I took the hand of the hired man and did the polka in the dark, if polka governs in a thing so marked . . .
>
> I find myself going back to some of Frost's most famous poems. "Mending Wall" is a fascinating fabrication, a metricalized, colloquial voice that breaks the vernacular over its lines, as theme synthesizes sound. As a first-wave modernist, Frost is at the center of the conflict between dialect and meter, traditional prosody and its others. This is one reason he is such an enduring poet – because he continues to speak to our enduring condition in poetry, our one-hundred-years-and – and still-counting *cris de vers* . . .
>
> Maybe Frost is not just "our" best-loved poet but also one of the most misread American poets. Else how to explain the image of Frost as the sage coiner of words of wisdom, who thinks that putting up walls will make your life better. There's something about the refinement of that poem that has precipitated an acceptance of it that flies in the face of its explicit content . . . It's so successful as to almost completely destroy its meaning, although of course it doesn't: the meaning is still there.[20]

Notes

1 Life

1. John Evangelist Walsh, *Into My Own: The English Years of Robert Frost* (New York: Grove Press, 1988), 84. Walsh provides the most detailed account of Frost's time in England.
2. Robert Graves, "The Truest Poet," *Sunday Times*, February 3, 1963, 26.
3. D. D. Paige, ed., *The Letters of Ezra Pound* (London: Faber, 1960), 16. Pound was writing to Harriet Monroe, the American editor of *Poetry*.
4. *Robert Frost and Sidney Cox: Forty Years of Friendship*, ed. William Evans (Hanover, N.H.: University Press of New England, 1963), 58.
5. Louis Mertins, *Robert Frost: Life and Talks-Walking* (Norman: University of Oklahoma Press, 1965), 177.
6. Letter to Gertrude McQuestern, undated. Boston University Library. Quoted in Jay Parini, *Robert Frost: A Life* (New York: Henry Holt, 1999), 144.

2 Contexts

1. Robert Frost to Lesley Francis Frost, 1934, *Family Letters of Robert and Elinor Frost*, ed. Arnold Grade (Albany: State University Press of New York, 1972), 161.
2. Ibid., 162.
3. Ibid., 163.
4. Interview by Harvey Breit with Frost in *The New York Times Book Review*, November 27, 1949.
5. William James, "What Pragmatism Means," *Pragmatism* in *William James: Writings 1902–1910*, ed. Bruce Kuklick (New York: Library of America, 1987), 509.
6. William James, "Pragmatism and Humanism," *Pragmatism* in *William James*, ed. Kuklick, 599.
7. Irving Babbitt, "Bacon and Rousseau" and "What is Humanism," *Literature and the American College* (Boston: Houghton, Mifflin and Company, 1908).
8. Josiah Royce, *The Spirit of Modern Philosophy* (New York: Houghton Mifflin, 1892), 274–275.

9. George Santayana, *The Sense of Beauty* (New York: Charles Scribner's Sons, 1896), 117.

10. John H. Timmerman, *Robert Frost and the Ethics of Ambiguity* (Lewisburg: Bucknell University Press, 2002) provides an interesting argument for the positive relationship and influence of Santayana on Frost's poetry and thought.

11. Santayana wrote in *Scepticism and Animal Faith* (New York: Charles Scribner's Sons, 1923), 52: "Every part of experience, as it comes, is illusion. And the source of this illusion is my animal nature, blindly laboring in a blind world. Such is the ancient lesson of experience itself, when we reflect upon experience and turn its illusions into instruction: a lesson which bird-witted empiricism can never learn, though it is daily repeated." Frost seemed to reject Santayana's extreme view of experience as producing merely a choice between illusions.

3 Works

1. One of the best full-length treatment's of Frost's prosody is Timothy Steele's "Across the Spaces of the Footed Line: the Meter and Versification of Robert Frost," in *The Cambridge Companion to Robert Frost*, ed. Robert Faggen (Cambridge: Cambridge University Press, 2001), 123–153.

2. For an extended look at Frost's sonnets see Richard C. Calhoun's "By Pretending They Are Not Sonnets," in *Roads Not Taken: Rereading Robert Frost*, ed. Earl Wilcox and Jonathan Barron (Columbia: University of Missouri Press, 2000), 217–235.

3. The last line of William Wordsworth's "My Heart Leaps Up" (1807).

4. Elizabeth Shepley Sergeant, *Robert Frost: The Trial By Existence* (New York: Holt, Rinehart and Winston, 1960), 325.

5. From a recorded talk, *Robert Frost Reads from His Own Work*, Carillion Records (1961), Yale Series of Recorded Poets. Produced by the Yale University Department of English and Audio Visual Center, ed. R. W. B. Lewis, recorded May 19, 1961 in the Pierson College Lounge, Yale University.

6. One of the first full-length discussions of Frost and the ancient pastoral tradition was John F. Lynen's *The Pastoral Art of Robert Frost* (New Haven: Yale University Press, 1964).

7. Lucretius, *On the Nature of the Universe*, trans. Ronald Lathem (London: Penguin Books, 1951), 148.

8. William Empson, *Some Versions of the Pastoral* (London: Chatto and Windus, 1935), 11–12.

9. Frost to F. S. Flint, July 6, 1913. The letter is reproduced in full in *Robert Frost on Writing*, ed. Elaine Barry (New Brunswick: Rutgers University Press, 1973), 82.

10. Ibid., 83.

11. For the best discussion of the history of the phrase in American culture see Brian Dippie's *The Vanishing American: White Indians and US Indian Policy* (Middletown: Wesleyan University Press, 1982).

12. Matthew Dennis, *Red, White, and Blue Letter Days* (Ithaca: Cornell University Press, 2002), pp. 81–118.

13. P. G. Wiggin, "French Canadians in New England," *The New York Times*, October 13, 1901.

14. See Helen Bacon's discussion of this poem in relation to Euripides and the Dionysiac lore of Maenadism in "Frost and the Ancient Muses," in *The Cambridge Companion to Robert Frost*, ed. Faggen, 75–100.

15. *Wisdom: Conversations with the Elder Wise Men of Our Day*, ed. James Nelson (New York: W. W. Norton, 1958), 16. This interview was conducted in 1952 by Bela Kornitzer at Frost's home in Ripton, Vermont.

16. Unpublished letter from Frost to Theodore "Ted" Baird, a member of the Amherst College English Department, October 16, 1946. Amherst College Archives. Frost was responding to an essay Baird had sent him, "Darwin and the Entangled Bank," published in *The American Scholar* (1946). Baird praised Darwin's writing as being as good as Carlyle's. Frost makes specific reference to Darwin's journal entry for January 20, 1833 about "Yammerschooner," a Fuegian word for "give me," and "Lampalagua," the name of a boa constrictor. The other two American works to which Frost refers are Thoreau's *Walden* and Richard Henry Dana's *Two Years Before the Mast*.

17. See George Monteiro's "The Facts on Frost," *South Carolina Review*, Fall 1989, 87–96. Monteiro provides an interesting discussion of how Frost's account of a spider's behavior as accounted in J. Fabre (whom Frost read) may diverge from some aspects of Frost's poem.

18. B. J. Sokol, "Bergson, Instinct, and Frost's 'The White-Tailed Hornet,'" *American Literature* 62, no. 1 (1990), 44–45.

19. George Monteiro, "Robert Frost's Solitary Singer," *New England Quarterly*, March 1971, 134–40.

20. Robert Faggen, *Robert Frost and the Challenge of Darwin* (Ann Arbor: University of Michigan Press, 2001), 53–62.

21. See William H. Pritchard's "Diminished Nature," *Massachusetts Review*, Spring 1960, 475–92.

22. Czeslaw Milosz, *Road-Side Dog* (New York: Farrar, Straus & Giroux, 1998), 21.

23. For differing recent discussions about Frost and science see Robert Bernard Hass, *Going by Contraries: Robert Frost's Conflict with Science* (Charlottesville: University Press of Virginia, 2002); Faggen, *Robert Frost and the Challenge of Darwin*; and Guy Rotella, "Comparing Conceptions: Frost and Eddington, Heisenberg, and Bohr," *American Literature* 59, no. 2 (1987), 167–89.

24. Henry David Thoreau, "Walking," in *Great Short Works of Henry David Thoreau*, ed. Wendell Glick (New York: Harper and Row, 1982), 304.

25. Richard Proctor, *Our Place Among the Infinities* (New York: D. Appleton, 1876), 9–10.

26. Ibid., 5–6.

27. Ibid., 34.

28. See Jonathan Barron's essay on Wordsworth's "The Ruined Cottage" and Frost's "The Black Cottage": "A Tale of Two Cottages," in *Roads Not Taken*, ed. Wilcox and Barrow, 132–151.

4 Reception

1. Norman Douglas, *The English Review*, June 14, 1913, 505.
2. F. S. Flint, *Poetry and Drama*, June 13, 1913, 250.
3. Ezra Pound, *Poetry*, May 2, 1913, 72–74.
4. Ezra Pound, *Poetry*, December 5, 1914, 127–130.
5. Amy Lowell, *The New Republic*, February 2, 1915, 81–82.
6. R. P. Blackmur, "The Instincts of a Bard," *The Nation*, 142, June 24, 1936, 817–819.
7. Rolfe Humphries, "A Further Shrinking," *New Masses*, 20, August 1, 1936, 42.
8. Malcolm Cowley, "The Case Against Mr. Frost," *The New Republic*, September 11, 18, 1944, 312–313, 345–347.
9. Yvor Winters, "Robert Frost, Or, the Spiritual Drifter as Poet," in *The Function of Criticism* (Denver: Alan Swallow, 1957), 160.
10. Ibid., 187.
11. Randall Jarrell, "'Tenderness and Passive Sadness,'" *New York Times Book Review*, June 1, 1947, 4.
12. Lionel Trilling, "A Speech on Robert Frost: A Cultural Episode," *Partisan Review*, Summer 1959.
13. W. H. Auden, *The Dyer's Hand* (New York: Vintage Books, 1948), 353.
14. Katherine Kearns, *Robert Frost and a Poetics of Appetite* (Cambridge: Cambridge University Press, 1994), 2.
15. Adam Kirsch, "Subterranean Frost," *The New York Sun*, February 12, 2007.
16. Seamus Heaney, "Above the Brim," in Joseph Brodsky, Seamus Heaney, and Derek Walcott, *Homage to Robert Frost* (New York: Farrar, Straus & Giroux, 1996), 77. Heaney has also written of Frost's work elsewhere in his prose, especially *The Government of the Tongue* and *The Redress of Poetry*.
17. See especially Muldoon's poem "The More One Has the More One Wants." Muldoon has included an extensive and provocative essay on "The Mountain" in his collection *The End of the Poem* (New York: Farrar, Straus & Giroux, 2006).
18. Derek Walcott, "The Road Taken," in Joseph Brodsky, Seamus Heaney, and Derek Walcott, *Homage to Robert Frost* (New York: Farrar, Straus & Giroux, 1996), 104.
19. Czeslaw Milosz, "Robert Frost," *Milosz's ABC's*, tr. Madeline Levine (New York: Farrar, Straus & Giroux, 2001), 400.
20. Charles Bernstein, *The Antioch Review*, 62, no. 1 (Winter 2004), 134–135.

Guide to further reading

I. Works by Robert Frost

Collected Prose of Robert Frost, ed. Mark Richardson. Cambridge, Mass.: Harvard University Press, 2008. A definitive, annotated edition of all of Frost's prose.

Concordance to the Poetry of Robert Frost, ed. Edward C. Lathem. New York: Henry Holt, 1971. A useful concordance to Lathem's 1969 edition of the *Complete Poems of Robert Frost*.

The Family Letters of Robert and Elinor Frost, ed. Arnold Grade. Albany: State University of New York Press, 1972. An important collection of Frost's letters.

The Letters of Robert Frost to Louis Untermeyer, ed. Louis Untermeyer. New York: Holt, Rinehart, and Winston, 1963. A valuable collection of Frost's correspondence, though expurgated by Untermeyer and lacking an index.

The Notebooks of Robert Frost, ed. Robert Faggen. Cambridge, Mass.: Harvard University Press, 2007. Frost's notebooks provide a rich mine on topics as diverse as poetics, science, religion, politics, and history.

Robert Frost: Collected Poems, Prose, and Plays, ed. Richard Poirier and Mark Richardson. New York: Library of America, 1995. An excellent comprehensive edition of Frost's work, including all of the published poems.

Selected Letters of Robert Frost, ed. Lawrance Thompson. New York: Holt, Rinehart and Winston, 1964. To date, the only available collection of Frost's letters, though hardly definitive.

II. Interviews with Frost

Cook, Reginald L. *Robert Frost: A Living Voice*. Amherst: University of Massachusetts Press, 1974. A rich account of numerous talks and lectures given by Frost provided by his friend and Middlebury professor.

Francis, Robert. *Frost: A Time to Talk: Conversations and Indiscretions*. Amherst: University of Massachusetts Press, 1971. An interesting perspective on Frost from a friend and fellow poet.

Lathem, Edward Connery, ed. *Interviews with Robert Frost.* New York: Holt,
    Rinehart and Winston, 1966. A rich resource of glimpses into Frost's
    thinking from the beginning of his career as a published writer to shortly
    before his death.
Mertins, Louis. *Robert Frost: Life and Talks-Walking.* Norman: University of
    Oklahoma Press, 1965. A younger poet and long-time friend of Frost's
    recounts their conversations.
Smythe, Daniel. *Robert Frost Speaks.* New York: Twayne Publishers, 1966.

III.   Biographies and memoirs

Anderson, Margaret Bartlett. *Robert Frost and John Bartlett: The Record of a
    Friendship.* New York: Holt, Rinehart, and Winston, 1963. An account of
    Frost's significant friendship with his former student.
Burnshaw, Stanley. *Robert Frost Himself.* New York: G. Braziller, 1986. A poet and
    Frost's editor gives his striking portrait of Frost.
Cox, Sidney. *A Swinger of Birches: A Portrait of Robert Frost.* Introduction by
    Robert Frost. New York: New York University Press, 1957. Cox, an
    English professor, met Frost in 1911, and was an early advocate of his
    work.
Francis, Lesley Lee. *The Frost Family's Adventure in Poetry: Sheer Morning
    Gladness at the Brim.* Columbia: University of Missouri Press, 1994.
    Frost's granddaughter provides a fascinating account of her family's
    education by poetry based on family letters and journals.
Meyers, Jeffrey. *Robert Frost: A Biography.* New York: Houghton Mifflin, 1996. A
    hastily researched biography that focuses superficially on the more
    troubled aspects of Frost's later personal life, presented better in the
    work of Donald Sheehy.
Muir, Helen. *Frost in Florida: A Memoir.* Miami: Valiant Press, 1995. An overview
    of the many winters Frost spent in Florida, by a journalist who knew
    him.
Newdick, Robert. *Newdick's Season of Frost: An Interrupted Biography of Robert
    Frost,* ed. William A. Sutton. Albany: State University of New York Press,
    1976. The first attempt at an official biography of Frost, interrupted by
    Newdick's death in 1939.
Parini, Jay. *Robert Frost: A Biography.* New York: Henry Holt, 1999. A thoughtful,
    balanced biography of the poet as a devoted father and demanding artist
    which also gives a particularly rich account of his early years.
Pritchard, William H. *Robert Frost: A Literary Life Reconsidered.* New York:
    Oxford University Press, 1984. A biography of Frost, addressing carefully
    his literary context and the limits of what we can know about the
    relationship between his life and work.
Reeve, E. D. *Robert Frost in Russia.* Boston: Little, Brown, 1964. A fascinating
    account of Frost's 1962 ambassadorial trip to the Soviet Union and

meeting with Russian poets and Kruschev by the translator who accompanied him.

Sergeant, Elizabeth Shepley. *Robert Frost: The Trial by Existence.* New York: Holt, Rinehart and Winston, 1960. A critical biography of Frost with which Frost cooperated. It includes valuable comments by Frost about his life and work.

Thompson, Lawrance. *Robert Frost: The Early Years, 1874–1915.* New York: Holt, Rinehart and Winston, 1966. The first of three volumes of the official biography of Robert Frost. The first two were completed by Thompson. Although the biography remains an invaluable resource, Thompson grew single-minded in his hatred of his subject. He tended to regard material favoring his subject with suspicion and welcome uncritically material and accounts contributing to his ever-growing negative view of Frost as a monster, particularly toward his family.

Robert Frost: The Years of Triumph, 1915–1938. New York: Holt, Rinehart, and Winston, 1970. The second and Pulitzer Prize-winning volume of the official biography.

Thompson, Lawrance, and R. H. Winnick. *Robert Frost: The Later Years, 1938–1963.* New York: Holt, Rinehart and Winston, 1976. Thompson died before the completion of this volume, which was completed by his assistant.

Walsh, John Evangelist. *Into My Own: The English Years of Robert Frost.* New York: Grove Press, 1988. An illuminating study of Frost's years in England, where he published his first two books and encountered Pound, Yeats, and Thomas.

IV. Criticism

Bagby, George. *Robert Frost and the Book of Nature.* Knoxville: University of Tennessee Press, 1993. An interesting study of Frost's taking nature as edifying text and scripture.

Barron, Jonathan and Earl Wilcox, eds. *Roads Not Taken: Rereading Robert Frost.* Columbia: University of Missouri Press, 2001. A groundbreaking collection of essays on many aspects of Frost's poetry.

The Robert Frost Review. Published annually by the Robert Frost Society.

Barry, Elaine, ed. *Robert Frost on Writing.* New Brunswick, N.J.: Rutgers University Press, 1973. A useful assembly of Frost's letters and essays on the subject of writing and poetics with a provocative introduction by the editor.

Brodsky, Joseph, Seamus Heaney, and Derek Walcott. *Homage to Robert Frost.* New York: Farrar, Straus & Giroux, 1996. A collection famous for revealing the range of Frost's global reach and the often surprising and contradictory reactions his work produces.

Brower, Reuben. *The Poetry of Robert Frost: Constellations of Intention.* New York: Oxford University Press, 1963. A sturdy, new critical study of Frost's poetry with an emphasis on his Emersonian alignment.

Budd, Louis and Edwin Cady, eds. *On Frost: The Best* from *American Literature.* Durham, N.C.: Duke University Press, 1991. Major essays on Frost which have appeared in this journal.

Cook, Reginald L. *The Dimensions of Robert Frost.* New York: Rinehart, 1958. An insightful general study by the Middlebury professor who knew the poet and his work well.

Cox, James M., ed. *Robert Frost: A Collection of Critical Essays.* Englewood Cliffs, N.J.: Prentice-Hall, 1961.

Cramer, Jeffrey S. *Robert Frost Among His Poems: A Literary Companion to the Poet's Own Biographical Contexts and Associations.* Jefferson, N.C.: McFarland, 1996. An invaluable guide for tracking the bibliographical history of Frost's poems and books.

Faggen, Robert. *Robert Frost and the Challenge of Darwin.* Ann Arbor: University of Michigan Press, 1997. Places Frost's poetry in the context of the tensions between science and faith that emerged from the nineteenth and continued into the twentieth century. Regards Frost as much more congenial to science than some critics had thought.

Faggen, Robert, ed. *The Cambridge Companion to Robert Frost.* Cambridge: Cambridge University Press, 2001. A collection of essays on key topics in Frost studies including biography, pastoral, prosody, politics, economics, and gender.

Gerber, Philip L., ed. *Critical Essays on Robert Frost.* Boston: G. K. Hall, 1982.

Jarrell, Randall. *No Other Book: Selected Essays,* ed. Brad Leithauser. New York: Farrar, Straus & Giroux, 1999. Paperback edn., HarperCollins, 1999. Jarrell's essays contain his illuminating studies of Frost's poetry, including his extensive meditation on "Home Burial."

Hass, Robert Bernard. *Going by Contraries: Robert Frost's Conflict with Science.* Charlottesville: University Press of Virginia, 2002. An insightful study of Frost's handling of twentieth-century biology and physics.

Hoffman, Tyler. *Robert Frost and the Politics of Poetry.* Hanover, N.H.: University Press of New England, 2001. A study that places Frost's theory of "the sound of sense" within the contexts of literary and cultural politics.

Jost, Walter. *Rhetorical Investigations: Studies in Ordinary Language Criticism.* Charlottesville: University Press of Virginia, 2004. A complex study of ordinary language criticism and rhetoric in "Home Burial," "Snow," "Death of the Hired Man," and "The Code."

Kearns, Katherine. *Robert Frost and a Poetics of Appetite.* Cambridge: Cambridge University Press, 1994. An engaging study of the erotic in Frost's poetry, particularly the tension between attitudes of masculinity and femininity, order and chaos.

Kemp, John C. *Robert Frost and New England: The Poet as Regionalist.* Princeton: Princeton University Press, 1979. Explores deeply the symbolism of location and New England in Frost's poetry.

Kilcup, Karen L. *Robert Frost and Feminine Literary Tradition.* Ann Arbor: University of Michigan Press, 1998. Focuses on the women writers who

inspired Frost, including Sarah Orne Jewett, Lydia Sigourney, and Mary
    Wilkins Freeman.
Lentricchia, Frank. *Robert Frost: Modern Poetics and the Landscapes of Self.*
    Durham, N.C.: Duke University Press, 1975. An important study of
    Frost's relationship to pragmatism and other philosophical
    traditions.
Lynen, John F. *The Pastoral Art of Robert Frost.* New Haven, Conn.: Yale University
    Press, 1964. An important early study of Frost's working in the pastoral
    mode.
Mauro, Jason. "Frost and James: The Gaps I Mean." *South Carolina Review,* (2)28
    (1996), 112–120. A subtle essay that reveals the skeptical depths of
    Frost's thinking about pragmatism.
Monteiro, George. *Robert Frost and the New England Renaissance.* Lexington:
    University Press of Kentucky, 1988. A lively and insightful study of
    Frost's dialogue with Emerson, Thoreau, and others.
Oster, Judith. *Toward Robert Frost: The Reader and the Poet.* Athens: University of
    Georgia Press, 1991. A reader-response approach to the poetry,
    providing provocative readings of the poems.
Poirier, Richard. *Robert Frost: The Work of Knowing.* New York: Oxford University
    Press, 1977. A landmark study that emphasized the great degree of
    literary intelligence and criticism within Frost's poetry.
Richardson, Mark, ed. *The Ordeal of Robert Frost.* Urbana: University of Illinois
    Press, 1997. This study reveals Frost's struggle to maintain his artistic
    integrity while also remaining accessible to a reading public.
Rotella, Guy. *Reading and Writing Nature.* Boston: Northeastern University Press,
    1991. Places Frost in the context of several modern poets – Stevens,
    Bishop, and Moore, and the idea of nature.
Sabin, Margery. "The Fate of the Frost Speaker," *Raritan,* 2 (Fall 1982), 128–139.
    A significant statement about the importance of sound and voice in
    Frost's poetry.
Sheehy, Donald G. "The Poet as Neurotic: The Official Biography of Robert
    Frost." *American Literature,* October 1986, 393–409. One of the most
    important critical essays written on Frost and the Thompson biography.
    "(Re) Figuring Love: Robert Frost in Crisis, 1938–1942." *New England
    Quarterly,* June 1990, 179–231. A fascinating essay on the relationship
    between Frost and Kathleen Morrison.
Tharpe, Jac, ed. *Frost: Centennial Essays,* vols. I–III. Jackson: University Press of
    Mississippi, 1976–78. Three volumes of essays on a wide range of
    topics.
Timmerman, John H. *Robert Frost and the Ethics of Ambiguity.* Lewisburg:
    Bucknell University Press, 2002. An interesting study of Frost's debt to
    Santayana, going against the usual thinking that sees Frost as entirely
    antagonistic to the philosopher.
Tuten, Lewis and John Zubizarreta, ed. *The Robert Frost Encyclopedia.* Westport,
    Conn.: Greenwood. 2001.

Wagner, Linda W., ed. *Robert Frost: The Critical Reception.* New York: Burt
    Franklin and Company, 1977. A useful collection of the major reviews of
    Frost's books.
Wilcox, Earl, ed. *His "Incalculable" Influence on Others: Essays on Robert Frost in
    Our Time.* English Literary Studies Monograph no. 63. Victoria, B.C.:
    University of Victoria Department of English, 1994.

Index

Abercrombie, Lascelles 7, 8
Akhmatova, Anna 12
Aristotle 37–39, 112
Arnold, Matthew 116, 134
Auden, W. H. 167–168

Babbitt, Irving 22
Bacon, Francis 22, 138
Bacon, Helen 140
Barron, Jonathan 171
Bartlett, John 8, 18, 26
Beard, Theodore 116
Bergson, Henri 7, 22, 24, 28
Bernstein, Charles 173–174
Binyon, Laurence 7
Bion 49
Bishop, Elizabeth 169
Blackmur, R. P. 165, 166
Blake, William 118
Bohr, Niels 9
Braithwaite, William Stanley 28
Bridges, Robert 7
Brodsky, Joseph 173
Brooke, Rupert 7
Brower, Reuben 169–170
Browning, Robert 15, 134
Bryant, William Cullen 16
Bunyan, John 143
Burnshaw, Stanley 1
Burrell, Carl 3, 86

Carlyle, Thomas 28, 116
Catullus 19
Chekhov, Anton 169

Colum, Padraic 10
Cook, Reginald 20
Cournos, John 29
Cowley, Malcolm 166
Cox, Sidney 8, 27, 29, 67, 163
cummings, e.e. 13, 172, 173

Dana 19
Dante 16, 36, 57, 134, 142, 145
Darwin, Charles 19–22, 28, 53, 80, 90,
    114, 115, 116–117, 122, 124, 127,
    129, 139–140, 171
De la Mare, Walter 7
Dickinson, Emily 16, 18, 164
Donne, John 15
Doolittle, Hilda, *see* H. D.
Douglas, Norman 162

Eaton, Walter Prichard 29
Eliot, T. S. 1, 10, 11, 13, 17, 19, 25, 27,
    148, 164
Emerson, Ralph Waldo 3, 15, 16, 17,
    20–21, 22, 39, 69, 127, 136, 154,
    166–167, 169–170, 172
Empson, William 63
Epstein, Jacob 7

Faggen, Robert 170–171
Flint, F. S. 7, 8, 64, 70, 162, 163
Ford, Ford Madox 7, 14, 163
Frost, Carol 5, 9, 11
Frost, Elinor 2, 4, 5, 6, 9, 10, 16, 98,
    133, 162
Frost, Elliot 4, 5, 98, 120

Frost, Irma 5, 10
Frost, Isabelle 2–3
Frost, Jeanie 2, 9, 10
Frost, Lesley 5, 11, 17
Frost, Marjorie 5, 10
Frost, Robert
  "Accidentally on Purpose" 161
  "Acquainted with the Night" 36,
    144, 145
  "After Apple-Picking" 34, 44–46, 64,
    83, 144
  "The Aim Was Song" 138, 145–146
  "Arrival Home" 64
  "At Woodward's Gardens" 114
  "The Ax-Helve" 9, 20, 58, 63, 65, 70,
    83–86, 168
  "The Bear" 114
  "Bereft" 133–134
  "Birches" 31, 42–44, 93, 155
  "The Black Cottage" 14, 20, 23, 53,
    64, 67, 154–155, 171
  "A Blue Ribbon at Amesbury" 5,
    90–91
  "Blueberries" 34, 58, 64, 110–112
  "The Bonfire" 9, 123
  A Boy's Will 4, 6, 7–8, 14, 17, 39, 40,
    51, 53, 56, 64, 65, 66, 102, 136,
    137, 162–163, 165
  "Build Soil" 60, 166
  "The Census-Taker" 53, 148
  "Choose Something Like a Star" 142
  "The Code" 64, 70–74
  Collected Poems (1930) 10, 58, 165
  Collected Poems (1939) 26
  "Come in" 112, 173
  Complete Poems (1949) 11
  "A Considerable Speck" 113
  "The Constant Symbol" 36, 37–38
  "A Cow in Apple Time" 67
  "The Death of the Hired Man" 35,
    64, 98, 102–103, 144, 170
  "The Demiurge's Laugh" 20, 56,
    137–138, 143
  "Departmental" 114
  "Desert Places" 32, 144, 166

  "Design" 113, 117–119, 128, 168,
    170
  "Directive" 11, 53, 143, 147–149,
    167, 170, 172
  "Door in the Dark" 48
  "The Draft Horse" 33
  "A Dream of Julius Caesar" 3
  "A Drumlin Woodchuck" 114
  "Dust of Snow" 35
  "Education by Poetry" 9, 25, 37, 44,
    46, 145, 146–147
  "The Egg and the Machine" 114
  "An Equalizer" 61
  "The Falls" 4
  "The Fear" 64, 98, 104–105, 170
  "The Fear of God" 149
  "The Figure a Poem Makes" 26, 30,
    47
  "For Once, Then, Something" 35,
    112–113
  "Forgive, O Lord, my little jokes on
    Thee" 161
  "A Fountain, a Bottle, a Donkey's
    Ears and Some Books" 16, 53, 65
  "From Iron" 67
  A Further Range 10, 61, 114, 128,
    165–166
  "The Future of Man" 139–140
  "The Generations of Men" 53, 58,
    108–109, 148, 168
  "The Gift Outright" 11, 17
  "Ghost House" 51–53, 148
  "The Grindstone" 65
  "The Hill Wife" 92, 103
  "Home Burial" 35, 53, 64, 98–102,
    105, 168, 170, 172, 173
  "The Housekeeper" 5, 14, 35, 64, 65,
    88–92
  "A Hundred Collars" 14, 58, 63, 64,
    70, 74, 78–81
  "Hyla Brook" 36, 114–115
  In the Clearing 12, 39, 40, 47, 59, 67,
    136, 138, 161
  "In the Home Stretch" 32, 53, 98,
    109

"In winter in the woods alone" 59

"Into My Own" 51, 143

Introduction to E. A. Robinson's *King Jasper* 8, 10, 18

"It takes all sorts of in and outdoor schooling" 14, 40

"Kitty Hawk" 35, 138

"La Noche Triste" 3

"The Last Mowing" 41

"The Lesson for Today" 153–154

Letter to *The Amherst Student* 25, 47, 60, 112, 116

"A Lone Striker" 61

"Love and a Question" 102

"Maple" 92, 95–98

A Masque of Mercy 11, 37–39, 158–161

A Masque of Reason 11, 134, 157–158, 160

"Mending Wall" 2, 14, 31–32, 63, 67–70, 113, 172, 173–174

"The Most of It" 11, 34, 131–132, 155–156, 168

"The Mountain" 20, 35, 58, 63, 64, 70, 74–77, 172

Mountain Interval 9, 56, 64, 115, 165

"Mowing" 35, 39–41, 56, 66

"My Butterfly" 4

"The Need of Being Versed in Country Things" 53, 113, 120–121, 128

"Neither out Far Nor in Deep" 168

"Never Again Would Birds' Song Be the Same" 11, 128, 130–131, 132

"New Hampshire" 19

New Hampshire 9, 64, 92, 132, 165

North of Boston 8, 14, 17, 26, 56, 57, 64, 66, 67, 70, 78, 79, 110, 162, 163–164, 165, 169

"On a Bird Singing in Its Sleep" 128

"On Extravagance" 159

"The Oven Bird" 35, 113, 128–129

"Pan with Us" 54–56, 145

"The Pasture" 47, 59

"Paul's Wife" 65, 92–93

"The Pauper Witch of Grafton" 35, 65, 92

"Petra and its Surroundings" 77

"Pod of the Milkweed" 121–122, 123

"Poverty and Poetry" 61

"The Prerequisites" 41, 44

"The Prophets Really Prophesy as Mystics, the Commentators Merely by Statistics" 136

"Provide, Provide" 61, 168

"A Question" 149

"Range Finding" 123–124

"The Road Not Taken" 16, 140, 141–143, 147, 165

"A Roadside Stand" 61, 62–63

"The Rose Family" 48, 95

"Rose Pogonias" 53

"The Self-Seeker" 58, 65, 86–88

Selected Poems (1928) 10

"A Semi-Revolution" 61

"A Servant to Servants" 35, 58, 65, 92, 98, 105–108

"Sitting by a Bush in Broad Sunlight" 138, 146

"Snow" 65, 144

"Spring Pools" 115

"A Star in a Stone-Boat" 170

"The Star-Splitter" 149–153

"Stars" 149

Steeple Bush 11, 149, 167

"Stopping by Woods on a Snowy Evening" 33, 140, 144, 145, 165

"The Subverted Flower" 11, 132

"Summering" 4

"To a Moth Seen in Winter" 11, 119–120

"Tree at My Window" 51

"The Trial by Existence" 138, 140–141, 158, 170

"Triple Bronze" 67

"The Tuft of Flowers" 41, 63, 66–67

Twilight 4, 162

"Two Look at Two" 132

"Two Tramps in Mud Time" 60, 61–62, 63

Frost, Robert (*cont.*)
  "An Unhistoric Spot" 4
  "The Vanishing Red" 81–83
  "The Vantage Point" 53–54
  "West-Running Brook" 24, 48–49,
    98, 156–157, 170
  West-Running Brook 10, 48, 64, 114,
    115, 165
  "The White-Tailed Hornet" 114,
    124–127, 129
  "Wild Grapes" 92, 93–95
  "The Witch of Coos" 63, 70, 92, 104,
    108, 169
  A Witness Tree 11, 61, 120, 132
  "The Wood Pile" 53, 143, 147
Frost Jr., William Prescott 2–3
Frost Sr., William Prescott 3, 5

Galton, Francis 90
George, Henry 2
Gibson, Wilfred 7, 8
Graves, Robert 7
Guay, Napoleon 70

Hardy, Thomas 135, 168
Hass, Robert Bernard 171
Hawthorne, Nathaniel 59
H. D. (Hilda Doolittle) 163
Heaney, Seamus 172
Hemingway, Ernest 11
Hesiod 55
Hicks, Granville 165
Holmes, Oliver Wendell 21
Horace 15
Howells, William Dean 163
Hulme, T. E. 7, 8, 14
Humphries, Rolfe 166
Huxley, Aldous 15

James, William 5, 6, 21–22, 24, 28, 154,
    169–170
Jarrell, Randall 1, 167–168, 173
Jeffers, Robinson 173
Jefferson, Thomas 23, 57, 78,
    154

Kearns, Katherine 170
Keats, John 15
Kemp, John C. 170
Kennedy, John F. 1, 11–12
Khruschev, Nikita 12
Kilcup, Karen 170
Kirsch, Adam 171

Lanier, Sidney 28
Lee, Robert E. 2
Lentricchia, Frank 169
Lewis, Cecil Day 57
Leyendecker, J. C. 79
Longfellow, Henry Wadsworth 16, 17,
    171
Lowell, Amy 163–164, 166
Lowell, James Russell 164
Lowell, Robert 167, 169
Lucretius 15, 19, 55
Lynen, John 170

Marlowe, Christopher 6
Marvell, Andrew 15, 41, 50
Meiklejohn, Alexander 9
Melville, Herman 19, 113, 135, 137
Michaud, Regis 16
Milosz, Czeslaw 135, 173
Milton, John 6, 15, 57, 134, 159
Monro, Harold 7
Monteiro, George 170
Moodie, Isabelle, *see* Frost, Isabelle
Moore, Marianne 13
Morrison, Kathleen (Kay) 10–11
Morrison, Theodore 10
Muldoon, Paul 172
Munsterberg, Hugo 5

Newdick, Robert 1
Nietzsche, Friedrich 172
Nitchie, Geroge 169
Nutt, David 6, 162

Olds, George Wilson 10
Oster, Judith 170
Ovid 15, 113, 163

Paley, William 117
Palmer, George Herbert 5
Parini, Jay 1
Pascal, Blaise 144
Pater, Walter 164
Peirce, Charles Sanders 21
Pestalozzi, Johann Heinrich 6
Plato 6, 37–39, 112, 140
Poe, Edgar Allen 3, 15
Poirier, Richard 169–170
Pope, Alexander 15
Porter, Jane 3
Pound, Ezra 7–8, 11, 13, 14, 17–18, 25, 27, 39, 56, 148, 163, 164, 166
Prescott, William H. 3
Pritchard, William 1
Proctor, Richard 3, 19, 150

Reed, Richard 17
Reichert, Rabbi Victor 11, 158–159
Richardson, Mark 170
Robinson, Edwin Arlington 8, 10, 16, 18, 27, 41, 169
Rogers, Walter M. 80
Roosevelt, Theodore 58, 79
Rousseau, Jean Jacques 6, 22, 38, 50, 150–153
Royce, Josiah 5, 22, 23
Russell, George (AE) 10

Santayana, George 5, 22, 23–24
Sergeant, Elizabeth Shepley 1
Shakespeare, William 3, 4, 15, 48, 95
Shaler, Nathaniel Southgate 5
Shelley, Percy Bysshe 43
Sheridan, Richard 6
Smart, Christopher 15
Sophocles 1, 171, 172
Sokol, B. J. 126
Spencer, Herbert 6, 28
Steele, Timothy 171

Stein, Gertrude 48, 95
Stevens, Wallace 13, 24, 25, 112, 161, 169, 173
Sullivan, John L. 19
Swedenborg, Emanuel 154
Swinburne, Algernon Charles 26

Taft, William Howard 80
Tennyson, Alfred Lord 15, 26, 134
Theocritus 49, 57
Thomas, Edward 7
Thompson, Lawrance 1, 2, 169
Thoreau, Henry David 20, 57, 116, 127, 136, 143, 156, 166–167
Trilling, Lionel 1, 168, 171, 173
Tvardovsky, Andrei 12

Untermeyer, Louis 110, 122

Virgil 15, 49, 55, 56, 57, 66, 114
Voznesensky, Andri 12

Walcott, Derek 172
Waller, Edmund 95
Walsh, John Evangelist 1
Ward, Susan Hayes 4, 162
White, Elinor Miriam, *see* Frost, Elinor
Whitehead, Alfred North 38
Whitman, Walt 18, 136, 164
Whittier, John Greenleaf 164
Wilcox, Earl 171
Williams, William Carlos 13, 163, 172
Winters, Yvor 166–167, 169
Wordsworth, William 15, 20, 28, 38, 41, 50, 57, 69, 74–75, 77, 116, 154, 172
Wright, Chauncey 21

Yeats, W. B. 6, 7, 8, 10, 14, 24, 148, 159, 168, 172
Yevtushenko, Yevgeny 12

The Cambridge Introductions to Literature

AUTHORS

Jane Austen Janet Todd

Samuel Beckett Ronan McDonald

Walter Benjamin David Ferris

J. M. Coetzee Dominic Head

Joseph Conrad John Peters

Jacques Derrida Leslie Hill

Emily Dickinson Wendy Martin

George Eliot Nancy Henry

T. S. Eliot John Xiros Cooper

William Faulkner Theresa M. Towner

F. Scott Fitzgerald Kirk Curnutt

Michel Foucault Lisa Downing

Robert Frost Robert Faggen

Nathaniel Hawthorne Leland S. Person

Zora Neale Hurston Lovalerie King

James Joyce Eric Bulson

Herman Melville Kevin J. Hayes

Sylvia Plath Jo Gill

Edgar Allen Poe Benjamin F. Fisher

Ezra Pound Ira Nadel

Jean Rhys Elaine Savory

Shakespeare Emma Smith

Shakespeare's Comedies Penny Gay

Shakespeare's History Plays Warren Chernaik

Shakespeare's Tragedies Janette Dillon

Harriet Beecher Stowe Sarah Robbins

Mark Twain Peter Messent

Virginia Woolf Jane Goldman

W. B. Yeats David Holdeman

Edith Wharton Pamela Knights

Walt Whitman M. Jimmie Killingsworth

TOPICS

The American Short Story Martin Scofield

Creative Writing David Morley

Early English Theatre Janette Dillon

English Theatre, 1660-1900 Peter Thomson

Francophone Literature Patrick Corcoran

Modernism Pericles Lewis

Modern Irish Poetry Justin Quinn

Narrative (second edition) H. Porter Abbott

The Nineteenth-Century American Novel Gregg Crane

Postcolonial Literatures C. L. Innes

Russian Literature Caryl Emerson

The Short Story in English Adrian Hunter

Theatre Historiography Thomas Postlewait

Theatre Studies Christopher Balme

Tragedy Jennifer Wallace

CPSIA information can be obtained at www.ICGtesting.com
Printed in the USA
BVOW071951081111

275628BV00004B/127/P